A Concise Companion to

Twentieth-century American Poetry

Praise for *A Concise Companion to Twentieth-century American Poetry*

"If I had to recommend a single book on the culture of twentieth-century American poetry to students or colleagues, I would choose Stephen Fredman's *Concise Companion*. Fredman wisely decided to treat the entire century as a whole rather than adopting the usual Modernist/Postmodernist division or treating decades and poets separately. From the opening 'Wars I Have Seen' to the final treatment of philosophy and theory in US poetry, Fredman's contributors carefully examine the intersecting worlds of our poetry – the New York art world, the impact of various diasporas, and the curious intersections with politics, gender, and religion. Yet the poetry itself always comes first, and no reader can fail to profit from these clearly written, concise, and truly expert chapters."

Marjorie Perloff, Stanford University

"This book offers a fresh and comprehensive reading of modern American poetry in several important ways. It takes in the whole of the twentieth century instead of dividing into decades like the 1920s and 1930s or into periods labelled Modernism and Postmodernism. Moreover, instead of focusing on individual poets, the successive chapters relate an often overlapping range of poets to the crucial and defining cultural issues within which the poetry took form and direction and to which the poetry spoke. Stephen Fredman has assembled an extraordinary group of critics to write the chapters. There is nothing else like this rich and trenchant book in the field of modern poetry."

Albert Gelpi, Stanford University

Also available in the Blackwell Concise Companions to Literature and Culture series

The Restoration and Eighteenth Century — Edited by Cynthia Wall

The Victorian Novel — Edited by Francis O'Gorman

Modernism — Edited by David Bradshaw

Postwar American Literature and Culture — Edited by Josephine G. Hendin

Feminist Theory — Edited by Mary Eagleton

A Concise Companion to Twentieth-century American Poetry

Edited by Stephen Fredman

BLACKWELL PUBLISHING
350 Main Street, Malden, MA 02148-5020, USA
9600 Garsington Road, Oxford OX4 2DQ, UK
550 Swanston Street, Carlton, Victoria 3053, Australia

First published 2005 by Blackwell Publishing Ltd

3 2006

Library of Congress Cataloging-in-Publication Data

A concise companion to twentieth-century American poetry / edited by Stephen Fredman.
p. cm.—(Blackwell concise companions to literature and culture)
Includes bibliographical references and index.
ISBN-13: 978-1-4051-2002-9 (hardcover : alk. paper)
ISBN-13: 978-1-4051-2003-6 (pbk. : alk. paper)
ISBN-10: 1-4051-2002-9 (hardcover : alk. paper)
ISBN-10: 1-4051-2003-7 (pbk. : alk. paper)
1. American poetry—20th century—History and criticism—Handbooks, manuals, etc. 2. United States—Intellectual life—20th century—Handbooks, manuals, etc. I. Fredman, Stephen, 1948– II. Series.

PS323.5.C574 2005
811′.509—dc22

2004025183

A catalogue record for this title is available from the British Library.

Set in 10/12pt Meridien
by Graphicraft Limited, Hong Kong
Printed and bound in Singapore
by Fabulous Printers Pte Ltd

The publisher's policy is to use permanent paper from mills that operate a sustainable forestry policy, and which has been manufactured from pulp processed using acid-free and elementary chlorine-free practices. Furthermore, the publisher ensures that the text paper and cover board used have met acceptable environmental accreditation standards.

For further information on
Blackwell Publishing, visit our website:
www.blackwellpublishing.com

Contents

Notes on Contributors

Maria Damon teaches poetry and poetics at the University of Minnesota. She is the author of *The Dark End of the Street: Margins in American Vanguard Poetry*, and coauthor of *The Secret Life of Words* (with Betsy Franco) and *Literature Nation* (with Miekal And).

Michael Davidson is Professor of Literature at the University of California, San Diego. He is the author of *The San Francisco Renaissance*, *Ghostler Demarcations: Modern Poetry and the Material Word*, and *Guys Like Us: Citing Masculinity in Cold War Poetics*. He is the editor of *The New Collected Poems of George Oppen*. He has published eight books of poetry.

Alan Filreis is Kelly Professor of English, Faculty Director of the Kelly Writers House, and Director of the Center for Programs in Contemporary Writing at the University of Pennsylvania. He is the author of *Wallace Stevens and the Actual World* (1991), *Modernism from Right to Left* (1994), and numerous articles on modernism and the literary left. He is editor of Ira Wolfert's *Tucker's People*, and *Secretaries of the Moon: The Letters of Wallace Stevens and Jose Rodriguez Feo*. His new book is entitled *The Fifties' Thirties: Anticommunism and Modern Poetry, 1945–60*.

Stephen Fredman has taught at the University of Notre Dame since 1980, and is presently Professor and Chair of the English Department. He is the author of three books of criticism, *Poet's Prose: The Crisis in American Verse* (1983, 1990), *The Grounding of American Poetry: Charles*

Olson and the Emersonian Tradition (1993), and *A Menorah for Athena: Charles Reznikoff and the Jewish Dilemmas of Objectivist Poetry* (2001), three books of translation, and a book of poetry.

Alan Golding is Professor of English at the University of Louisville, Kentucky, where he teaches American literature and twentieth-century poetry and poetics. He is the author of *From Outlaw to Classic: Canons in American Poetry* (1995) and of numerous essays on modernist and contemporary poetry. His current projects include *Writing the New Into History*, which combines essays on the history and reception of American avant-garde poetics with readings of individual writers, and *Isn't the Avant-Garde Always Pedagogical*, a book on experimental poetics and pedagogy. He also coedits the Wisconsin Series on Contemporary American Poetry.

David Herd is Senior Lecturer in English and American Literature at the University of Kent, UK, and coeditor of *Poetry Review*. His book of criticism, *John Ashbery and American Poetry*, was published in 2000. His book of poems, *Mandelson! Mandelson! A Memoir*, is to be published in 2005.

Lynn Keller is Professor of English at the University of Wisconsin-Madison. She is the author of *Re-Making it New: Contemporary American Poetry and the Modernist Tradition* (1987) and *Forms of Expansion: Recent Long Poems by Women* (1997). With Cristanne Miller, she coedited *Feminist Measures: Soundings in Poetry and Theory* (1994). With Alan Golding and Adalaide Morris, she coedits the University of Wisconsin Press Series on Contemporary North American Poetry.

A. Robert Lee, formerly of the University of Kent at Canterbury, UK, is Professor of American Literature at Nihon University, Tokyo. He has held frequent visiting professorships at universities in the USA including University of Virginia, Northwestern, University of Colorado, and Berkeley. His recent books include *Multicultural American Literature: Black, Native, Latino/a and Asian American Fictions* (2003), *Postindian Conversations*, with Gerald Vizenor (2000), *Designs of Blackness: Mappings in the Literature and Culture of Afro-America* (1998), and the essay collections *Herman Melville: Critical Assessments* (2001), *The Beat Generation Writers* (1996), and *Other Britain, Other British: Contemporary Multicultural Fiction* (1995).

Peter Middleton is a Professor of English at the University of Southampton, UK, and the author of *The Inward Gaze* (with Tim Woods), *Literatures of Memory*, and *Distant Reading: Performance, Readership and Consumption in Contemporary Poetry*, as well as a volume of poetry, *Aftermath*.

Cristanne Miller is W. M. Keck Distinguished Service Professor of English at Pomona College in California. She is the author of *Emily Dickinson: A Poet's Grammar* (1987), *Marianne Moore: Questions of Authority* (1995), and *Cultures of Modernism: Marianne Moore, Mina Loy, and Else Lasker-Schüler: Gender and Literary Community in New York and Berlin* (2005). With Lynn Keller, she coedited *Feminist Measures: Soundings in Poetry and Theory* (1994).

Peter Nicholls is Professor of English and American Literature at the University of Sussex, UK. He is the author of *Ezra Pound: Politics, Economics and Writing* (1984), *Modernisms: A Literary Guide* (1995), and of many articles and essays on twentieth-century literature and theory. He has coedited (with Giovanni Cianci) *Ruskin and Modernism* (2001) and is editor of the journal *Textual Practice*.

Rowan Ricardo Phillips is Assistant Professor of English and Codirector of the Poetry Center at SUNY, Stony Brook. He was a finalist for the 2004 Walt Whitman Award of the Academy of American Poets. His work has appeared in *The Kenyon Review, The Harvard Review, The New Yorker, The Iowa Review*, and other journals.

Brian M. Reed is Assistant Professor of English at the University of Washington, Seattle. He has written articles on the poets Susan Howe, Ezra Pound, Carl Sandburg, and Rosmarie Waldrop, and he has coedited, with Nancy Perloff, a collection of art-historical essays titled *Situating El Lissitzky: Vitebsk, Berlin, Moscow*. His first book, *Hart Crane: After His Lights*, is forthcoming.

Acknowledgments

The editor and publisher gratefully acknowledge the permission granted to reproduce the copyright material in this book:

E. E. Cummings "next to of course god America i" is reprinted from *Complete Poems 1904–1962*, by E. E. Cummings, edited by George J. Firmage, by permission of W. W. Norton & Company. Copyright © 1991 by the Trustees for the E. E. Cummings Trust and George James Firmage.

Unpublished material held in the George Oppen archive at the Mandeville Special Collections, University of California at San Diego, is reprinted by permission of Linda Oppen of the George Oppen archive. This is cited in chapter 1 as UCSD, followed by collection number, box number, file number.

Extract from "Poet" by Genevieve Taggard, is reprinted with kind permission of Judith Benét Richardson.

Chronology

1872
Birth of **Paul Laurence Dunbar**

1873
Birth of **Lola Ridge**

1874
Birth of **Robert Frost**, **Amy Lowell**, **Gertrude Stein**

1875
Birth of **Alice Dunbar-Nelson**

1878
Birth of **Carl Sandburg**

1879
Birth of **Vachel Lindsay**, **Wallace Stevens**

1882
Birth of **Mina Loy**; death of **Ralph Waldo Emerson**

1883
Birth of **William Carlos Williams**

1885
Birth of **Ezra Pound**, **Elinor Wylie**

1886
Birth of **Hilda Doolittle (H. D.)**; Death of **Emily Dickinson**

1887
Birth of **Robinson Jeffers**, **Marianne Moore**

1888
Birth of **T. S. Eliot**, **John Crowe Ransom**

1889
Birth of **Conrad Aiken**

1890
Birth of **Claude McKay**

1891
Death of **Herman Melville**

1892
Birth of **Archibald MacLeish**, **Edna St Vincent Millay**; death of **Walt Whitman**; final edition of **Walt Whitman's** ***Leaves of Grass*** published

1894
Birth of **E. E. Cummings**, **Charles Reznikoff**, **Jean Toomer**

1899
Birth of **Hart Crane**, **Allen Tate**

1900
Birth of **Yvor Winters**

1901
Birth of **Sterling Brown**, **Laura (Riding) Jackson**

1902
Birth of **Arna Bontemps**, **Kenneth Fearing**, **Langston Hughes**; **Edwin Arlington Robinson's** *Captain Craig* published; **President McKinley assassinated**

1903
Birth of **Countee Cullen**, **Lorine Niedecker**; **Wright brothers' pioneer flight**

1904
Birth of **Louis Zukofsky**

1905
Birth of **Stanley Kunitz**, **Robert Penn Warren**; **Einstein's first paper on relativity**

1906
Death of **Paul Laurence Dunbar**

1907
Birth of **W. H. Auden**

1908
Birth of **George Oppen**, **Theodore Roethke**; **Ezra Pound's** ***A Lume Spento*** and ***A Quinzaine for this Yule*** published

1909
Ezra Pound's *Personae of Ezra Pound* and *Exultations of Ezra Pound* published; **Ford introduces Model T**

1910
Birth of **Charles Olson**

1911
Birth of **Elizabeth Bishop**, **Kenneth Patchen**

1912
Birth of **John Cage**, **William Everson**; **Amy Lowell's** *A Dome of Many-Colored Glass*, **Ezra Pound's** *Ripostes* published; **the Titanic sinks**; **founding of** *Poetry: A Magazine of Verse*

1913
Birth of **Carlos Bulosan**, **Charles Henri Ford**, **Robert Hayden**, **Muriel Rukeyser**, **Delmore Schwartz**; **Robert Frost's** *A Boy's Will*, **William Carlos Williams's** *The Tempers* published; **Ford Company introduces assembly line**; **69th Regiment Armory Art Exhibition**

1914
Birth of **John Berryman**, **David Ignatow**, **Randall Jarrell**, **Weldon Kees**, **William Stafford**; **Robert Frost's** *North of Boston*, **Vachel Lindsay's** *The Congo and Other Poems*, **Amy Lowell's** *Sword Blades and Poppy Seed*, **Gertrude Stein's** *Tender Buttons* published; **outbreak of World War I**

1915
Birth of **Ruth Stone**; **Edgar Lee Masters'** *Spoon River Anthology*, **Ezra Pound's** *Cathay* published; **D. W. Griffith's** *Birth of a Nation*; **sinking of the Lusitania**; **Labor leader Joe Hill convicted of murder and executed**

1916
Birth of **John Ciardi**; **H. D.'s** *Sea Garden*, **Amy Lowell's** *Men, Women, and Ghosts*, **Carl Sandburg's** *Chicago Poems* published; **Einstein's General Theory of Relativity published**

1917
Birth of **Gwendolyn Brooks**, **Robert Lowell**; **T. S. Eliot's** *Prufrock and Other Observations*, **Vachel Lindsay's** *The Chinese Nightingale and Other Poems*, **Edward Arlington Robinson's** *Merlin* published; **Associated Press publishes the "Zimmerman Telegram," United States enters World War I.**

1918
Birth of **William Bronk**, **Mary Tallmountain**; **Lola Ridge's** *The Ghetto and Other Poems* published; **Wilson issues Fourteen Points plan**

1919
Birth of **Robert Duncan**; **John Crowe Ransom's** *Poems About God* published; **Versailles Treaty**

1920
Birth of **Charles Bukowski**, **Barbara Guest**, **Howard Nemerov**; **Edna St Vincent Millay's** *A Few Figs from Thistles* and *Aria da Capo*, **Ezra Pound's** *Hugh Selwyn Mauberly* and *Umbra*, **William Carlos Williams's** *Kora In Hell: Improvisations* published; **Chicago "Black Sox" scandal**; **American women achieve the right to vote**

1921
Birth of **Mona Van Duyn**, **Richard Wilbur**; **Marianne Moore's** ***Poems***, **Elinor Wylie's** ***Nets to Catch the Wind*** published

1922
Birth of **Jack Kerouac**, **Jackson Mac Low**; **T. S. Eliot's** ***The Waste Land***, **E. E. Cummings's** ***The Enormous Room***, **William Carlos Williams's** ***Spring and All*** published

1923
Birth of **James Dickey**, **Alan Dugan**, **Anthony Hecht**, **Denise Levertov**, **James Schuyler**, **Louis Simpson**, **Philip Whalen**; **Roberts Frost's** ***New Hampshire***, **Edna St Vincent Millay's** ***The Harp-Weaver and Other Poems***, **Wallace Stevens's** ***Harmonium*** published

1924
Birth of **Cid Corman**; **Emily Dickinson's** *Collected Poems* **(first published edition)**, **Robinson Jeffers,** *Tamar and Other Poems*, **Marianne Moore,** ***Observations*** published; **André Breton's "First Surrealist Manifesto"** published

1925
Birth of **Robin Blaser**, **Bob Kaufman**, **Kenneth Koch**, **Maxine Kumin**, **Jack Spicer**; death of **Amy Lowell**; **H. D.'s** *Collected Poems*, **Ezra Pound's** ***A Draft of XVI Cantos*** published; **Scopes Monkey Trial**

1926
Birth of **A. R. Ammons**, **Paul Blackburn**, **Robert Bly**, **Robert Creeley**, **Allen Ginsberg**, **James Merrill**, **Frank O'Hara**, **W. D. Snodgrass**; **Hart Crane's** ***White Buildings***, **Langston Hughes's** ***The Weary Blues*** published

1927
Birth of **John Ashbery**, **Larry Eigner**, **Galway Kinnell**, **Philip Lamantia**, **Philip Levine**, **W. S. Merwin**, **James Wright**; **E. A. Robinson's** *Tristram*, **Carl Sandburg's** *The American Songbag* published; **Lindbergh's first transatlantic flight**; **execution of Sacco and Vanzetti**; *The Jazz Singer*, **first sound film**

1928
Birth of **Ted Joans**, **Anne Sexton**; death of **Elinor Wylie**; **Countee Cullen's** *Ballad of the Brown Girl*, **Archibald MacLeish's** *The Hamlet of A. MacLeish*; **Carl Sandburg's** *Good Morning, America* published

1929
Birth of **Ed Dorn**, **Kenward Elmslie**, **Adrienne Rich**; **Conrad Aiken's** *Selected Poems*, **Countee Cullen's** *The Black Christ and Other Poems*, **Vachel Lindsay's** *The Litany of Washington Street* published; **Valentine's Day Massacre in Chicago**; **"Black Tuesday" stock market crash**; **"Second Surrealist Manifesto" published**; **opening of the Museum of Modern Art, New York**

1930
Birth of **Gregory Corso**, **Gary Snyder**; **Hart Crane's** *The Bridge*, **T. S. Eliot's** *Ash-Wednesday*, **Ezra Pound's** *A Draft of XXX Cantos* published; **television begins in the USA**; **photo flashbulb invented**

1931
Death of **Vachel Lindsay**; **Conrad Aiken's** *Preludes for Memnon* published; **Louis Zukofsky publishes "Objectivists" issue of** ***Poetry*****, the Scottsboro Boys case establishes African Americans' right to serve on juries**

1932
Birth of **David Antin**, **Sylvia Plath**; death of **Hart Crane**; **Sterling A. Brown's** *Southern Road*, *An "Objectivist's" Anthology* published; **Lindbergh baby kidnapped**; **Presidential candidate Franklin D. Roosevelt announces New Deal**

1933
Birth of **Etheridge Knight**; **E. A. Robinson's** *Talifer* published; **Adolf Hitler appointed Chancellor**; **Roosevelt becomes President**; **Prohibition repealed**

1934
Birth of **Amiri Baraka**, **Wendell Berry**, **Diane di Prima**, **Audre Lorde**, **N. Scott Momaday**, **Sonia Sanchez**, **Mark Strand**, **John Wieners**; **George Oppen's** *Discrete Series*, **Ezra Pound's** *Eleven*

New Cantos XXXI–XLI, **Louis Zukofsky's** *First Half of "A"-9* published; **Public Enemy number one, John Dillinger, shot and killed; radioactivity discovered**

1935
Birth of **Russell Edson, Clayton Eshleman, Robert Kelly, Joy Kogawa, Mary Oliver, Tomás Rivera, Charles Wright**; death of **Alice Dunbar Nelson, Edwin Arlington Robinson; E. E. Cummings'** *No Thanks* and *Tom,* **Muriel Rukeyser's** *Theory of Flight,* **Wallace Stevens's** *Ideas of Order* published

1936
Birth of **Lucille Clifton, Jayne Cortez, Marge Piercy; Robert Frost's** *A Further Range,* **Genevieve Taggard's** *Calling Western Union,* **Allen Tate's** *The Mediterranean and Other Poems* published; **Spanish Civil War begins**

1937
Birth of **Kathleen Fraser, Susan Howe, Alicia Ostriker, Diane Wakoski; Robinson Jeffers's** *Such Counsels You Gave Me,* **Muriel Rukeyser's** *Mediterranean,* **Wallace Stevens's** *The Man With The Blue Guitar* published; *Kenyon Review* **founded**

1938
Birth of **Michael S. Harper, Charles Simic**; death of **James Weldon Johnson; E. E. Cummings's** *Collected Poems,* **Muriel Rukeyser's** *U. S. 1,* **Delmore Schwartz's** *In Dreams Begin Responsibilities* published

1939
Birth of **Clark Coolidge**; death of **Sigmund Freud; Muriel Rukeyser's** *A Turning Wind* published; **Spanish Civil War ends; World War II begins**

1940
Birth of **Fanny Howe, Angela de Hoyos, Robert Pinsky; Ezra Pound's** *Cantos LII–LXXI,* **Yvor Winters'** *Poems* published

1941
Birth of **Toi Derricotte, Robert Hass, Lyn Hejinian, Simon Ortiz, Tino Villanueva**; death of **Lola Ridge; Marianne Moore's** *What*

Are Years, **Theodore Roethke's** *Open House*, **Louis Zukofsky's** *55 Poems* published; **Pearl Harbor invasion marks the United States's entrance into WWII**

1942
Birth of **Gloria Anzaldúa**, **Haki Mahubuti**, **Sharon Olds**; **Langston Hughes's** *Shakespeare in Harlem*, **Randall Jarrell's** *Blood for a Stranger*, **Wallace Stevens's** *Parts of the World* and *Notes Towards a Supreme Fiction* published

1943
Birth of **Nikki Giovanni**, **Louise Glück**, **Michael Palmer**, **Quincy Troupe**; **T. S. Eliot's** *Four Quartets* published; **Zoot Suit riots in Los Angeles**; **Benito Mussolini forced to resign**

1944
H. D.'s *The Walls Do Not Fall*, **Kenneth Rexroth's** *The Phoenix and the Tortoise*, **Melvin B. Tolson's** *Rendezvous with America* published

1945
Birth of **Alice Notley**, **Anne Waldman**; **Gwendolyn Brooks's** *A Street in Bronzeville*, **Gertrude Stein's** *Wars I Have Seen* published; **Adolf Hitler commits suicide**; **V-E Day – Germany surrenders to Allies, atomic bomb is dropped on Japanese cities of Hiroshima and Nagasaki, Japan surrenders to Allies**

1946
Death of **Countee Cullen**, **Gertrude Stein**; **Elizabeth Bishop's** *North and South*, **Robert Lowell's** *Lord Weary's Castle*, **James Merrill's** *The Black Swan*, **William Carlos Williams's** *Paterson* **(Book I)**, **Louis Zukofsky's** *Anew* published

1947
Birth of **Ai**, **Rae Armantrout**, **Yusef Komunyakaa**, **Nathaniel Mackey**; **Robert Duncan's** *Heavenly City, Earthly City* published; **Jackie Robinson becomes first African-American major league baseball player**

1948
Birth of **Leslie Marmon Silko**; death of **Claude McKay**; **Ezra Pound's** *The Pisan Cantos*, **Theodore Roethke's** *The Lost Son and Other Poems*, **William Carlos Williams's** *Paterson* **(Book II)**, **Louis**

Zukofsky's ***A Test of Poetry*** published; **the United States formally recognizes the state of Israel**

1949
Birth of **Victor Hernandez Cruz, C. D. Wright; Gwendolyn Brooks's** ***Annie Allen*****, Kenneth Rexroth's** ***The Signature of All Things*****, Muriel Rukeyser's** ***The Life of Poetry*****, William Carlos Williams's** ***Paterson*** **(Book III)** published; **USA joins NATO; Mao Zedong proclaims the People's Republic of China**

1950
Birth of **Charles Bernstein, Carolyn Forché**; death of **Edna St Vincent Millay; Charles Olson's "Projective Verse"** published; **Korean War begins when North Korean forces cross the 38th Parallel into South Korea**

1951
Birth of **Gloria Bird, Jorie Graham, Joy Harjo, Garrett Hongo, Tato Laviera, Ray A. Young Bear; Langston Hughes's** ***Montage of A Dream Deferred*****, Robert Lowell's** ***The Mills of the Kavanaughs*****, Adrienne Rich's** ***A Change of World*****, Theodore Roethke's** ***Praise to the End!*****, William Carlos Williams's** ***Paterson*** **(Book IV)** published; **Julius and Ethel Rosenberg are executed**

1952
Birth of **Jimmy Santiago Baca, Rita Dove, David Mura, Gary Soto; Robert Creeley's** ***Le Fou*****, Robert Duncan's** ***Fragments of a Disordered Devotion*****, Frank O'Hara's** ***A City Winter, and Other Poems*****, Kenneth Rexroth's** ***The Dragon and the Unicorn*** published

1953
Birth of **Ana Castillo, Mark Doty**; death of **Edgar Lee Masters; Robert Creeley's** ***The Immoral Proposition*****, Charles Olson's** ***In Cold Hell, In Thicket, The Mayan Letters***, and ***The Maximus Poems 1–10*** published

1954
Birth of **Lorna Dee Cervantes, Sandra Cisneros, Thylias Moss; William Carlos Williams's** ***The Desert Music and Other Poems*** published; **the McCarthy Hearings begin, Brown vs. Board of**

Education case – Supreme Court rules unanimously that segregated schools are unconstitutional

1955
Birth of **Marilyn Chin, Cathy Song**; death of **Weldon Kees, Wallace Stevens; Elizabeth Bishop's** *Poems: North and South – A Cold Spring*, **Emily Dickinson's** *Collected Poems* **(Johnson Edition), Lawrence Ferlinghetti's** *Pictures of the Gone World*, **Adrienne Rich's** *The Diamond Cutters and Other Poems*, **William Carlos Williams's** *Journey to Love* published; **Rosa Parks refuses to give up her seat on a Montgomery, Alabama city bus; AFL-CIO established through merger**

1956
Death of **Carlos Bulosan; John Berryman's** *Homage to Mistress Bradstreet*, **Gregory Corso's** *Gasoline*, **Allen Ginsberg's** *Howl and Other Poems*, **Charles Olson's** *The Maximus Poems 11–21*, **Richard Wilbur's** *Things of this World: Poems* published; **Black Mountain College closes**

1957
Denise Levertov's *Here and Now*, **Wallace Stevens's** *Opus Poshumous* published; **Soviet Union launches Sputnik, first artificial satellite**

1958
Lawrence Ferlinghetti's *A Coney Island of the Mind*, **Theodore Roethke's** *The Waking*, **William Carlos Williams's** *Paterson* **(Book V)** published

1959
Ted Joans's *Jazz Poems*, **Robert Lowell's** *Life Studies*, **Gary Snyder's** *Riprap*, **W. D. Snodgrass's** *Heart's Needle* published; **Fidel Castro defeats Batista**

1960
Robert Duncan's *The Opening of the Field*, **Randall Jarrell's** *The Woman at the Washington Zoo*, **Galway Kinnell's** *What a Kingdom It Was*, **Frank O'Hara's** *Second Avenue*, **Charles Olson's** *The Distances* and *The Maximus Poems (1–22)*, **Sylvia Plath's** *The Colossus* published; **U2 spy plane shot down over Soviet Union, Kennedy and Nixon debates televised**

1961
Death of **H. D. (Hilda Doolittle), Kenneth Fearing; Amiri Baraka's** *Preface to a Twenty Volume Suicide Note,* **Paul Blackburn's** *The Nets,* **John Cage's** *Silence,* **Alan Dugan's** *Poems,* **Allen Ginsberg's** *Kaddish and Other Poems,* **H. D.'s** *Helen in Egypt* published; **Berlin Wall begun, Russian Cosmonaut Yuri Gagarin becomes first human to orbit the earth, USA launches first astronaut, Alan Shepard**

1962
Death of **E. E. Cummings, Robinson Jeffers; John Ashbery's** *The Tennis Court Oath,* **Robert Bly's** *Silence in the Snowy Fields,* **George Oppen's** *The Materials,* **Charles Reznikoff's** *By the Waters of Manhattan: Selected Verse,* **William Carlos Williams's** *Pictures from Brueghel and Other Poems* published; **Cuban Missile Crisis**

1963
Death of **Robert Frost, Sylvia Plath, Theodore Roethke, William Carlos Williams; Amiri Baraka's** *Blues People: Negro Music in White America,* **Allen Ginsberg's** *Reality Sandwiches,* **Adrienne Rich's** *Snapshots of a Daughter-in-Law: Poems, 1954–1962,* **Theodore Roethke's** *Sequence, Sometimes Metaphysical,* **Louis Simpson's** *At the End of the Open Road: Poems,* **William Carlos Williams's** *Paterson: I–V* published; **Martin Luther King Jr. delivers "I Have a Dream" speech, black church in Birmingham, Alabama is bombed, John F. Kennedy assassinated in Dallas**

1964
A. R. Ammons's *Expressions at Sea Level,* **Amiri Baraka's** *The Dead Lecturer,* **John Berryman's** *77 Dream Songs,* **Robert Duncan's** *Roots and Branches,* **Robert Lowell's** *For the Union Dead,* **Frank O'Hara's** *Lunch Poems,* **Charles Reznikoff's** *Testimony* published; **President Johnson signs the Civil Rights Act of 1964, Gulf of Tonkin resolution passed, authorizing aggression against North Vietnamese**

1965
Death of **T. S. Eliot, Randall Jarrell, Jack Spicer; A. R. Ammons's** *Tape for the Turn of the Year,* **Elizabeth Bishop's** *Questions of Travel,* **Charles Olson's** *Human Universe and Other Essays,* **George**

Oppen's *This In Which,* **Sylvia Plath's** *Ariel* published; **USA bombs North Vietnam, Malcolm X assassinated**

1966
Birth of **Sherman Alexie**; death of **Mina Loy, Frank O'Hara, Delmore Schwartz; Adriennne Rich's** *Necessities of Life,* **Robert Duncan's** *Of the War: Passages 22–27* published

1967
Death of **Langston Hughes, Dorothy Parker, Carl Sandburg, Jean Toomer; Paul Blackburn's** *The Cities,* **John Cage's** *A Year from Monday,* **Robert Creeley's** *Words,* **Ed Dorn's** *The North Atlantic Turbine,* **Robert Lowell's** *Near the Ocean* published; **Six-Day War in Israel, the "Summer of Love" in San Francisco, Thurgood Marshall sworn in as first African-American Supreme Court justice**

1968
Death of **Yvor Winters; Robert Duncan's** *Bending the Bow,* **Allen Ginsberg's** *Planet News,* **Galway Kinnell's** *Body Rags,* **Charles Olson's** *The Maximus Poems IV, V, VI,* **George Oppen's** *Of Being Numerous* published; **Martin Luther King Jr. assassinated, Robert Kennedy assassinated**

1969
Death of **Jack Kerouac; James Merrill's** *The Fire Screen,* **N. Scott Momaday's** *The Way to Rainy Mountain* published; **Neil Armstrong, first man to walk on the moon, Woodstock Music Festival**

1970
Death of **Lorine Niedecker, Charles Olson; Amiri Baraka's** *It's Nation Time,* **Robert Duncan's** *Tribunals Passages 31–35,* **Lorine Niedecker's** *My Life by Water: Collected Poems 1936–1968* published

1971
Death of **Paul Blackburn; Jayne Cortez's** *Festivals and Funerals,* **Galway Kinnell's** *The Book of Nightmares,* **Adrienne Rich's** *The Will to Change: Poems, 1968–1970,* **Jerome Rothenberg's** *Poems for the Game of Silence* published; **New York Times prints first installment of the Pentagon Papers, Nixon visits China**

1972
Death of **John Berryman**, **Marianne Moore**, **Kenneth Patchen**, **Ezra Pound**; **A. R. Ammons's** *Collected Poems 1951–1971*, **David Antin's** *Talking*, **Michael Palmer's** *Blake's Newton*, **Syvia Plath's** *Winter Trees*, **Louis Zukofsky's** *"A" 24* published; **Israeli athletes held hostage at Munich Olympics**

1973
Death of **Conrad Aiken**, **W. H. Auden**, **Arna Bontemps**; **John Cage's** *M*, **Nikki Giovanni's** *Black Judgment*, **Robert Lowell's** *History*, *Lizzie and Harriet*, and *The Dolphin*, **Adrienne Rich's** *Diving into the Wreck: Poems, 1971–1972* published; **Watergate Hearings**, **oil embargo**

1974
Death of **John Crowe Ransom**, **Miguel Piñero**, **Anne Sexton**; **A. R. Ammons's** *Sphere*, **Jerome Rothenberg's** *Poland/1931*, **Gary Snyder's** *Turtle Island*, **Diane Wakoski's** *Trilogy* published; **President Nixon resigns and is pardoned by President Ford**

1975
John Ashbery's *Self-Portrait in a Convex Mirror*, **Ed Dorn's** *Slinger*, **Louise Glück's** *The House on Marshland*, **Susan Howe's** *Chanting at the Crystal Sea*, **Charles Olson's** *The Maximus Poems, Volume Three*, **Robert Pinsky's** *Sadness and Happiness* published; **Vietnam War ends**

1976
Death of **Charles Reznikoff**; **David Antin's** *talking at the boundaries*, **Charles Bernstein's** *Parsing*, **Elizabeth Bishop's** *Geography III*, **James Merrill's** *Divine Comedies* published

1977
Death of **Robert Lowell**; **Jayne Cortez's** *Mouth on Paper*, **Robert Lowell's** *Day By Day* published

1978
Death of **Louis Zukofsky**; **Lawrence Ferlinghetti's** *Landscapes of Living and Dying*, **Allen Ginsberg's** *Mind Breaths: Poems 1971–1976*, **Lyn Hejinian's** *Writing is an Aid to Memory*, **Susan Howe's** *Secret History of the Dividing Line*, **Audre Lorde's** *The*

Black Unicorn, **James Merrill's** *Mirabell: Books of Number*, **Charles Reznikoff's** *Testimony: The United States 1885–1915* **(complete edition)**, **Jerome Rothenberg's** *A Seneca Journal* published

1979
Death of **Elizabeth Bishop**, **Allen Tate**; **Jimmy Santiago Baca's** *Immigrants in Our Own Land*, **John Cage's** *Empty Words*, **Ana Castillo's** *The Invitation*, **Yusef Komunyakaa's** *Lost in the Bonewheel Factory* published; **Accident at Three Mile Island nuclear power plant**

1980
Death of **Robert Hayden**, **James Wright**; **Charles Bernstein's** *Controlling Interests*, **Louise Gluck's** *Descending Figure*, **Lyn Hejinian's** *My Life*, **Audre Lorde's** *The Cancer Journals* published

1981
John Ashbery's *Shadow Trains*, **William Bronk's** *Life Supports*, **Michael Palmer's** *Notes for Echo Lake* published; **Sandra Day O'Connor confirmed as first female Supreme Court justice**

1982
Death of **Archibald MacLeish**; **Charles Bukowski's** *Love is a Dog from Hell*, **Jayne Cortez's** *Firespitter*, **Susan Howe's** *Pythagorean Silence*, **James Merrill's** *The Changing Light at Sandover*, **Alicia Ostriker's** *A Woman Under the Surface* published

1983
John Cage's *X*, **Robert Duncan's** *Ground Work: Before the War*, **Charles Olson's** *The Maximus Poems* **complete edition** published.

1984
Death of **George Oppen**, **Tomás Rivera**; **David Antin's** *tuning*, **Ana Castillo's** *Women Are Not Roses*, **Yusef Komunyakaa's** *Copacetic*, **Michael Palmer's** *First Figure*, **Sonia Sanchez's** *homegirls and handgrenades* published

1985
Charles Bernstein's *Content's Dream*, **James Merrill's** *Late Settings*, **Marge Piercy's** *My Mother's Body* published

1986
Death of **Bob Kaufman**, **John Ciardi**; **Yusef Komunyakaa's** *I Apologize for the Eyes in My Head*, **Audre Lorde's** *Our Dead Behind Us* published

1987
Sandra Cisneros's *My Wicked, Wicked Ways*, **Robert Duncan's** *Ground Work II: In The Dark* published; **Wall Street stock market crash**, **Iran-Contra hearings**

1988
Death of **Robert Duncan**, **Miguel Piñero**; **Ana Castillo's** *My Father Was a Toltec: Poems*, **Yusef Komunyakaa's** *Dien Cai Dau*, **Michael Palmer's** *Sun* published

1989
Death of **Sterling Brown**, **Robert Penn Warren**; **Jimmy Santiago Baca's** *Black Mesa Poems*, **N. Scott Momaday's** *The Ancient Child*, **Jerome Rothenberg's** *Khurbn & Other Poems* published; **Exxon Valdez oil spill**, **USA invades Panama**, **Berlin Wall comes down**

1990
Louise Glück's *Ararat*, **Susan Howe's** *Singularities* published; **Iraq invades Kuwait**

1991
Death of **Laura (Riding) Jackson**, **Etheridge Knight**, **James Schuyler**; **Charles Bernstein's** *Rough Trades*, **Lyn Hejinian's** *Oxota: A Short Russian Novel* published; **Gulf War**

1992
Death of **John Cage**, **Audre Lorde**; **Jimmy Santiago Baca's** *Working in the Dark*, **Charles Bernstein's** *A Poetics*, **Lyn Hejinian's** *The Cell*, **Yusef Komunyakaa's** *Magic City* published

1993
Death of **William Stafford**; **David Antin's** *what it means to be avant-garde*, **Sherman Alexie's** *I Would Steal Horses* published; **NAFTA passed**

1994
Death of **Charles Bukowski**, **William Everson**, **Mary Tallmountain**; **Charles Bernstein's** *Dark City*, **Lyn Hejinian's** *The Cold of Poetry* published

1996
Death of **Larry Eigner**; **Sherman Alexie's** *Water Flowing Home*, **Jayne Cortez's** *Somewhere in Advance of Nowhere* published

1997
Death of **Allen Ginsberg**, **David Ignatow**, **Denise Levertov**

1999
Death of **William Bronk**, **Ed Dorn**

2000
Death of **Gwendolyn Brooks**

Introduction

Stephen Fredman

In the twenty-first century, when US poetry is being read and taught around the globe, it becomes crucial to present readers with the major contexts for situating the poetry and for appreciating the issues to which it responds. Although there have been many studies of the contexts of American poetry prior to World War II, this book innovates by giving a view of the entire century's poetry and its concerns. Each chapter, commissioned specifically for this volume, explores a particular context, such as feminism, visual art, philosophy, or immigration, discussing how its topic evolves over the course of the century and how the poetry responds to it. This allows the contributors to compare and contrast poetry from various points in the century, while maintaining a balance between outlining a context and engaging in commentary on individual poems. A signal feature of the volume is the overlapping that occurs among the essays: the discussion of poets and poems in different contexts makes apparent the multidimensional nature of poetic engagements with the world. Each essay concludes with suggestions for further reading and the volume includes a chronology of major events and publication dates.

Although poetry had been composed in the geographical area that became the United States for hundreds of years by Native Americans, and since the seventeenth century by European immigrants and African captives, it wasn't until the nineteenth century, in the throes of creating a nation-state after the Revolutionary War, that writers set out to produce a specifically "American" poetry. The loudest call came from Ralph Waldo Emerson in a number of his essays, especially in "The Poet," where he observed that "the experience of each new age requires a new confession, and the world seems always waiting for its poet" (Emerson, 1983, p. 450). In Emerson's view, the poet that America was waiting for would have an entirely new subject matter, for "Our log-rolling, our stumps and their politics, our fisheries, our Negroes, and Indians, our boasts, and our repudiations, the wrath of rogues, and the pusillanimity of honest men, the Northern trade, the Southern planting, the western clearing, Oregon and Texas, are yet unsung. Yet," he rhapsodizes, "America is a poem in our eyes; its ample geography dazzles the imagination; and it will not wait long for metres" (p. 465). In 1844 this claim for America's fitness as poetic material was sheer prophecy, but already by 1855 the waiting ceased when Walt Whitman published the first edition of *Leaves of Grass*, whose central poem, "Song of Myself," invented a national "self" that was at once an expression of individual experience and a witness to the geographical, social, sexual, racial, and occupational diversity of the expanding nation. Emerson as thinker and Whitman as poet represent two indispensable voices in the formation of an American poetry, voices heard loud and clear by other poets throughout the next century-and-a-half. The other indispensable nineteenth-century poet who followed in Emerson's wake was Emily Dickinson. Less concerned, perhaps, with creating a national self than Emerson or Whitman, she has had nonetheless a profound impact upon poets in the second half of the twentieth century through her pyrotechnic use of language and her probing explorations of the most intimate and most cosmic of dilemmas.

The desire to create a national literature is not enough to guarantee that such a literature will arise, and even if it does it won't happen overnight. With the older European states as its only models for national culture, the new United States craved self-sufficiency but felt itself at a distinct disadvantage because of its very newness. The key ingredient for creating culture that the nation lacked was tradition – in fact, defiance of tradition was one of its hallmarks. Without a tradition built up over centuries of common experience, though, the new poem comes into a seemingly barren world unprepared to accept it; William Carlos Williams portrays this condition symbolically in "Spring and All" (1922) when he writes of human and seasonal birth, "They enter the new world naked,/ cold, uncertain of all/ save that they enter." The barrenness of American culture has been an abiding concern for its poets, who feel chilled to the bone when they enter it and find no ready ground cultivated to accept them. Wherever their ancestors came from and no matter how long they or their families have been resident in the United States, American poets have not had the status accorded poets in more traditional societies, where the foundational importance of poetry is taken for granted, its centrality to the national character guaranteed. In every generation, starting with Emerson, American poets exhibit an anxious need to invent American poetry, as though it had never existed before. This very need to invent, to attempt a new cultural grounding, has become one of the hallmarks of the poetry, which is always trying to explain itself to readers or trying to find analogies to other cultural practices that will grant it legitimacy.

For American poetry, then, an understanding of its cultural location is absolutely crucial. The poetry, no matter how brilliantly accomplished, cannot stand on its own because it has not yet occupied the position of national centrality to which it aspires. The present volume gives readers the tools for "placing" twentieth-century American poetry, for understanding the cultural work it does and the cultural milieus of which it partakes. The 12 chapters can be divided into three groups. The first three chapters consider the struggle to create a national mission for poetry, looking at its relations to war, to British poetry, and to the academy. The next six chapters set the poetry into a variety of the social worlds it both arises from and addresses: feminism, the queer city, New York art, the blues, immigration and migrancy, and communism and anticommunism. The last three chapters place the poetry within the world of ideas, showing how it stands in relation to mysticism, science and technology, and philosophy and theory.

This book chooses to engage the entire century, rather than its first or second half, out of a conviction that the issues faced by American poets during this time have not changed very much. The subject matter of each of the chapters is as pertinent to the late century as it is to the early century, and there is much to be gained by taking a synoptic view rather than one that divides the century and its poetry into modern and postmodern periods. The standard narrative of the literary history of twentieth-century American poetry posits a time of radical innovation in the first two decades, fatefully truncated by World War I; a consolidation of gains during the twenties; a detour into political activism in the thirties and early forties; a final flowering of the great modernists after World War II; a postmodern break with the modernists beginning in the fifties; a poetic response to war again in the sixties; and from the seventies onward the rise and consolidation of three trends – the creative writing workshop, the "identity" poetries (feminist, racial, and ethnic), and the Language Poetry movement with its commitment to theory. This narrative awards primacy to a select circle of modernist poets – Robert Frost, Gertrude Stein, Ezra Pound, T. S. Eliot, H. D., William Carlos Williams, Wallace Stevens, and Marianne Moore – and views everyone who emerges simultaneously or subsequently as deriving from these masters. By taking the long view of the century, we can see that these poets derive their primacy not necessarily from an incommensurable greatness but from having been the first poets to confront the social contexts that would continue to obtain for US poets throughout the century, such as the terrors of modern warfare, the transformative power of science and technology, the rise of feminism and of queer urban enclaves, the shocks of competing ideologies, the radical discoveries of modern art, and the pull of mystical religions and modern philosophies.

What these early modernists were disdainful of, or just plain blind to, were many of the social shifts in population occurring in the United States and their cultural impact: the Northern migration of African Americans to the cities and the attendant burst of creativity during periods such as the Harlem Renaissance and the Black Arts movement; and the repeated waves of immigration to the United States, with entirely new populations bringing their former traditions into the American poetry they created. The critics who have made the modernists and the period around World War I central to the literary history of the twentieth century have also overlooked to a surprising extent the crucial fulcrum that World War II has been for American culture. Rather than seeing the war as merely a dividing line between modernism and postmodernism, we need to recognize the extent to which this devastating war changed American life. When we take into account the four hundred thousand Americans killed in the war and combine that with the unending impact of the Holocaust and the atomic bombings, World War II emerges as the central trauma of the century for the United States, casting a shadow upon the political, emotional, and linguistic resources of the poetry of the second half of the century in ways still to be fully articulated. And of course the other outcome of the war was a regnant United States, a superpower in an entirely new relationship of increasing dominance with respect to the rest of the world. By looking at the entire century of American poetry and the compelling contexts in which it was written, we can begin to give a more balanced assessment of the poetry and a clearer account of how it fits into the world.

In the first chapter of our study, "Wars I Have Seen," Peter Nicholls points out how instrumental wars have been in creating and constituting nationhood. During the twentieth century, the language of war became increasingly in the United States the language of the state – a purposefully confusing and self-justifying Orwellian rhetoric that poets have identified and analyzed and sought to counter with their own linguistic means. In response to World War I, poets such as Ezra Pound, E. E. Cummings, and Archibald MacLeish employed distanced ironies to deplore the high-flown rhetoric that led so many innocents to their death. The poets of World War II began to write of a phenomenon that has continued to occupy poets of the Vietnam War and subsequent wars, which involves another kind of distance – that of pilots in bombers or civilians in front of television screens, observing murderous destruction in a weird air of unreality.

If war has applied one kind of nearly constant pressure to the language of American poetry, then British poetry can be seen as applying a similarly ubiquitous pressure on the self-conception of American poetry, for British poetry represents the tradition of English-language poetry to which US poets are always comparing themselves. David Herd, in "Pleasures at Home: How Twentieth-Century American Poets Read the British," discusses the centrality of Emerson in defining an independent American poetry by borrowing British Romantic terms. Emerson created a Romantic image of American culture founded in innocence and optimism, connected spiritually with nature, and guided by the Poet, whose imaginative capacity makes him (or her) the great interpreter of experience and the prophetic proponent of the culture's values. Emerson not only aligned American poetry with British and German Romantic tenets, he also proposed that US poets become original "readers" of British poetry, creatively turning against it for their own purposes, and thus inaugurated a line of revisionist reading that continues into the present. Herd shows how twentieth-century poets have followed Emerson both by creative appropriation from British poetry and by resisting it through severe revisionist readings.

The third chapter to look at the general situation of US poetry, Alan Golding's "American Poet-Teachers and the Academy," investigates the ambivalent dealings poets have had with universities, one of the most important sites of reception, evaluation, and increasingly production of modern poetry. The great nineteenth-century figures Emerson, Whitman, and Dickinson all disdained the restrictions of "school" and the institutional inculcation of knowledge. During the twentieth century, many poets sought to use the classroom to pass on to other poets and readers their notions of craft and their attitudes toward poetry and culture. Golding discusses the most critical moments in the relationship of poetry to the academy, beginning with Ezra Pound's alternative to the academy, the "Ezuversity," conducted both in person and via letters and essays, and continuing through the Fugitives, who governed the reading of poetry for half a century with their New Criticism, Charles Olson's avant-garde academy at Black Mountain College after World War II, the anthology wars of the sixties, the resistance to the academy by African-American poets, and the concentration of poetry within the academy in the last three decades of the century through creative writing workshops and poet-theorists.

The first of the chapters to focus upon social contexts for the poetry is Lynn Keller and Cristanne Miller's "Feminism and the Female Poet," which gives a rich and detailed survey of women's writing and of the feminist issues to which it responds. Keller and Miller point out how active women poets in the United States were in the birth of modernism and how closely involved these same poets were with social issues and gender politics. Women poets criticized the "feminine" stereotypes of the age, portraying as beautiful such qualities as toughness, harshness, intellectuality, and thorniness. Because women poets were active in social and racial causes during the Depression, and then women worked in factories during World War II, the isolation and conformism that set in after the war had severe consequences both for political feminism and for women poets. With the rebirth of the women's movement in the sixties, feminist poets such as Adrienne Rich came to the fore, embodying the new slogan that "the personal is political."

The exploration of the lives of women poets and the communities they created is picked up in Maria Damon's "Queer Cities," particularly with reference to Paris, but also in the two other cities that Damon considers in depth, New York and San Francisco. Because the United States was not hospitable to queer communities in the early part of the century, Paris became the central venue for lesbian coteries in particular. New York had multiple queer cultures, from the Harlem Renaissance through the New York School and the Beats, and San Francisco has also been home to the Beats, the San Francisco Renaissance, the Gay Liberation poets, and ethnic queer poets. In addition to discussing the queer poetry scenes, Damon posits a tradition in American poetry of the urban queer national epic, reaching from

Whitman's *Leaves of Grass* to Hart Crane's "The Bridge," Gertrude Stein's *The Making of Americans,* Allen Ginsberg's "Howl" and "Wichita Vortex Sutra," Rich's "Atlas of a Difficult World," Robert Duncan's "Passages," and Tony Kushner's *Angels in America*.

Brian Reed, in "Twentieth-Century Poetry and the New York Art World," focuses upon one city, New York, in order to consider the ways in which the restless experimentation of its visual art provided a goad to experimentation in poetry, as well as discussing how it hosted an appreciative intellectual community in which poetry could flourish alongside art, music, dance, and theater. Poets influenced by the New York art scene have moved past the standard model of the lyric poem as the heightened utterance of an individual speaker in order to try a great variety of linguistic experiments. The successive breakthroughs of Dada – with its blurring of distinctions between art and the world; of Surrealism – with its techniques of automatic writing and random visual composition; of Abstract Expressionism – with its gestural spontaneous style; of John Cage's revolutionary use of chance in composing music and poetry; and of the further intrusions into daily life of Conceptual and Performance Art – all these breakthroughs provided fertile examples and encouragement to experimental poets both within and beyond New York City.

New York has also provided poets with aesthetic models through acting as home to the performance of blues and jazz. Rowan Ricardo Phillips, in "The Blue Century: Brief Notes on Twentieth-Century African-American Poetry," shows how the example of the blues as aesthetic object, and the blues singer and jazz instrumentalist as spokespersons for African-American experience and as emblems of its achievements, have had a profound effect upon African-American poetry during the century. Drawing attention to how at the turn of the century Paul Dunbar prepares in his dialect poems for an incorporation of the oral element of the blues, Phillips goes on to show how poets such as Langston Hughes, Sterling Brown, Robert Hayden, Gayl Jones, Yusef Komunyakaa, and Michael Harper make use of this oral element, with its extensive repetition and its empathic connection to an audience, in creating poetry that addresses the aesthetic and social needs of African Americans at specific moments during this tumultuous century.

African-American poetry is one of the ethnic poetries treated in A. Robert Lee's "Home and Away: US Poetries of Immigration and Migrancy." Lee points to immigration as the central social fact of US culture, and contends that the timelines of immigration and internal migration are the central memories mined by much of American poetry. In the United States, Europeans met native peoples, Asians met Mexicans and other Latin Americans, and peoples of the Caribbean met other former African slaves. Within the United States there is also a history of constant migration – of Europeans and Asians crossing the continent in opposite directions, of Native Americans marched in forced migrations to reservations, and of African Americans flooding northward in the Great Migration. Among poets of European descent, Lee focuses upon the immigrant poetries of German Americans, Irish Americans, Italian Americans, and Jewish Americans; he draws comparisons to these poetries when discussing the immigrant and migrant poetries of Asian Americans, Chicanos, Puerto Ricans, Cubans, African Americans, and Native Americans.

Much of ethnic poetry is characterized by political radicalism, for ethnic poets have taken an active role in attempting to secure the rights and welfare of those with whom they identify and often of other stereotyped and oppressed peoples as well, causing them to participate in large-scale political movements such as those chronicled by Alan Filreis in "Modern Poetry and Anticommunism." Filreis notes that there were eras during the century when political poetry was celebrated and others when it was shunned, with the thirties being the prime example of the former and the fifties of the latter. From the vantage point of the fifties, whose perspective has not yet fully been superseded, anyone who wrote with ideological confidence and explicitness was by definition "antipoetic." Filreis demonstrates that modernist experimental form and radical political critique were not inimical to one another in the thirties, as the anticommunists of the fifties contended, but that these two qualities could be very effective participants in an exploratory poetry that speaks to social issues.

The ideological contention outlined in Filreis's chapter makes a useful transition to the concerns of the last three chapters, which focus upon the ways American poets have situated themselves with reference to religious, scientific, and philosophical ideas. In "Mysticism: Neo-paganism, Buddhism, and Christianity," I look at the three most prevalent forms of mysticism among American poets, asking why mysticism has appealed to so many poets. There are a variety of answers. One is that mystical beliefs question so many of the basic tenets held by a capitalistic, rationalistic, mechanistic American society and that mysticism proposes instead countercultural criticisms, values, and lifestyles. A second answer is that occult symbols offer poets many-layered objects with great potential for poetic use; Kabbalah, the Jewish occult system, for example, places tremendous magical efficacy in words and even in letters. Thirdly, mysticism lends an esoteric stance to much of the avant-garde US poetry, whose various movements often require of readers a kind of initiation before being able to comprehend the poetry.

Another form of knowledge that requires initiation is science, the subject of Peter Middleton's "Poets and Scientists." Since science is the most prestigious form of knowledge in our era, poets must take cognizance of it, either by trying to imitate it in some way or by proposing, as the poets engaged with mysticism do, alternative ways of knowing; some poets do both. The poetic responses to science that Middleton recounts run a gamut from alluding to its theories and inventions by way of images and metaphors, to engaging in close "scientific" observation, to trying to imitate science by performing experiments and offering theory through poetry, to finding poetic equivalents for what it feels like to live in the new world the physical and biological sciences have opened up, to finally responding negatively to science as soul-deadening, as complicit in war and destruction, or as ideologically driven.

Mystical and scientific scrutiny of language have been significant contributors toward the philosophical preoccupation with language as an object in twentieth-century American poetry. In "Philosophy and Theory in US Modern Poetry" Michael Davidson notes how modern poetry places a value on words as pure force or nondiscursive object, thus joining with modern philosophy in an obsession with discovering the powers and limits of language. Mounting a full-scale synopsis of poetry's relationship with philosophy and theory during the century, Davidson notes four particular moments of philosophical crisis. The first was early in the century when the question of solipsism, the relation of the "I" to other minds and to the objects of the world, was especially pressing. The second moment was the crisis of capitalism during the Great Depression, which placed Marxism and populism in the forefront of poetic concerns. The third crisis was that of the "linguistic turn," which posited the made-up nonessential nature of the words and concepts we employ and called into question the notion of "voice" in poetry and the sense of a unitary "I." At the century's end a "cultural turn" occurred, which examines the cultural placement of the poet and celebrates concepts like hybridity, diaspora, performance, collaboration, signifyin(g), and electronic virtuality.

The rich mix of topics and poets discussed in this book gives a multifaceted introduction to one of the most exciting and influential bodies of literature written during the last century. A companion of this size cannot, however, cover every possible topic of interest to twentieth-century American poets, nor can it even mention all of the worthy poets among the thousands published during the century – let alone consider in great depth the work of any one particular poet. Instead, we hope to provide provocative readings of poems and their contexts that will equip and motivate readers for further exploration.

Reference

Emerson, Ralph Waldo (1983). "The Poet." In Joel Porte (ed.), *Essays and Lectures*. New York: Library of America, pp. 445–68.

Chapter 1

Wars I Have Seen

Peter Nicholls

Early in 2003, Sam Hamill, poet and editor of Copper Canyon Press, was one of a number of writers invited by the President's wife Laura Bush to a symposium on "Poetry and the American Voice." Mrs Bush intended the gathering to discuss and celebrate the "American voices" of Walt Whitman, Langston Hughes, and Emily Dickinson. Hamill wasn't alone in the disgust he felt at the timing of this event so soon after the President's announced policy of "Shock and Awe" against Iraq. He quickly composed a letter to "Friends and Fellow Poets" in which he asked writers to register their opposition to the war by contributing a poem to his website. In the space of not more than a month, he had received 13,000 poems. From his huge electronic manuscript, Hamill quarried the contents of a condensed anthology, *Poets Against the War*, published later that year. As it happened, Hamill wasn't the only one to enlist poetry for this purpose; the same year saw the publication of Todd Swift's *100 Poets Against the War* of which its publisher, Salt, claims that it "holds the record for the fastest poetry anthology ever assembled and disseminated; first planned on January 20, 2003 and published in this form on March 3, 2003."

These two projects alone tell us a lot about the level of animus directed against Bush and his bellicose supporters, but they also raise some interesting questions about the means adopted to channel this feeling. Certainly, the response to Hamill's email circular is surprising for the sheer volume of contributions it produced, but at the same time *not* so surprising, perhaps, in its choice of poetry as the appropriate vehicle of public dissent. For poetry, while increasingly a marginalized medium, is still popularly regarded as an appropriate, sometimes even a therapeutic, response to certain types of widely felt political outrage. And war has always seemed to occasion poetry as both its compensation and its negative reflection. Indeed, the respective languages of war and poetry have been bound together in interacting cycles of attraction and repulsion. On the one hand, the poetic idiom presents itself as more accurate, more authentic, more expressive of those human values so systematically trampled on in war; on the other hand, it is poetry which has so regularly been ransacked for the memorable tropes of political demagogy. This is the "High Diction" of which Paul Fussell speaks in his seminal *The Great War and Modern Memory* (1975), and while there is little significant twentieth-century American poetry in the heroic mode after the World War I writings of Alan Seeger and Joyce Kilmer, we do find that American political rhetoric is increasingly dependent on the tropes of a phoney poetic sublime: Shock and Awe, the threat of "an attack/ that will unleash upon Iraq// levels of force that have never been/ imagined before, much less seen" (quoted in Geoff Brock's poem "Poetry & the American Voice" in Hamill 2003: 42), the promise of "unbelievable" force in the lead-up to the attack on Fallujah, and so on. Increasingly, US military operations have been given not the random names they had previously received, but names associating hyperbolic cosmic force with absolute rightness: Urgent Fury (Grenada), Just Cause (Panama), Desert Storm (the Gulf), Instant Thunder (the air operation in the Gulf), Infinite Justice (Afghanistan), and Enduring Freedom (the war on terror) (Sieminski 1995). These are, we might say, pseudo-performatives which cultivate the apocalyptic tone to conflate means and ends.

There is something at once risible and deadly in the use of such language. As a version of Orwellian "doublespeak," this deployment of words to project final desired outcomes – victory, conciliation – while at the same time hinting in its transitivity at the force needed to achieve them has created a mechanically rationalistic language in which American agency works apparently selflessly and with great scruple to achieve what is now called in a wonderfully circular phrase "preemptive defense." There is no attempt to conceal the serpentine movements of government "logic" here, for you are either inside this discourse or not, and the surgically drawn line that divides those sectors is almost childishly plain. In April 2003, for example, Bush visited wounded soldiers from the war in Iraq: "I reminded them and their families," he said, "that the war in Iraq is really about peace"

(Stauber and Rampton 2003). Only a little massaging was needed here – Bush's tactful "reminder" to these damaged troops and his insidiously persuasive "really" – to elide the gap between war and peace. It is often said that in contrast to earlier statesmen it is not this President's tabletalk that is prized but rather his many blunders and slips. At the same time, though, there is a growing realization that this use of "empty language," as one commentator in *The Nation* recently called it, might reveal strategy rather than gullibility (Brooks 2003).

In reading such speeches, one is likely to experience a kind of linguistic claustrophobia. This is a discourse hermetically sealed; it has no outside and renders itself impervious to any kind of test. And if the verbal sleight of hand is more perceptible when it comes to telling us that war is "really" about peace, it seems increasingly the case that wartime discourse is "really" little different from peacetime discourse. War, it seems, is continuous and unrelenting, confirming Emmanuel Levinas's proposition that "The peace of empires issued from war rests on war" (Levinas 1969: 22). In other words – and this seems to me a perception of particular relevance to the poets I shall discuss here – "the state and war are structurally inseparable." It's hardly a novel idea: Daniel Pick, whose phrase this is, traces it to Hegel for whom, he says, "The state is not the alternative to war, but the formation which could only be realized in war. It is in war that a state constitutes itself as subject" (Pick 1993: 234). Twentieth-century American fiction, of course, has been fascinated with variations on this axiom, projecting surreal fantasies of paranoia and conspiracy, and in some cases (Thomas Pynchon's *Vineland*, for example) suggesting that the American state is actually at war with its own citizens. The poets' approach to these questions has necessarily been different, though Allen Ginsberg's *Howl* (1956) is there to remind us of a parallel vision of America as war zone, with those who were "burned alive in their innocent flannel suits on Madison Avenue amid blasts of leaden verse & the tanked-up clatter of the iron regiments of fashion and the nitroglycerine shrieks of the fairies of advertising & the mustard gas of sinister intelligent editors, or were run down by the drunken taxicabs of Absolute Reality" (Ginsberg 1995: 129).

The great images of *Howl* are images of confinement and enclosure – "the crossbone soulless jailhouse and Congress of sorrows . . . Robot apartments! Invisible suburbs! Skeleton treasuries! Blind capitals! Demonic industries! Spectral nations! Invincible mad-houses! Granite cocks! Monstrous bombs!" (Ginsberg 1995: 131–2). Ginsberg's "howl" is against not only these literal spaces of miserable confinement, but against a closed language which can be broken open only by something as primitive and inchoate as a howl. And by closure here I mean exactly what Roland Barthes meant when he wrote of totalitarianism as a world in which:

> *definition*, that is to say the separation between Good and Evil, becomes the sole content of all language, there are no more words without values attached to them, so that finally the function of writing is to cut out one stage of a process: there is no more lapse of time between naming and judging, and the closed character of language is perfected, since in the last analysis it is a value which is given as explanation of another value. (Barthes 1968: 24)

If we tend to associate developments in American poetry, from Modernism through the New American Poetry to Language Poetry, with the discovery of a variously conceived "open form," then surely one way to understand the urgency of this is in relation to an evolving war-speak which has become, increasingly, a more continuously spoken state-speak. This circular rhetoric first came into its own during the Vietnam conflict. Describing it as a language "self-enclosed in finality," poet Thomas Merton observed that "One of the most curious things about the war in Vietnam is that it is being fought to vindicate the assumptions upon which it is being fought" (Merton 1969: 113, 114–15). With a language that is also, as Jeffrey Walsh puts it, "heavy with nouns, bloated with abstractions, and swarmed over with polysyllables" (Walsh 1982: 216), we are likely to miss the simple moves by which opposites conjoin and responsibility is displaced.

When public language becomes openly deceptive and self-legitimating it is inevitable that a gulf will open up between political rhetoric and an apparently more authentic literary language. Especially in time of war, "poetry" seems to offer itself as a medium which by its very nature occupies some sort of higher moral ground, gesturing toward the cultural values presently threatened by the forces of barbarism. The idea of poetry as a means by which we *see* things more clearly, in an ethical light, is closely linked to the conception of poetic language as a medium capable of freeing us from the tautological confinement of war-speak. If poetry allows us to penetrate the dense "fog of war," to borrow the title of Errol Morris's very pertinent movie, it is arguably because it makes available a particular type of thinking which counters that of war – poetic thinking, we might say, recalling Heidegger's distinction between "essential" and "calculative" modes. Of course, much of the poetry written about war never attains that level, remaining trapped in the same kind of binary logic as the war-speak it opposes. This is probably why irony has proved such an important resource to poets dealing with this kind of subject matter, for irony may at once invert a system of conventional values and seem to position the poet outside it. Certainly, in the small amount of poetry produced by American poets about World War I, irony was a dominant mode. One thinks, of course, of Pound's "Hugh Selwyn Mauberley", with its corrosive elegy to "a myriad" who died "For an old bitch gone in the teeth,/ For a botched civilization" (Pound 1990: 188), and of E. E. Cummings' parody of war-speak:

> "why talk of beauty what could be more beaut-
> iful than these heroic happy dead
> who rushed like lions to the roaring slaughter
> they did not stop to think they died instead
> then shall the voice of liberty be mute?"
>
> He spoke. And drank rapidly a glass of water. (Cummings 1968: 268)

Different types of venom are expressed here, but in each case irony seems the only effective response to the degraded language of the "liars in public places," as Pound calls them, whose rhetoric of phoney sublimity, leeched from the classics, drives the innocent toward slaughter. Archibald MacLeish's fine poem "Memorial Rain," an elegy for his brother, similarly frames political rhetoric, weaving between the words of the US Ambassador to France and an evocation of the landscape in which the poet's brother is buried. We hear alternately the Ambassador and the poet:

> – Dedicates to them
> This earth their bones have hallowed, this last gift
> A grateful country –
>
> Under the dry grass stem
> The words are blurred, are thickened, the words sift
> Confused by the rasp of the wind, by the thin grating
> Of ants under the grass, the minute shift
> And tumble of dusty sand separating
> From dusty sand. The roots of the grass strain,
> Tighten, the earth is rigid, waits – he is waiting . . .
> (MacLeish 1933: 135–6)

Each of these poems seeks in different ways to show the limits of political rhetoric and each speaks at a temporal distance from the war. In each, the writer is powerfully aware of the way that poetry and the rhetoric of war have shamefully consorted in the past, and the result is a kind of antipoetic mode, Pound forcing the elegant epigrammatic form of *Mauberley* to spit out contemptuously the "old men's lies," while Cummings mocks the pentameter (splitting "beaut-iful" across two lines, for example), and MacLeish evokes an uncompromisingly harsh antipastoral. A certain distance is necessary, it seems, if poetry is to be wrenched away from the state which customarily embraces it in time of war. And a certain distance is needed, too, if the war is to be clearly *seen* for what it is. Pound, for example, an expatriate and noncombatant, published *Cathay* in 1915, using the late Ernest Fenollosa's notes to create poems like "Song of the Bowmen of Shu" and "Lament of the Frontier Guard," poems which exhibit, as Hugh Kenner long ago remarked, "a sensibility responsive to torn Belgium and disrupted London" (Kenner 1971: 202). These are poems of distances and "desolate fields" (Pound 1990: 137), which powerfully evoke the loneliness and disorientation of war even as they take their models from a remote and ancient culture.

The poems of *Cathay* certainly remain, as Kenner says, "among the most durable of all poetic responses to World War I," though Pound's sweeping chronological detour would never again seem quite appropriate to the challenge of writing about war. Indeed, with World War II, it was the very question of distancing which became for many writers a primary concern. How and from where do we see a war? This is one of the conundrums posed by Gertrude Stein's *Wars I Have Seen*, first published in 1945. It's a title quite devoid of hyperbole: Stein was born in 1874, and her lifetime, as she reminds us, spanned the Spanish–American War, the Russo-Japanese War, the Boer War, the Chinese–Japanese War, the two Balkan wars, the Abyssinian War, the Spanish Civil War, as well as the two world wars (Stein 1945: 43, 64, 72). Enough wars, certainly, to give the observer some authority, though, as she says, "It is funny about wars, they ought to be different but they are not" (p. 11). Stein's title neatly addresses itself to the problems attached to writing about war. Wars *I* Have Seen – it's a point of view at once relative and self-emphasizing, at once involved and detached. Stein is as suspicious of the first person plural, the national "we," as she is of what Malcolm Cowley had called the "spectatorial attitudes" of some of those who had written about World War I (Cowley 1934: 38). In Stein's case, though, the "seeing" is being done by someone apparently immersed in domestic routine – "Yesterday," she says, "I went my usual twelve kilometres to get some bread and cake" (p. 137) – but someone who is also able to reflect on the ways in which the present war has "put an end an entire end to the nineteenth century" (p. 20). The faux-naïf simplicity of Stein's style perfectly catches the unreality of wartime existence, with quirky observations undermining conventional wisdoms: so, for example, she tells us that America is "the oldest country in the world and the reason why was that she was the first country to enter into the twentieth century" (p. 257); and she ponders, too, "how nice it will be to have those happy days come back when vegetables grew not in the ground but in tins" (p. 39).

These playful inversions of logic are crucial to Stein's way of seeing war. For if we have finally "killed" the nineteenth century, as she puts it (p. 16), that means that we are no longer tied to the obviousness of literary realism and can begin to understand that "life is not real it is not earnest, it is strange which is an entirely different matter" (p. 44). Stein draws a distinction between World War I, which, she says, belongs to the nineteenth century and has a "legendary" aspect, and World War II which is not "legendary" at all (p. 20; see also Rose 1993: 16–18). Her way of then projecting this as a parallel distinction between conventional literary realism and modernist "strangeness" might strike us initially as perverse. The point, though, is that Stein sees war by writing about it, which is very different from seeing war *and then* writing about it. It is not so much the local perceptions of wartime experience that matter – though these are acutely registered – but the way in which Stein's language challenges at a minutely local level the logical machinations of war-speak. "Certainly," she writes, "Certainly nobody no not anybody thinks that this war is a war to end war. No not anybody, no well no certainly nobody does think about it, they only think about this war ending, they cannot take on the future, no really not, certainly not as warless certainly not as a future. Better get through this war first" (p. 187). For all the emphatic repetition of "certainly," the passage demonstrates, of course, that there is actually no certainty at all outside the purely propagandist talk of a "war to end all wars." For war, Stein observes, has become structurally necessary, an effect of the nineteenth century's ferocious commitment to "progress":

> . . . the North Pole was found and the South Pole was found, and the work of Christopher Columbus was over, and so the nineteenth

> century which had undertaken to make science more important than anything by having finished the work of Christopher Columbus and reduced the world to a place where there was only that, forced the world into world wars to give everybody a new thing to do as discoveries being over science not being interesting because so limiting there was nothing to do to keep everybody from doing everything in the same way . . . (Stein 1945: 64–5).

This process, says Stein, has "made the world all one" (p. 64), a seamless totality which the idiosyncratic style of *Wars I Have Seen* sets out to challenge by offering linguistic and existential alternatives to the monolithic conformism of "everybody doing everything in the same way." Accordingly, like Hemingway in *A Farewell to Arms,* Stein sees the local detail of war, not its supposedly grand design, and her customary fondness for "error" and "errancy" here directs her eye not to the politicians' narrative of war, but to the confusions and blunders that characterized the actual "theater of war" ("'theater' is good," remarked Pound in *The Pisan Cantos,* "There are those who did not want/ it to come to an end" – Pound 1986: 491).

War as theater, war as cinema in Paul Virilio's more recent formulation: these analogies stress the spectacular nature of combat and its "perceptual logistics." In American poetry, however – as the ambiguity that attaches to Stein's notion of "seeing" might suggest – the connection between war and visuality is far from straightforward. In writing by World War II combatants it is less the exteriorization of war as theater than the self-estrangement of the individual actors that is the issue. The "growing derealization of military engagement," as Virilio calls it (Virilio 1989: 1), becomes a key experience of this war through the development of aerial combat. The act of seeing, now technologically mediated, produces a new form of self-alienation. The speaker sees himself as other, most grotesquely in Randall Jarrell's famous "The Death of the Ball Turret Gunner" where he has already died, his remains "washed out of the turret with a hose" (Shapiro 2003: 88). Less luridly, James Dickey in "The Firebombing" sees himself as another person, only partially recognizable:

> some technical-minded stranger with my hands
> Is sitting in a glass treasure-hole of blue light
> Having potential fire under the undeodorized arms
> Of his wings (Shapiro 2003: 153)

while William Stafford writes of dropping bombs

from five
miles high, the flower of smoke and fire
so far there is no sound. No cry
disturbs the calm through which we fly (Shapiro 2003: 95)

The bomber is "like a god," as Lowell has it in one poem (Shapiro 2003: 119), but as William Meredith writes in "Love Letter From an Impossible Land," "issues drop away/ Like jettisoned bombs, and all is personal fog" (Shapiro 2003: 137).

While James Mersmann has claimed in his *Out of the Vietnam Vortex* that "Resignation is the dominant temper of World War II poetry" (Mersmann 1974: 15), this seems far from the case in Harvey Shapiro's excellent anthology from which I've quoted these examples. Indeed, the "geometries of distance," to borrow Robert Duncan's phrase from his "A Spring Memorandum: Fort Knox" (Shapiro 2003: 129), are often acutely explored in poems that try to grasp the unreality of deploying weapons, and the lack of articulation between self and machine. As Levinas puts it, the violence of war consists partly in making people "play roles in which they no longer recognize themselves" (Levinas 1969: 21). Such self-estrangement is there in Duncan's poem as he recalls the "unreal clarity" of the target on a firing range – "death/ we see there painted as precisely as a medieval rose" – while Kenneth Koch writes:

As machines make ice
We made dead enemy soldiers, in
Dark jungle alleys, with weapons in our hand
That produced fire and kept going straight through
I was carrying one (Shapiro 2003: 213)

The stunned idiom that measures this estrangement is of a piece with the general sense of war not as a strategic operation but as confusion – Koch, for example, dedicates one poem "To Carelessness" (Shapiro 2003: 210), partly because the landmine he steps on was "badly wired," but also because he values this evidence of human weakness in a world so governed by mechanistic thinking. Howard Nemerov writes in darker vein:

Remembering that war, I'd near believe
We didn't need the enemy, with whom
Our dark encounters were confused and few
And quickly done, so many of our lot
Did for themselves in folly and misfortune. (Shapiro 2003: 141)

Poems such as these attempt to turn the logic of war back on itself – in Nemerov's poem, for example, it is the rhetoric of collective unity, of "us" and "ours," that progressively unravels. In "An Essay at War," Duncan, with the Korean conflict in view, poses the question of unity in a different way:

> The war is a mineral perfection, clear,
> unambiguous evil   within which
> our delite, our life, is the flaw,
> the contradiction? (Duncan 1968: 23)

The war is figured here as some kind of absolute totality, disrupted only by the "contradiction" that turns out to embody "All that we valued" (p. 11) (note the final question mark which disputes any alternative propositional closure). Duncan suggests that poetic language – our now apparently anachronistic "delite" – acquires authenticity from the act of speaking against the language of war and thereby exposes the necessary "flaw" in an otherwise impeccably circular logic. As for Stein, the "flaw" is produced not just by seeing war but by seeing it through writing, an optic which also, as the Language poets would later confirm, allows us to see the writing itself.

The assumptions at work here, shared in different ways by poets such as Charles Olson, Robert Creeley, George Oppen, and Louis Zukofsky, return us inevitably to the primary influence all four shared – Ezra Pound – who, when Duncan wrote these lines, was confined in St Elizabeth's hospital, pending his eventual fitness to stand trial for treason. The "case" of Pound – one can hardly avoid that phrasing – is too well known to need lengthy exposition here, but in any consideration of American war poetry it is an inevitable point of reference. For it was Pound, *the* proponent of linguistic accuracy and clear-sightedness, who ultimately made the fatal mistake of dreaming of a sort of symbiotic relation between poetic language and the language of the state, a relation that might eradicate the necessary "flaw" of which Duncan spoke. Pound's classic injunction to "Make It New" was progressively elided with the "continuous revolution" of Italian fascism, and *The Cantos* came to internalize both the Manichean thinking of conspiracy theory and the bellicose rhetoric of war-speak – both failings that Pound constantly attributed to the governments of Britain and the United States in his wrathful wartime broadcasts, but which reappeared with a terrible inevitability in his own rhetorical "war" against usury. (It was precisely this being "at war against war" for which Duncan would later criticize Denise Levertov – see Perloff 1998: 211–12.) In this context it is hard not to remember the acutely judged moment in Pasolini's film, *Saló or 120 Days of Sodom*, where the camera rises from a scene of blackshirt violence in a courtyard to an upper floor window from which issues the crackling radio voice of Pound, urging his auditors to an appreciation of Confucian order. It's a moment difficult to forget, since it intersects so closely with the opening of *The Pisan Cantos*, which Pound audaciously revised to begin with a long lament for the death of Mussolini in which images from Confucius are prominent. With this note struck at the opening, the rest of the sequence intermittently registered Pound's continuing ideological commitment to the "enormous dream" of the fascist state, and for all its lyric fineness showed the usual binaristic limits of war-speak (the twist here, of course, though few readers wanted to grasp it, was that the "barbarians" vilified in *The Pisan Cantos* were the Allies). So while the elegiac dimension of the sequence lamented the casualties of war – Pound was particularly disturbed by news of damage to the Tempio Malatestiano in Rimini – and even while he was writing at the *end* of the war, the poem's political investments meant that he could seek ethical certainty only through a continuing rhetoric of conflict. "Seeing" war here meant conflating totality with design, thereby achieving a kind of cognitive mastery fundamentally at odds with those moments of more minute vision in which Pound at Pisa famously attended to natural detail.

It is precisely the possibility of another kind of seeing that has galvanized the poets most influenced by Pound, a seeing which once again Levinas seems to signal when he declares that "ethics is an optics. But it is a 'vision' without image, bereft of the synoptic and totalizing objectifying virtues of vision, a relation or an intentionality of a wholly different type" (Levinas 1969: 23). Different poets have explored this possibility in different ways. Duncan, for example, was drawn to the "unwarlike" side of Pound as romantic visionary, stressing as his predecessor's most important insight the view that "All ages are contemporaneous" (Duncan 1995: 99), and that "the contemporary opens upon eternity in the interpenetration of times" (p. 124). In face of war – Duncan would write powerfully of the Vietnam conflict in the sequence called *Tribunals* – myth offers a means of establishing relationship, so that mythic contemporaneity becomes the ground for what he calls "the community of the poem" (p. 170), the poem as an expression of "the communality we have with all men, our interdependence everywhere in life" (Duncan 1963: 41).

George Oppen sought similarly to establish poetry as a medium of relationship rather than of hierarchy and authority. For him, as for Duncan, it was the spectacle of Pound's war-speak that had to be avoided at all cost. Several of Oppen's poems – for example, "Of Hours" and "The Speech at Soli" – confront that problem directly. In the first, Oppen remembers "Burying my dogtag with H/ For Hebrew in the rubble of Alsace" (Oppen 2002: 218). He had been seriously wounded there in 1945 when, as he tersely reported in a letter, "88mm shell landed in a foxhole: Three of us were in that fox-hole" (Oppen 1990: 203). Of the three, only Oppen, his body pitted with shrapnel, would live to be haunted by the attack. The experience was for him, he later said, a definitive "ur-scene" (Oppen UCSD: 16, 17, 1) and it would figure as a commanding presence in his postwar writing. In "Of Hours," this traumatic memory is embedded in an address to Pound as the father-figure who failed to learn the lesson of his own famous line, "What thou lovest well remains" and who is finally seen walking home "Unteachable" (Oppen 2002: 217–19). In "The Speech at Soli," Pound is again reproached for the willed nature of his seeing, as Oppen reinflects Canto CXV's "I cannot make it cohere": "war in incoherent/ sunlight it will not/ cohere it will NOT" (Oppen 2002: 239). The war that Oppen himself had seen was supremely "incoherent" and is thus graspable in retrospect only in a language that renounces any authoritative point of view or totalizing vision, a language of "holes" and "pitfalls," as he describes it in "Of Hours."

In contrast to Pound's way of seeing war, then, Oppen's involves a moment of acknowledged blindness, a moment in which, as Levinas has it, we experience "the surplus of being over the thought that claims to contain it" (Levinas 1969: 27). Oppen's "ur-scene" thus never comes completely into view, blocked as it is by the trauma of injury and by the guilt he apparently felt for being unable to rescue another wounded man in the foxhole (McAleavey 1985: 309). So in the great serial poem, "Of Being Numerous," for which Oppen was awarded the Pulitzer Prize in 1969, various reminiscences of men and places in the war seem to be focused in some peculiarly oblique lines:

> Under the soil
> In the blind pressure
> The lump,
> Entity
> Of substance
> Changes also. (Oppen 2002: 176)

An earlier unpublished version of these lines renders them less enigmatic:

> Under the sea, under the deep
> Soil hidden
> In the black
> And heavy depths,
> Lump, accretion,
> Is one's brother. (Oppen UCSD: 16, 22, 22)

The poem as a whole is haunted by thoughts of death but here it is as if Oppen almost literally buries a dead comrade, removing mention of his "brother" and leaving the body as just an unrecognizable "lump" in the final version.

Such conflicted memories of World War II intersect with the poem's powerful stand against the Vietnam war:

> It is the air of atrocity,
> An event as ordinary
> As a President.
>
> A plume of smoke, visible at a distance
> In which people burn.

There is, he continues:

> Insanity in high places,
> If it is true we must do these things
> We must cut our throats (Oppen 2002: 173)

The directness of these lines differs tellingly from the contorted passage about burial. In contrast to the madness of the Vietnam war in which, Oppen says, "the casual will/ Is atrocious" (p. 173), World War II remains cryptic, at once a so-called "good war" in which, as it happened, Oppen had chosen to fight, *and* the source of a trauma, personal and cultural, which now haunts the new conflict. At the time that he was completing "Of Being Numerous," Oppen remarked that "If we launch that 'general war in Asia,' I think I will have to give this up again" (Oppen UCSD: 16, 19, 12). He had already given up writing during the Depression and had not returned to it until the late 1950s. Now he found again that "I perhaps cannot write poetry in war time. I couldn't before, and perhaps cannot now. I become ashamed, I become sick with shame" (UCSD: 16, 19, 12). Oppen's "sickness" is produced in part by a sense of deadly repetition, of the traumatic experience of Alsace occurring again, bringing back what he called the "guilt of that foxhole" (Oppen 1974: 5). While the Vietnam war can be "seen," as it were, in that terrible image of "A plume of smoke, visible at a distance/ In which people burn," World War II has a sort of belated force, continuing to deliver traumatic memories from a distance and refusing to come into the clear focus that might allow it to be forgotten.

This distinction, which is not, of course, meant to suggest a qualitative comparison of incomparable events, may speak to a more general sense of what Robert Bly calls "the sudden new change in the life of humanity" after World War II (quoted in Walsh 1982: 116). Among contemporary poets Charles Bernstein has expressed this view most systematically in an essay called "The Second War and Postmodern Memory," where he argues that "the psychological effects of the Second War are still largely repressed and that we are just beginning to come out of the shock enough to try to make sense of the experience" (Bernstein 1992: 193). While for Bernstein, born in 1950, the war seems "an historical event, something past and gone," the Holocaust, he says, "each year . . . seems nearer, more recent" (p. 194). And although Bernstein is weighing the effect of World War II on what is written after it, he is not, he insists, talking about " 'war poetry' in the sense of poems about the war; they are notoriously scarce and beside the point I want to make here" (p. 200). When it comes to representation, he says, "Only the surface of the war can be pictured." A different poetics is needed if we are to grasp the deeper meanings of the Holocaust, for the Second War differs fundamentally from the First: in the Second War, says Bernstein, "the malaise is not locatable as the official event of the war, the battles; the whole of everyday life has lost its foundations" (p. 204). Oppen had already spoken (after Michael Heller) of the need "to save the commonplace" (Oppen 2002: 270) and in some of his late poems, such as "The Occurrences," with its talk of the "survivor," there are related but oblique intimations of the Holocaust. It is the obliquity that must be emphasized, for while, as Virilio says, military engagement is increasingly a visual spectacle, its attendant derealization makes it ever harder to "see" in an ethical sense.

For Bernstein, this might exemplify what he regards as a general shift from the New American Poetry onwards, a shift from what I've called "seeing" wars as actual events to a poetics that finds in acts of linguistic precision and discrimination an ethical counter to what he terms "the grammar of control and the syntax of command" (Bernstein 1992: 202). War as a particular historical event recedes, even as the language in which its aims are articulated figures increasingly as an all-enclosing linguistic environment whose limits poetry must ceaselessly define. So in recent American poetry, Bernstein argues, we find a countervailing emphasis on "particularity, the detail rather than the overview, form understood as eccentric rather than systematic, process more than system, or if system then system that undermines any hegemonic role for itself" (p. 210). It's not surprising that Gertrude Stein is often thought of as a progenitor of Language writing, since what Bernstein describes here could apply equally to her way of "seeing" wars. The difference is, perhaps, that for Bernstein the poet is no longer bound to write about wars directly, since the Enlightenment values so fatally discredited in the Second War – values associated with "patriarchy, authority, rationality, order, control" (p. 198) – are ever present to us in their degraded form and continue to "manipulate and dominate us" in "everyday" language (p. 202). Just as Stein's "I" played serious games with the logic of normal ways of seeing war, so poetry is here proposed as a critical act that illuminates the political and social dimensions of language hitherto obscured by its assumed transparency. Recent American poetry thus draws on the insights of an earlier modernism, but, as Bernstein notes, in doing so it gives them what he calls "an entirely different psychic registration" (p. 205), interrogating the fetish of authority that characterizes some of their best-known expressions.

The terms of Bernstein's essay help to point up an increasingly noticeable divergence between the different strands of war-writing in America. On the one hand, there is the huge body of poetry produced by Vietnam veterans (see Chattarji 2001). Many of these are poems of everyday horror, poems of wounding, guilt, and protest that, for the most part, derive their moral charge from their clear-sighted presentation of life and death and from the bitter irony with which they address the administration that had sent them there. These poems are frequently moving in their sensitivity to nuance and detail in a world more attuned to destruction and apocalyptic force. The best of them – by John Balaban and W. D. Erhart, for example – are also responsive to the landscape and ancient culture of the country (Balaban writes: "In Vietnam, poets brushed on printed silk/ those poems about clouds, mountains, and love./ But now their poems are cased in steel" – Erhart 1985: 17), and the tendency to journalistic description, too much in evidence in many of the anthologies, is often curbed by pithy reflections on the soldiers' role. In "Relative thing," for example, Erhart writes;

> We are the ones you sent to fight a war
> You didn't know a thing about.
>
> It didn't take us long to realize
> The only land that we controlled
> Was covered by the bottoms of our boots. (Erhart 1985: 95)

Many of these poems certainly strike home, though to read through the big anthologies of them is to be made strongly aware of their time-bound quality. The repetition is relentless and true to fact – burning bodies, mutilation, fear, and disillusion – but it tends to fix the historical events of Vietnam as a series of frozen images.

This perhaps explains why other, more clearly major poets have responded to the challenge not so much by writing *about* war as by somehow internalizing it within their work or even by not looking directly at it at all (Kenneth Koch remarked of one of his protest poems, that "the parts that were about the war actually kept sort of being rejected by the poem," quoted in Herd 2000: 124). In similar vein, one critic has said of Duncan's *Passages* sequence, "these are not anti-war poems, but war poems, studies in struggle" (Reid 1979: 169), and it is indeed the case that while Duncan names and excoriates the "betrayers of public trust," Lyndon Johnson chief among them, he does so in a highly charged context of Dantescan and mythological allusion that deliberately recalls Pound's "Hell Cantos." The "struggle" is waged in and with language, recapitulating a sort of primal contest of powers that, for Duncan, informs the practice of writing itself. As he remarks in the preface to *The Years as Catches*, "The War itself and the power of the State I dimly perceived were not only a power over me but also a power related to my own creative power but turnd [sic] to purposes of domination, exploitation and destruction" (quoted in Reid 1979: 169). For Duncan, this contest of powers is typically perceived in cosmic, almost Blakean terms, which designedly give less historical specificity to the ongoing war.

Few poets would deploy Duncan's inflated cosmic perspectives, but others would find ways of writing about the war without confronting its historical detail directly. For the noncombatant, Vietnam was of course the first real TV war; images of it were increasingly mediated and experienced as remote and unreal. Louis Zukofsky's "A-18," for example, which can be read, as Bob Perelman puts it, "as voicing a sincere though distant opposition to the Vietnam War," regularly quotes from TV and the press (Perelman 1994: 205). The mediatedness of war now gives a new twist to the theatrical metaphor, making it ever harder to "see" war in any meaningful sense – pondering the unreality of infant death in Vietnam, Denise Levertov writes in "Advent 1966" that

> because of this my strong sight,
> my clear caressive sight, my poet's sight I was given
> that it might stir me into song,
> is blurred. (Levertov 1970: 4)

For some poets, and Levertov is one, the task of poetry is to find, or perhaps in some sense to recover, a simple, undamaged language, the language, as she puts it in "Life at War," of

> humans, men who can make;
> whose language imagines *mercy,*
> *lovingkindness*; we have believed one another
> mirrored forms of a God we felt as good –
> who do these acts, who convince ourselves
> it is necessary; these acts are done
> to our own flesh; burned human flesh
> is smelling in Viet Nam as I write. (Levertov 1967: 230)

Charles Olson was fond of quoting Heraclitus's view that "Man is estranged from that with which he is most familiar" (Olson 1970: 25); Levertov's lines are perhaps more self-reflexive, proposing that a culture of war has forced us to live in a language in which we cannot recognize ourselves. In "Wichita Vortex Sutra," Allen Ginsberg thus observes mordantly that

> The war is language,
> language abused
> for Advertisement,
> language used
> like magic for power on the planet:
> Black magic language,
> formulas for reality. . . . (Ginsberg 1995: 401)

Hence the push to what I earlier called "poetic thinking," to a language freed from the closure of end–means logic and the finality of war-speak.

Not all poets, of course, have fought state power, as have Duncan and Ginsberg, with the counterpower of bardic eloquence. As Bernstein suggests, many have instead cultivated a particularity of vision as the basis for ethical discrimination and as a way of recovering a necessary sense of human scale in the face of war-speak's phoney sublimities. Of the Language poets, some, like Bob Perelman and Bernstein himself, have found in humor a way of achieving that scale, forcing familiar rhetorics to implode in a sordid mass of cliché and hyperbole – "the stately violence of the State," by which Perelman characterizes World War II, thus reveals itself as heartless farce, "a classic war," he sums up, "punctuated by Hiroshima" (Perelman 1986: 45).

While Language poetry was fundamentally shaped in the rhetorical crucible of the Vietnam years, it often seems that it is World War II that still exerts a primary influence. For poets such as Lyn Hejinian and Susan Howe, that war is forever associated with a rending of family ties. In the opening prose section of Howe's *The Europe of Trusts*, for example, she recalls how her childhood was enmeshed with the events of the war and how her father, "a man of pure principles, quickly included violence in his principles, put on a soldier suit and disappeared with the others into the thick of the threat to the east called the West" (Howe 1990a: 10). More tentatively, Hejinian opens *My Life* with "A moment yellow, just as four years later, when my father returned home from the war, the moment of greeting him, as she stood at the bottom of the stairs, younger, thinner than when he had left, was purple – though moments are no longer so colored" (Hejinian 1987: 7). These moments of departure and return inaugurate a history – Howe remembers a visit to Buffalo Zoo with her father before he enlisted, "a treasured memory of togetherness," she says, but one also infected by a violence to come, as she watches "Three bears running around rocks as if to show how modern rationalism springs from barbarism" (Howe 1996: 3). For Howe – and this is the main motive behind all her writing – the past is an immediate force, it is what "never stops hurting" (Howe 1990a: 26), the inscription of a loss that can never be made good. As a result, the wars she has seen – and her work gives sight of many – abolish completely the objectivity normally associated with the contemplative gaze. As she puts it: "If to see is to *have* at a distance, I had so many dead Innocents distance was abolished. Substance broke loose from the domain of time and obedient intention. I became part of the ruin. In the blank skies over Europe I was strife represented" (Howe 1990a: 12). With that breakdown of contemplative distance goes a parallel suspicion about the language of historical record. History, for Howe as for Walter Benjamin, is the story told by the victors, and her explorations of American violence have been premised on, as she says, "A recognition that there is another voice, an attempt to hear and speak it" (Howe 1990b: 192). That other voice lies at a far remove from the slick logics of political speech – it is a broken voice, "a stammering even," she says, "Interruption and hesitation used as a force." In recognizing this voice of the other, Howe seeks thus to derive an ethical language from the ruins of an authoritarian one.

Lyn Hejinian's aim in her recent work has been comparable, though where Howe has sought to keep her own poetic language at the threshold of meaning, shattering the historical record into a rubble of verbal bits and pieces, Hejinian seems to have moved in the opposite direction in works like the recent *A Border Comedy*, where the language is playful and apparently discursive, offering the poem as a kind of dialogic, social space. The concern here is not with war as such, though the calculated strangeness of Hejinian's poetic thinking, where fantasies freely masquerade as aphorisms, seems tacitly to invoke an absent "political" language against which it speaks. Not war, then, nor its tautological language of fixed terms, but a thinking which for Hejinian is once again prefigured in Stein's work, with its commitment to "beginning again and again" (Hejinian 2000a: 102). Stein, says, Hejinian, "invented a mode of iteration to indicate not recurrence but phenomenological *occurrence*, the perpetual coming into being through accumulated instances of the person that is" (Hejinian 2000a: 289). This "coming into being," as Hejinian calls it, is at once our coming into social being and the appearance of the poem which announces it as something new and unexpected. Hejinian's thinking here is much influenced by her reading of Hannah Arendt's *The Human Condition* and particularly by a passage in that book where Arendt speaks of what she calls "the space of appearance" as "the space where I appear to others as others appear to me, where men exist not merely like other living or inanimate beings but make their appearance explicitly" (Arendt 1998: 198–9). In another recent work called *Happily*, Hejinian declares that "Logic tends to force similarities but that's not what we mean/ By 'sharing existence'" (Hejinian 2000b: 15). Poetic thinking undermines that logic, she would say, inasmuch as the open form of the poem allows thought to be grasped as something "happening" rather than as something always already enclosed in its own doom-laden logic. That logic – the logic of war-speak – will no doubt be forever with us, but Hejinian's work seeks out its limits, realizing in its deepest instincts that – in the words of Denise Levertov – "nothing we do has the quickness, the sureness,/ the deep intelligence living at peace would have" (Levertov 1967: 230). In a warlike world, we continue to need that conditional tense that poetry at its best delivers.

References and Further Reading

Arendt, Hannah (1998). *The Human Condition*, 2nd edn. Chicago: University of Chicago Press.

Barthes, Roland (1968). *Writing Degree Zero*, trans. Annette Lavers and Colin Smith. New York: Hill and Wang.

Bernstein, Charles (1992). *A Poetics*. Cambridge, MA and London: Harvard University Press.

Brooks, Renana (2003). "A Nation of Victims," <http://www.thenation.com/doc.mhtml?i=20030630&s=brooks&c=1>

Chattarji, Subarno (2001). *Memories of a Lost War: American Poetic Responses to Vietnam*. Oxford: Clarendon Press.

Cowley, Malcom (1934). *Exiles Return: A Literary Odyssey of the 1920s*. London: Bodley Head.

Cummings, E. E. (1968). *Complete Poems*, vol. 1. London: MacGibbon & Kee.

Duncan, Robert (1963). "From the Day Book: Excerpts from an Extended Study Of H.D.'S Poetry," *Origin*, 10 (July), 1–47.

— (1968). *Derivations*. London: Fulcrum Press.

— (1995). *A Selected Prose*, ed. Robert J. Bertholf. New York: New Directions.

Erhart, W. D. (ed.) (1985) *Carrying the Darkness: The Poetry of the Vietnam War*. Lubbock, TX: Texas Tech University Press.

Fussell, Paul (1975). *The Great War and Modern Memory*. Oxford: Oxford University Press.

Ginsberg, Allen (1995). *Collected Poems 1947–1985*. Harmondsworth, UK: Penguin.

Hamill, Sam (ed.) (2003). *Poets Against the War*. New York: Thunder's Mouth Press.

Hejinian, Lyn (1987) *My Life*. Los Angeles: Sun & Moon Press.

— (2000a). *The Language of Inquiry*. Berkeley, Los Angeles, and London: University of California Press.

— (2000b). *Happily*. Sausalito, CA: The Post-Apollo Press.

— (2001). *A Border Comedy*. New York: Granary Books.

Herd, David (2000) *John Ashbery and American Poetry*. Manchester, UK: Manchester University Press.

Howe, Susan (1990a). *The Europe of Trusts*. Los Angeles: Sun & Moon Press.

— (1990b). "Encloser." In Charles Bernstein (ed.), *The Politics of Poetic Form: Poetry and Public Policy*. New York: Roof Books, pp. 175–96.

— (1996). *Frame Structures: Early Poems 1974–1979*. New York: New Directions.

Kenner, Hugh (1971). *The Pound Era*. Berkeley and Los Angeles: University of California Press.

Levertov, Denise (1967). *Poems 1960–1967*. New York: New Directions.

— (1970). *Relearning the Alphabet*. New York: New Directions.

Levinas, Emmanuel (1969). *Totality and Infinity: An Essay on Exteriority*, trans. Alphonso Lingis. Pittsburgh, PA: Duquesne University Press.

MacLeish, Archibald (1933). *Poems 1924–1933*. Boston and New York: Houghton Mifflin Company.

McAleavey, David (1985). "The Oppens: Remarks Towards Biography," *Ironwood*, 26: 309–18.

Mersmann, James F. (1974). *Out of the Vietnam Vortex: A Study of Poets and Poetry Against the War*. Lawrence: University Press of Kansas.

Merton, Thomas (1969). "War and the Crisis of Language." In Robert Ginsberg (ed.), *The Critique of War*. Chicago: Henry Regnery Company, pp. 99–119.

Charles Olson (1970). *The Special View of History*. Berkeley: Oyez.

Oppen, George (1974). "Non-resistance, etc. Or: Of the Guiltless," *East End*, 3 (1): 5.

— (1990). *Selected Letters*, ed. Rachel Blau DuPlessis. Durham, NC and London: Duke University Press.

— (2002). *New Collected Poems*, ed. Michael Davidson. New York: New Directions.

Perelman, Bob (1986). *The First World*. Great Barrington, MA: The Figures.

— (1994). *The Trouble with Genius: Reading Pound, Joyce, Stein and Zukofsky*. Berkeley, Los Angeles, and London: University of California Press.

Perloff, Marjorie (1998). *Poetry On and Off the Page: Essays for Emergent Occasions*. Evanston, IL: Northwestern University Press.

Pick, Daniel (1993). *War Machine: The Rationalisation of Slaughter in the Modern Age*. New Haven, CT and London: Yale University Press.

Pound, Ezra (1986). *The Cantos*. London: Faber and Faber.

— (1990). *Personae: The Shorter Poems*, revised edn. by Lee Baechler and A. Walton Litz. New York: New Directions.

Reid, Ian W. (1979). "The Plural Text: 'Passages'." In Robert J. Bertholf and Ian W. Reid (eds.), *Robert Duncan: Scales of the Marvelous*. New York: New Directions, pp. 161–80.

Rose, Jacqueline (1993). *Why War?* Oxford: Blackwell.

Shapiro, Harvey (ed.) (2003). *Poets of World War II*. New York: The Library of America.

Sieminski, Gregory C. (1995). "The Art of Naming Operations," *Parameters: US Army War College Quarterly*, Autumn: 81–98.

Stauber, John and Sheldon Rampton (2003). "The Fog of War Talk," <http://www.alternet.org/story/16497/>

Stein, Gertrude (1945). *Wars I Have Seen*. New York: Random House.
Swift, Todd (ed.) (2003) *100 Poets Against the War*. Cambridge, UK: Salt Publishing.
Virilio, Paul (1989). *War and Cinema: The Logistics of Perception*, trans. Patrick Camiller. London and New York: Verso.
Walsh, Jeffrey (1982). *American War Literature 1914 to Vietnam*. London and Basingstoke, UK: Macmillan Press.

Chapter 2

Pleasure at Home: How Twentieth-century American Poets Read the British

David Herd

I

We need to go back a bit.

American poetry was inaugurated by Ralph Waldo Emerson in 1836. There had, of course, been poetry written in America before 1836 – by William Cullen Bryant, say, or John Greenleaf Whittier, or Edgar Allen Poe – but it wasn't until Emerson declared America's cultural independence in 1836 with his anonymously published essay *Nature* that the possibility, one might say the project, of American poetry was born. As he put it, at the beginning of his essay,

> Our age is retrospective. It builds the sepulchres of the fathers. It writes biographies, histories, and criticism. The foregoing generations beheld God and nature face to face; we, through their eyes. Why should not we also enjoy an original relation to the universe? Why should not we have a poetry of insight and not of tradition, and a religion by revelation to us, and not the history of theirs?
>
> . . . The sun shines to-day also. There is more wool and flax in the fields. There are new lands, new men, new thoughts. Let us demand our own works and laws and worship. (Emerson 2001: 27)

The "eyes" here, the "eyes" through which "we," the Americans, behold "God" and "nature" are, from one point of view, British. Emerson, in other words, in inaugurating American literature was, in

"Nature" and other essays of the late 1830s and 1840s, formulating a question that American poets would be asking themselves long into the next century: how to read the British? More than this, in his essays of this period Emerson arrived at responses (not answers) to this question that have been informing American poetry ever since. To understand, therefore, how "Twentieth-century American poets read the British" we need to go back a bit.

American writing, its poetry in particular perhaps, was, as Emerson rightly saw it, in awe of its European, especially its British, forbears. Such awe, one might better call it reverence, for another nation's literary conventions made it impossible for the new nation to establish what Emerson termed "an original relation to the universe." What was needed, therefore, prior even to a new way of writing, was a new way of reading. What America had, in 1836, was a "poetry of . . . tradition." A tradition, as Emerson understood it, was a function of overly reverential reading habits. Before it could have the new writers it needed, America needed new readers. He set out this demand in his address to "The American Scholar," "An Oration Delivered before the Phi Beta Kappa Society at Cambridge, August 31, 1837" in which he argued explicitly for what he called "creative reading." The problem was – and of course this is always the problem – that, "Meek young men grow up in libraries believing in their duty to accept the views which Cicero, which Locke, which Bacon have given, forgetful that Cicero, Locke and Bacon were only young men in libraries when they wrote these books" (Emerson 2001: 59). As a mode of literary criticism this is, arguably, Puritan, and so, as such, arguably American: Emerson's insistence that readers not simply "accept" the authority of their writers articulates a mindset that had its origins in the Reformation's refusal to accept the authority of the priests. (This, anyway, is how the argument played out when Emerson made another address at Harvard, a year later, this time to the Divinity School.)

Emerson's demand was, it would seem, a clear one: creative – properly creative – American writing, required a creative, which is to say a nonreverential, reading of European, but especially British, literature. Except, of course, his demand – "Let us demand our own works and laws and worship" – wasn't clear, because Emerson himself (and who isn't?) was deeply in debt to the writers who had gone before him; his own thought, what he came to call *Transcendentalism,* for all its independence of mind – and it was independent-minded – and for all its American accent – and it clearly had an American accent – was very largely influenced by British Romanticism. Thus it is in the key works of British writing of the generation before his own that one finds the major tropes of Emerson's cultural project: a project governed by an image of American culture characterized by innocence and optimism, informed by a spiritual connection with nature, and guided by the figure of a Poet whose capacity for imagination rendered him central (if not necessarily recognized as such) to the culture's practices, linguistic and otherwise. Taking these in turn, "innocence" was Blake's optimistic early Romantic term (Blake, like, Emerson, would subsequently write about "Experience"), while "optimism" was a version, prolonged and teleological, of Wordsworthian joy; the divinity of "Nature" was Wordsworth's theme; the cultural centrality of the poet had been given fullest expression most recently by Shelley in his *Defense of Poetry* (a work that served as the model for the Emersonian essay-as-manifesto); and imagination was vaunted by Romantic writers generally, but most richly by Coleridge and Keats, as the presiding intellectual faculty.

Emerson thus told future American poets – twentieth-century American poets – two largely contradictory things about British poetry: that they should read it creatively, which is to say nonreverentially, and that Romanticism was the source. The effect of this, unavoidable as Emerson is for subsequent poets (he can be argued with and deviated from, but in his foundational capacity he cannot simply be dismissed), is that in their readings of British poetry twentieth-century American poets have had to organize themselves in relation to Romanticism. Which is not to say that all American poetry of the last century was an outgrowth of the British Romantic movement. It is to say that Romanticism was a central axis to that poetry, and that the decision to find a source elsewhere in British poetry was precisely that, an aesthetic decision. But one can perhaps go further, because among the many ways one might categorize twentieth-century American poetry would be in terms of its Romantics – those like Frost, Stevens, and Ginsberg, explicity writing within Romantic conventions – and its Readers – those like Pound, Olson, and Bernstein, who insist on creative reading as a central aspect of the creative act. Except, of course, that the dichotomy barely survives the saying of it: O'Hara, Ashbery, and Rich (not to mention Ginsberg and Olson) being hugely creative readers in the Romantic tradition. Even so, Emerson was America's first great reader of British poetry, and in his casting of his culture's poetic enterprise in terms of Romanticism, he left his twentieth-century successors with a series of decisions to make.

II

If there is a moment in twentieth-century American poetry when it is possible to establish a confident distinction in terms of Emerson's implicit Romanticism and his insistence on creative reading, it is in the beginning, with Robert Frost and Ezra Pound: a distinction mediated by the poets' respective attitudes to their immediate British contemporaries. At the beginning of "The Figure a Poem Makes," a short essay he wrote by way of an introduction to his *Collected Poems* of 1939, Frost himself put the distinction this way:

> Abstraction is an old story with the philosophers, but it has been like a new toy in the hands of the artists of our day . . . Granted no one but a humanist much cares how sound a poem is if it is only *a* sound. The sound is the gold in the ore. Then we will have the sound out alone and dispense with the inessential. We do till we make the discovery that the object in writing poetry is to make all poems sound as different as possible from each other, and the resources for that of vowels, consonants, punctuation, syntax, words, sentences, meter are not enough. We need the help of context-meaning-subject matter. All that can be done with words is soon told. So also with meters – particularly in our language where there are virtually but two, strict iambic and loose iambic. (Frost 1951: 17)

In broad outline Frost was a Wordsworthian poet. Metrically he recalled Wordsworth in sticking, as he implies, almost exclusively to iambics, strict or loose, his longer narrative poems, like Wordsworth's, being sustained by a skillfully varied blank verse. Not that a fidelity to blank verse identifies a poet as Wordsworthian (although a governing formal straightforwardness does more so). A fidelity to a certain straightforwardness of diction, on the other hand, is a strong link. In "The Figure a Poem Makes," Frost comments on his diction only indirectly, contesting that, among other things, the figure a poem makes is "the happy-sad blend of the drinking song." To present the drinking song as a model for the poem – Ezra Pound, it might be noted, never stood up for the drinking song – is to argue for a mode of address that in various ways, but not least in terms of diction, makes a direct appeal to a general audience. Like Wordsworth, Frost understood himself (after Wordsworth) as a "man speaking to men," from which it followed that his poems spoke, or were spoken – there is invariably a speaking voice in a Frost poem – in the language of ordinary Americans, where ordinary Americans meant the rural folk Frost encountered as a New England farmer. It is there, though, in the situation of the poet that Frost is most clearly gripped by the Wordsworthian imagination. To use his own terms (or term, the hyphens indicating features of a poem it is hard to separate out) the "context-meaning-subject matter" of Frost's work are invariably, and for all he means them to introduce variety to his work, directed by Wordsworthian values. The context of a Frost poem, therefore, is almost invariably either rural or natural, or both; the meaning, in the sense of a paraphrasable lesson (and a Frost poem is a frequently a cautionary tale of sorts), has very often to do with loss; while the subject matter, out of which the sense of loss flows, is characteristically (though not uniformly) rural poverty, or the cost of Modernity as measured by the desperation of rural lives.

Not that there aren't other Frosts, and not that Frost's relationship with British Romanticism should be thought uncomplicated. As the peculiar unredeemed savagery of "Out, Out – " indicates (and as poems like "Neither Out Far Nor In Deep" and "Design" spell out), Frost occupies a much bleaker, more tragic universe than any Romantic poet liked to envisage; his *Collected Poems*, for all their seeming homeliness, present a fundamentally alienated, largely joyless existence. It is as if, in Wordsworth, as mediated for him by Hardy, Frost found a set of conventions through which he was able to articulate his circumstances but in which he was never able quite fully to invest; "After Apple-Picking" is, among other things, a poem weary, not to say sated, with its own limited range of expression. But Frost was a poet of continuities, the more so, probably, because of his presiding bleakness, and not the least important of these continuities was the line running from British through American poetry.

Frost and Pound met in England in 1913, Frost, like Pound before him, having reached the conclusion that the best place for an American to make a poetic career – America lacking the necessary infrastructure for such a career of fellow poets, critics, publishers, and readers – was Britain. Motivated by a form of expatriatism – glad to find an American poet of obvious accomplishment – Pound's enthusiastic recommendation helped Frost to secure a publisher for his second book, *North of Boston*. He then reviewed his first book in less than ecstatic terms. "Frost's people are distinctly real. Their speech is real; he has known them. I don't much want to meet them, but I do know that they exist" (Myers 1996: 108). This double-gesture, boosting Frost and then putting him in his place, was entirely characteristic of Pound

– always, in his early career anyway, equally the enthusiast and the arbiter. Frost, however, was a special case for Pound. That he didn't want to meet his people was no doubt because he had met them before, not in Wordsworth only, but in the English Georgians, with whom Frost had affinities – witness his great friendship with Edward Thomas – and who for Pound stood at the end of a hopelessly outmoded poetic line: metrically, linguistically, context-meaning-subject matter-wise. Equally, though, Frost's Americans were among the reasons Pound left America. Witness his brimming, exhilarated address to his fellow artists – "O helpless few in my country,/ O remnant enslaved!" – in his early poem "The Rest" (Pound 1981: 46):

> You who cannot wear yourselves out
> By persisting to successes,
> You who can only speak,
> Who cannot steel yourselves into reiteration . . .
> Take thought:
> I have weathered the storm,
> I have beaten out my exile. (Pound 1981: 47)

Frost's people are not "The Rest"; "The Rest" are the artists Pound left behind him in America, and who continued to work, as he saw it, in conditions wholly unsuitable to art. Frost's people, rather, were those who thwarted "The Rest," villagers (metaphorically and otherwise, provincial folk) steeling themselves, like Frost's wall-mending neighbor, to reiteration. Pound's objective, as "The Rest" implies, in going to Britain, was, among other things, to decouple himself from America; or at least to decouple himself from a provincialism that he found in America and that he took to be antipathetic to art. It was a provincialism, which, though he would have named it differently, Frost had identified in British poetry. Pound agreed, and so in decoupling himself from his own culture, he sought to decouple, or at least to loosen, the link between American and British poetry; witness, for instance, his essay on "Vorticism."

"Vorticism," an early manifesto, though clearly concerned with creative practice – with common practices between the arts and with the practice of imagism in poetry – is not the less an argument for reading. Distinguishing himself from futurism, and from the Italian futurist Marinetti in paticular, Pound observes of "various men who agree with me": "We do not desire to evade comparison with the past. We prefer that the comparison be made by some intelligent person whose idea of 'the tradition' is not limited by the conventional taste of four or five centuries and one continent" (Pound 1980: 206). Pound was perfectly serious about this scope, his translations of ancient Chinese poetry, *Cathay*, coming out a year after the essay on "Vorticism." In particular, though, the limits and conventions that bothered him were those of British poetry. Thus imagism, "a sort of poetry where painting or sculpture seems as if it were just coming over into speech," is expressly defined against English modes:

> That other sort of poetry [imagism] is as old as the lyric and as honorable, but, until recently, no one had named it. Ibycus and Liu Ch'e presented the "Image." Dante is a great poet by reason of this faculty, and Milton is a wind-bag because of his lack of it. The "image" is the furthest possible remove from rhetoric. (Pound 1980: 200)

Imagism was a largely successful attempt to take the wind out of English poetry, where wind is both the figure for the inspiration that fuels the lyric self, and also the redundancies that Pound found in Milton in particular, but more generally in metrically conventional British poetry. A corrective to British poetic habits, an imagist poem was to offer "direct treatment of the 'thing'," so excluding the self that Wordsworth in particular had made central to poetry; "use no word that does not contribute to the presentation"; and to "compose in the sequence of the musical phrase, not in the sequence of the metronome" (Pound 1980: 2010), where metronome meant, primarily, the pentameter that had shaped British poetry for centuries, and that Frost had argued was the natural form of expression in English. What imagism also implied, however, was a doubly anti-Romantic mode of reading. For Pound, then, Romanticism was not the source. The sources, rather, were to be found, insofar as they could be found in British poetry, in nonlyric modes, in the dramatic monologues of Browning for instance, or in the Anglo-Saxon anonymity of "The Sea Farer." Nor, equally, should the manner of one's reading – the "how" rather than the "what" – be informed by the Romantics. When Pound urged poets to "Make it new," he meant not that they should seek desperately after originality, but that they should innovate with the intention of making certain values and virtues available again (hence the fact that, in his early career in particular, he read invariably with a view to translation). These values and virtues resided not in the poet, but in poetry, and not only in British poetry but in the poetry of at least two continents. Pound identified a provincialism in American poetry that had its roots in the provincialism of some strains of Romanticism. He read British poetry from a cosmopolitan viewpoint.

It is arguable – anyway it is being argued here – that in their starkly different poetries Frost and Pound provided twentieth-century American poetry with its two main alternative approaches to British poetry. Working differently out and away from Emerson, Frost and Pound established ways of writing that continue to shape and polarize American work. However, wherever one finds a major poet one finds also a major reader, and so in all the significant American Modernists one finds a singular relationship with British poetry. T. S. Eliot, like Pound, oriented himself in American poetry by resisting the Romantic model offered him by Emerson. Again the reorientation occurred in prose as well as poetry, Eliot's own great statement of what and how to read being "Tradition and the Individual Talent" – a manifesto of sorts, if only in the sense that a character from Henry James might issue a manifesto. The essay opens this way:

> In English writing we seldom speak of tradition, though we occasionally apply its name in deploring its absence. We cannot refer to "the tradition" or to "a tradition"; at most, we employ the adjective in saying that the poetry of So-and-so is "traditional" or even "too traditional". Seldom, perhaps, does the word appear except in a phrase of censure. (Eliot 1975: 37)

Perhaps the most striking feature of this authoritative opening is the pronoun. Where Pound wanted to loosen the link between American poet and British poet, or to step above and beyond both, Eliot wants to insist on a convergence. It is 1919, only seven years since he left Harvard, and already Eliot is insisting by his pronoun on a common identity. In doing so his argument, though it looks like it is squarely with, or within, "English" writing, is at least as much with or within "American." So whereas his complaint about the use of the word "tradition" makes some sense in an English, or British, context, it makes much more sense in an American one, and especially as an argument with Emerson. It was Emerson, after all, who insisted on the kind of nonreverential reading that most threatens a tradition; reverence, both in the hush of Eliot's prose, but also, as he says later in the essay, in the act of "surrender" necessary to the writing of poetry, being among the mental habits he wants to revisit. More to the point, what Emerson sought above all was that American poetry should have an "original relation to the universe," it being precisely this insistence on "originality" that Eliot wants to contest in his discussion of tradition.

> We dwell with satisfaction upon the poet's difference from his predecessors . . . Whereas if we approach a poet without this prejudice we shall often find that not only the best, but the most individual parts of his work may be those in which the dead poets, his ancestors, assert their immortality most vigorously. And I do not mean the impressionable period of adolescence, but the period of full maturity. (Eliot 1975: 38)

"Originality," "the poet's difference from his predecessors," is not the only Emersonian, and Romantic, value Eliot wants to reassess here. His sense of "adolescence" also implies a changing of the scale.

As a means of redirecting American poetry, and especially of reconstructing its relationship with British poetry, the term "adolescence" is perfectly pitched. It is a way of construing youth that breaks its hold on the poetic imagination. For Blake (as for Wordsworth), "youth" was all, everything that limited or impinged upon childhood, school for instance, carrying a clearly negative value. "The School Boy" complains:

> Ah! then at times I drooping sit,
> And spend many an anxious hour,
> Nor in my book can take delight,
> Nor sit in learning's bower,
> Worn thro' with the dreary shower. (Blake 1958: 57)

For Blake, as for Emerson, the "anxious hour" was the hour spent in the schoolroom. Thus as Blake's "School Boy" grows up to be Emerson's American Scholar, the issue remains the same: institutions, in their rules and conventions, produce distraction at best and the intellectual "meekness" Emerson spoke of at worst. Addressing nationhood as much as individuality, Emerson developed a literary and cultural project for America that turned constantly on synonyms for youthfulness: "There are new lands, new men, new thoughts." What was required, accordingly, of American poetry was originality.

Eliot's "adolescence" designates a slightly later moment, of course, than Blake ever had in mind, but in its impression of moodiness, in the fickle and feckless temperament it conjures up, it works hard to cast youth in its least admirable light. And this was crucial to Eliot, because what he was trying to articulate in "Tradition and the Individual Talent" was a mode of poetry that was as far as possible from the Romantic model; a model which, in its insistence on inspiration, made personal mood and emotion central, and so which, albeit at an elevated level, made poetry susceptible to whim.

> The point of view which I am struggling to attack is perhaps related to the metaphysical theory of the substantial unity of the soul: for my meaning is, that the poet has, not a "personality" to express, but a particular medium, which is only a medium and not a personality, in which impressions and experiences combine in peculiar and unexpected ways. (Eliot 1975: 42)

Eliot's argument with Romanticism goes deep. His object is not only to free the poetic imagination, American and otherwise, from the allure of "youth," but to distinguish it from personal development almost entirely. Like Pound he wanted to break radically with the sense that poetry was necessarily lyrical. It was to be thought of, rather, as impersonal, as a "medium," as a form of linguistic practice deeply informed by tradition. What resulted was *The Waste Land,* a poem whose creative operations, especially as they relate to British poetry, are as well caught by quoting from its footnotes as from the body of its text:

> III. The Fire Sermon
> 176. V. Spenser, *Prothalamion.*
> 192. Cf. *The Tempest,* I, ii.
> 196. Cf. Marvell, *To His Coy Mistress.*
> 197. Cf. Day, *Parliament of Bees:*
> "When of the sudden, listening, you shall hear,
> "A noise of horns and hunting, which shall bring
> "Actaeon to Diana in the spring,
> "Where all shall see her naked skin . . ." (Eliot 1961: 70)

Eliot's poetry and prose of the late 1910s and early 1920s, viewed from an American point of view, constituted an attempt to write a poetry not directed, via Emerson, by Romanticism. He reads British poetry against the Romantic grain, establishing a procedure that resists lyricism by surrendering the self to the medium of language. Poetry, for Eliot, is not so much emotion as reading recollected in tranquility. Even so the reading is creative, *The Waste Land*'s particular irreverence being to cut up the texts – *The White Devil, Antony and Cleopatra,* "To His Coy Mistress," *The Spanish Tragedy* – it thought most admirable, most wanted to shape the canon. Pound resisted Emerson, very largely, by reading above and beyond British literature. Eliot resisted Emerson by coming up with his own list. At which point William Carlos Williams threw his hands up in horror.

Williams begins chapter 25 of his autobiography with the following remark. "These," he writes, "were the years before the great catastrophe to our letters – the appearance of T. S. Eliot's *The Waste Land*" (Williams 1968: 146). In Williams the pronoun is not ambiguous. "Our letters" refers to American literature, it being Williams's express intention to write, as the title of his fictionalized study of American literary history had it, *In the American Grain*. *The Waste Land* was a catastrophe, as Williams saw it, in part because it insisted on a continuity between American and British literature, to the point even of refusing to recognize the former as a category in its right. But it wasn't only what Eliot read, and what he therefore expected others to read (or to have read) but the manner in which he absorbed his reading. In turning American poetry back to the British, Eliot, as Williams saw it, turned poetry back in on itself, Eliot's footnoted art lacking that drive out of the institutions and towards contemporary experience Emerson had sought to enshrine as an axiom of American poetry, and which Charles Olson would subsequently term its projective quality. This drive toward experience, and away from the conventions of literature, had its origins in Williams's own development in imagism, which movement's insistence on objects he subsequently transformed as the dictum "No ideas but in things," where the things were resolutely American, as was the writer's emphasis on them, Thoreau having previously insisted that the "Roots of letters are things." The roots of Eliot's letters were other letters, and largely British letters at that. For Williams this constituted a catastrophic misdirecting of American poetry.

Even so, the frame of Williams's poetry – the set of conventions out of which he developed and with which he argued – was Romantic. His major poem "To Elsie," for instance (from his post-*Waste Land* book *Spring and All*), though it doesn't sound it, and for all the unmetered, conversational, headlong rush of its syntax, and its insistence on dealing only with "The pure products of America," is a culturally independent poem unthinkable without Wordsworth. Like Frost, though he would very likely not have enjoyed the comparison, Williams is Wordsworthian in his "context-meaning-subject matter." This is discernible in "To Elsie," the poem being a casting about for the "peasant traditions" that might form a basis for American cultural expression. It is more apparent, however, in poems that prefigure "To Elsie." "Pastoral," for instance, finds the poet walking the back streets,

> admiring the houses
> of the very poor:
> roof out of line with sides
> the yards cluttered
> with old chicken wire, ashes,
> furniture gone wrong . . . (Williams 1976: 25)

In so far as this is Romantic poetry, then the Romanticism is audibly American, it being the ingenuity and self-reliance of the very poor that the poetic voice in large part admires. Centrally at issue, though, is the material, the diction of poetry, Williams, like Wordsworth, finding the stuff of poetry in local, working-class life and experience.

Except that in Williams's mind, in so far as it is part of a redirection of poetry toward the stuff and experience of American life, this lexical decision, the move towards the vernacular, was an anti-Romantic gesture. Witness the end of "To Elsie," where in his freewheeling way, Williams invites us to contemplate the dangers to American culture implicit in a poetry caught in another nation's rhetorical conventions:

> as if the earth under our feet
> were
> an excrement of some sky
>
> and we degraded prisoners
> destined
> to hunger until we eat filth
>
> while the imagination strains
> after deer
> going by fields of goldenrod in
>
> the stifling heat of September
> Somehow
> it seems to destroy us
>
> It is only in isolate flecks that
> something
> is given off

No one
to witness
and adjust, no one to drive the car. (Williams 1976: 57)

Here again the mood is of catastrophe: "Somehow/ it seems to destroy us." What "it" is would seem to be the imagination, or at least, that which the poetic imagination conventionally "strains after": the strains of "deer" and of "goldenrod," of the "stifling heat of September." What will destroy us, in other words, as Williams would have it here, where "us" means Americans, are others' words; the diction American poetry had inherited from British poetry, and that threatened, as he saw it, to occlude American experience.

Except to say that the "deer" Williams thought so destructive were, or had already become, American. Compare, or contrast, the end of "To Elsie" with the end of Wallace Stevens's "Sunday Morning":

We live in an old chaos of the sun,
Or old dependency of day and night,
Or island solitude, unsponsored, free,
Of that wide water, inescapable.
Deer walk upon our mountains, and the quail
Whistle about us their spontaneous cries;
Sweet berries ripen in the wilderness;
And, in the isolation of the sky,
At evening, casual flocks of pigeons make
Ambiguous undulations as they sink,
Downward to darkness, on extended wings. (Stevens 165: 25)

Same "deer"? Same "us"? "Sunday Morning" is a poem about religion, the poem's narrative voice entering into conversation with a woman who does not feel compelled to spend her Sunday mornings at church, but who in her nonattendance feels the absence of an ordering, a divine, presence. Such consolation as the poem has to offer in the face of a godless universe is to be found here, in the last stanza, and would seem, as it returns us to loosely iambic natural landscape, to revisit the conventions of Romanticism. But what kind of deer are those? And where are those mountains? And those pigeons flocking, ambiguously undulating, really how casual are they?

Stevens, with whom Williams was in respectful argument all his life, was much more clearly a poet in the Emersonian, which is to say the Romantic, tradition. But not as clearly as the end of "Sunday

Morning" would suppose. Writing always in the absence of a divine presence, Stevens sought consolation for the loss of universal order implied by the death of God in the ordering power of the imagination. And so while it doesn't look like it, the end of "Sunday Morning" is not Wordsworthian but Keatsian in spirit, where "Keatsian" means something like the closing couplet of "Fancy": "Let the winged Fancy roam,/ Pleasure never is at home." The key word here, in this American context, is "home." Whereas for Keats imagination, if not precisely the lesser faculty fancy, had the capacity to lead somewhere, toward truth and so revelation, for Stevens, in the absence of a sustainable metaphysics, the value of imagination lay in its capacity to construct the world even as the world was known to be chaotic. Imagination in Stevens, therefore, is always deeply ambivalent, always abstracting people as it does from the actuality of their landscapes. Stevens's poetry, in other words, unlike Williams's, is never quite at home, his landscapes, as in "Sunday Morning," being always works of the imagination; and in so far as Stevens understood the imagination to have been most fully explored by the Romantics, then for all the domestic placenames and the American slang, his poetry is never local. Instead it hovers above a self-consciously constructed world, which threatens always, as at the end of "Sunday Morning," and as in many of his most famous poems – "Domination of Black," "The Snow Man," "The Idea of Order at Key West" – to give way to "chaos," "darkness".

Marianne Moore's mountains, or rather her mountain, were, by contrast, peculiarly American. Like Williams, Moore understood that if American poetry was to enjoy "an original relation to the universe" it must exceed the limits of British poetic diction. "An Octopus," a poem that is not in fact about an octopus, but is about a mountain that reminds the poet of the shape of an octopus, presents its most sublimely Romantic of subjects not in terms of "deer" and "sweet berries" and "quail" but, very largely, in the verbatim terms of local guide books and government pamphlets (Moore 2003: 169). Arguably the most American of American modernists, Moore collaged the vernacular into her poems, and in doing so made herself almost unreadable in terms of the British.

III

In 1941 Randall Jarrell announced the death of Modernism.

> It Is The End Of The Line. Poets can go back and repeat the ride; they can settle in attractive, atavistic colonies along the railroad; they can repudiate the whole system, à la Yvor Winters, for some neo-classical donkey caravan of their own. But Modernism As We Know It – the most successful and influential body of poetry of this century – is dead. (Jarrell 1981: 81)

Jarrell's statement was in fact a question. How, he was asking his mid-century contemporaries, should poetry be written after Modernism? This was a tough question, but it concealed a still tougher one, Modernism, as Jarrell saw it, being the "final exploitation" of the tendency towards "experimentalism" and "originality" that had its source in Romanticism. This implied continuity was arguable, but Jarrell's sense that different modes of writing were now necessary was shared. Different writing demanded different reading.

In a general sense, how, what, but also where to read were questions that became central to American poetry during and in the years after World War II. This was, as Jarrell observed, "The Age of Criticism," the reading of literature having become fully professionalized in America for the first time with the expansion of the English department, and of all that goes on in the English department, in the 30 years or so before the war. The most professional readers were the so-called New Critics, and the question that most clearly defined New Criticism was how to read British poetry; the most polished and influential answer being provided by Cleanth Brooks's *The Well-Wrought Urn: Studies in the Structure of Poetry*. Brooks's studies – the word is right – were of Shakespeare, Milton, Herrick, Pope, Gray, Wordsworth, Keats, Tennyson, and Yeats. This is not an Emersonian list; there are no Americans here. Nor, more importantly, were the readings Emersonian. Brooks's opening chapter is entitled "The Language of Paradox," his opening statement making the carefully couched claim that "Few of us are prepared to accept the statement that the language of poetry is the language of paradox" (Brooks 1968: 3). Here's the pronoun problem again. Who is "us" as Brooks sees it? Academics? Students? Speakers of English? Americans? Actually, as the argument unfolds, it seems, as with Eliot, that Brooks's universalizing address works best in an American context. Thus, "The case of William Wordsworth, for instance, is instructive on this point. His poetry would not appear to promise many examples of the language of paradox. He usually prefers the direct attack" (Brooks 1968: 3). Brooks does not exclude Romanticism from his revisiting of British poetry, rather he reads it anti-Romantically, from the point of view of a figure, the paradox, which is much more characteristic of earlier British poets, the Metaphysicals especially. This too is an Eliotic maneuver, Eliot having directed attention away from the poetry of the turn of the nineteenth century, and toward the poetry of the seventeenth. Equally telling is the rhetorical opposition Brooks sets up in his reevaluation of Wordsworth; paradox being opposed to "the direct attack." With this opposition, Brooks presents a structure of judgment that means to elevate British poetry over American. Thus there has been, in British poetry (Wordsworth himself was writing against it) a tendency toward paradox, ambiguity, circumlocution, and irony; while there has also been, in American poetry (leading out of Wordsworth) a tendency precisely toward the direct attack: Pound looked back to Whitman, and forward to Williams, Zukofsky, Oppen, and Ginsberg, when he demanded a "direct treatment of the 'thing'." Brooks in particular, but New Criticism generally, read British poetry at the expense of American.

Such institutionalized reading gave rise to institutionalized writing habits, as in the historically self-conscious early poetry of Robert Lowell and John Berryman. Careful to get themselves a traditional education – Lowell at Kenyon College under John Crowe Ransom and Allen Tate, and Berryman at Cambridge (England) under I. A. Richards – both poets, in their work of the 1930s through to the early 1950s, sought a way of handling American subjects (where often this meant history) in a manner learned from their reading of the British. Among Modernists, Eliot was an important model for both poets; not the Eliot of *The Waste Land*, perhaps, but the Eliot of the essays and the later poetry. More important, though, among Modernist models, was the visionary grandiloquence of Hart Crane, Crane, as the imitations and emulations of *The Bridge* make clear, being the American Modernist most keen to maintain the sound and measure of the British grand style. Lowell, the more precociously gifted of the two, arrived at his own visionary style early, his second volume, *Lord Weary's Castle*, squaring up to the conflicts and implications of American religious history in a voice schooled in the compression Eliot so admired in seventeenth-century English poetry – compression, one supposes, as opposed to expansiveness – and the emphatic rhythms and insistent alliteration of Gerard Manley Hopkins. If anything, arguably, Berryman was the more serious reader of the two, witness – supposing this to be the criterion – his extensive and insightful essays on, in particular, Shakespeare. By the same token, and much more than early Lowell,

Berryman's early poems were themselves readerly. From his earliest publications in *Five Young American Poets* up until he found a mode he could live with in *The Dream Songs*, Berryman's writing, for all its accomplishment, amounted to an extended exercise: always formal (few poets wrote as many sonnets in the 1940s as Berryman), invariably somewhat awkward, Anglo-American in a most un-Emersonian way.

Happily, and in quite direct response to this studied revisiting of British poetry, there emerged in the period after World War II a generation (or two) of great, independent poet-readers – Charles Olson, Robert Duncan, Denise Levertov, Frank O'Hara, John Ashbery, Barbara Guest, Allen Ginsberg, Adrienne Rich, Susan Howe, Lyn Hejinian – for whom the question was how might it be possible to develop a model of the non- (or at least the much less) institutionalized, readerly poet. And one way or another, in correcting New Criticism, this post-modern project involved deepening readings of Romanticism.

With his first book, *Call Me Ishmael* (1977), a tensely brilliant account of the making of *Moby Dick*, Charles Olson established himself both as a major reader of American literature, and as a highly significant contributor to the critical project counterbalancing New Criticism, the documenting of the American Renaissance. But he was also a significant rereader of British poetry, his rereading, like Pound's, seemingly skirting Romanticism and, like Pound's, taking place in the manifestos that were a necessary accompaniment to his poetry. "Projective Verse," Olson's most important early statement of his poetics, begins with a presentation of "The NON-Projective":

> (or what a French critic calls "closed" verse, that verse which print bred and which is still pretty much what we have had, in English and American, and have still got, despite the work of Pound & Williams:
>
> it led Keats, already a hundred years ago, to see it (Wordsworth's, Milton's) in the light of "the Egotistical Sublime"; and it persists, at this latter day, as what you might call the private-soul-at-any-public-wall). (Olson 1997: 239)

The issue is directness. The poem, as Olson understands it, is "energy transferred from where the poet got it . . . by way of the poem itself, all the way over to the reader" (Olson 1997: 240). What this circuit excludes is the poet, the poet's self and self-absorption being among the ways in which that which the poem means to communicate is lost. Likewise form serves to close the poem, both to experience and to the reader. Olson's argument is for "COMPOSITION BY FIELD," a creative state that implies a pragmatic openness to the world, and from which it follows that "FORM IS NEVER MORE THAN AN EXTENSION OF CONTENT" (Olson 1997: 240). And nor, crucially, is rhythm. Trying to get at the essential energy of the poem, Olson moves via breath to the syllable, the syllable (as the rudimentary linguistic unit) being the shape the poet's breath first takes on becoming language, and being therefore the expression closest to the poem's inspiration (the object by which it was inspired). It is according to the syllable, therefore, as opposed to the metrical foot, that poetry should be composed, and it is from the syllable that Olson indicates his alternative history of British poetry. This history starts, not unpredictably, with the anonymous lyric "O western wynd, when wilt thou blow," but crucially takes in Shakespeare, Olson pausing to quote "If music be the food of love. . . ." It is a beautifully staged moment, Olson's projective argument allowing this most famous of speeches to be heard afresh, not as iambics, loose or strict, but as syllabics, form extending from content. British poetry, as Olson wants passionately to show us, is more open than we have been able to think.

Like Pound, Olson read British poetry against its own metrical grain. Unlike Pound, there is an Emersonianism, and so a Romanticism, running through his reading, his reworking of the trope of inspiration through the relation of form to content having its root in Emerson's injunction to "Ask the fact for the form," but also in Wordsworth's "gentle breeze." More than this, in his poetry, "In Cold Hell, In Thicket," say, it is clearly Olson's intention to strike "an original relation with the universe," where the universe is an American landscape, approached as if prior to its colonial possession; as if, again, for the first time.

Olson's committed reading of British and American poetry shaped and directed Black Mountain poetry and poetics. Frank O'Hara's seriously irreverent reading was central to the New York School. John Ashbery recalls that the second time he met O'Hara – the first had been at a party – was outside the Widener Library at Harvard, and O'Hara, who had a "knack for discovering unknown writers," was "carrying a stack of books by various writers I had never heard of, including Samuel Beckett, Jean Rhys and Flan O'Brien, who were in fact all but unknown in 1949" (Berkson and LeSueur 1978: 20). The stack of books became something like a formal principle for O'Hara, many of his poems casually naming (and thereby circulating) the books that had gone into the poem's making. "Memorial Day 1950," for instance, a beautiful, early autobiographia literaria, lists Stein, Auden, Rimbaud, Pasternak, and Apollinaire, and alludes to Stevens and Delmore Schwartz. This list is typical in being almost exclusively not British, O'Hara's stack of books being, among other things, a counter to Brooks's *Well Wrought Urn*. Sensing very early that after Modernism, American poetry required a new departure, O'Hara, like Pound before him, set about reading as voraciously as possible outside of the English tradition. It is a pleasure of O'Hara's poems that they name names, and that when, as is often the case, the name is of a writer or artist, one feels, not as in Eliot that one ought to have grappled with them already, but rather that it would be fun to try. Rarely, though, are English poets named or referred to, and when they are it is with an irreverence that Emerson could hardly have dreamed of. Thus "Post the Lake Poets Ballad" finds O'Hara, "Moving slowly sweating a lot/ . . . pushed by a gentle breeze/ outside the Paradise Bar on/ St. Mark's Place":

> a cheerful type who pretends to
> be hurt to get a little depth into
> things that interest me . . . (O'Hara 1991: 157)

Arguably O'Hara's great contribution to American literature was the reading he brought, and absorbed from outside of the British tradition. Even so he was always a Romantic. Always direct – he wrote in the understanding that "I could use the telephone instead of writing the poem" – O'Hara made joy a principle of writing, always moving on because life is short, and because

> the light seems to be eternal
> and joy seems to be inexorable
> I am foolish enough always to find it in wind. (O'Hara 1991: 162)

The questions Olson and O'Hara asked themselves were how, what, and where to read – O'Hara, like the authentic American scholar, was leaving the library when Ashbery caught him with his stack of books – as American poets after Modernism. The further question Adrienne Rich has asked is: what do these questions mean for a feminist American woman? Rich has written and lectured on her formative reading – in "When We Dead Awaken," for instance, or "Blood Bread and Poetry" – describing her experience of that formation in terms of "splitting." She names the poets she was taught and by whom her "style was formed" as Donne, Blake, Keats, Byron, Yeats, Auden, MacNeice, and Thomas. She names also the poets who were not available to her because "still buried by the academic literary canon": Elizabeth Barrett Browning, H. D. Muriel Rukeyser. She doesn't mention, but might, Gertrude Stein, Mina Loy, Lorine Niedecker, and Laura Riding. Rich's early, institutionalized reading, in other words, in British poetry, occluded British and American women poets, with the twofold effect that for many years she was obliged to write as if there were no body of women's poetry to draw on, and that therefore her experience as a woman was entirely separate from, unvoiced in and unvoicable by, her reading and writing. This is the "split," a state of being she first began adequately to articulate in "Snapshots of a Daughter-in-Law," a fragmented poem that proceeds largely by allusion, stitching together quotes – from Thomas Campion, say, or Samuel Johnson – in which women's writing is casually and devastatingly marginalized. The real force of the split, however, is that Rich remains deeply drawn to, cannot imagine doing without, that body of writing that threatened to exclude hers. A later poem, "Transcendental Etude," shows this better than "Snapshots of a Daughter-in-Law," drifting, as it does, while contemplating Vermont, into the familiar diction and power of the English line:

> But this evening, deep in summer
> the deer are still alive and free,
> nibbling apples from early laden-boughs
> so weighted, so englobed
> with already yellowing fruit
> they seem eternal, Hesperidian
> in the clear-tuned, cricket throbbing air. (Rich 1993: 87)

IV

The major theorist of American readings of British poetry is Harold Bloom. For Bloom (1973) what these readings, or misreadings, invariably betray is an anxiety of influence which is the condition of all poetry, but especially of American poetry, hence, as he would see it, Emerson's "demand." Except that as Pound's "image," Eliot's "tradition," Williams's "deer," and Olson's "syllables" show, and as, were there world enough and time, Ginsberg's "Blake," Ashbery's

"Rivers and Mountains," Susan Howe's scholarship, and Lyn Hejinian's theorizing would confirm, significant American poets have arrived at their own terms for the pleasures and difficulties of reading the British. Which reminds one in turn, as Emerson insisted, that the reader does well always to look beyond the institution.

References and Further Reading

Berkson, Bill and LeSueur, Joe (1978). *Homage to Frank O'Hara*. Berkeley, CA: Big Sky.

Blake, William (1958). *William Blake: A Selection of Poems and Letters*, ed. J. Bronowski. Harmondsworth, UK: Penguin.

Bloom, Harold (1973). *The Anxiety of Influence: A Theory of Poetry*. Oxford: Oxford University Press.

Breslin, James E. B. (1984). *From Modern to Contemporary: American Poetry, 1945–1965*. Chicago: University of Chicago Press.

Brooks, Cleanth (1968). *The Well Wrought Urn: Studies in the Structure of Poetry*. London: Dennis Dobson Ltd.

Eliot, T. S. (1961). *Selected Poems*. London: Faber and Faber.

— (1975). *Selected Prose of T. S. Eliot*, ed. Frank Kermode. London: Faber and Faber.

Emerson, Ralph Waldo (2001). *Emerson's Poetry and Prose*, ed. Joel Porte and Saundra Morris. New York: Norton.

Forbes, Deborah (2004). *Sincerity's Shadow: Self-Consciousness in British Romantic and Mid-Twentieth-Century American Poetry*. Cambridge, MA: Harvard University Press.

Frost, Robert (1951). *Complete Poems of Robert Frost*. London: Jonathan Cape.

Gelpi, Albert (1987). *A Coherent Splendour: The American Poetic Renaissance, 1910–1950*. Cambridge, UK: Cambridge University Press.

Golding, Alan (1995). *From Outlaw to Classic: Canons in American Poetry*. Madison: University of Wisconsin Press.

Jarrell, Randall (1981). *Kipling, Auden and Co.: Essays and Reviews, 1935–1964*. New York: Farrar, Straus, and Giroux.

Kenner, Hugh (1975). *A Homemade World*. New York: Knopf.

Longenbach, James (1987). *Modernist Poetics of History: Pound, Eliot and the Sense of the Past*. Princeton, NJ: Princeton University Press.

McGann, Jerome (1983). *The Romantic Ideology*. Chicago: University of Chicago Press.

Moore, Marianne (2003). *The Poems of Marianne Moore*, ed. Grace Schulman. London: Faber and Faber.

Myers, Jeffrey (1996). *Robert Frost: A Biography*. London: Constable.

O'Hara, Frank (1991). *The Selected Poems of Frank O'Hara*, ed. Donald Allen. Manchester, UK: Carcanet.

Olson, Charles (1977), *Call Me Ishmael.* Baltimore, MD: Johns Hopkins University Press.
— (1997). *Collected Prose,* ed. Donald Allen and Benjamin Friedlander. Berkeley: University of California Press.
Pound, Ezra (1980). *Ezra Pound and the Visual Arts,* ed. Harriet Zinnes. New York: New Directions.
— (1981). *Selected Poems.* London: Faber and Faber.
Rich, Adrienne (1993). *Adrienne Rich's Poetry and Prose,* ed. Barbara Gelpi and Albert Gelpi. New York: Norton.
Stevens, Wallace (1965). *Selected Poems.* London: Faber and Faber.
Vendler, Helen (1980). *Part of Nature, Part of Us.* Cambridge, MA: Harvard University Press.
Williams, William Carlos (1968). *The Autobiography of William Carlos Williams.* New York: MacGibbon and Kee.
— (1971). *In the American Grain.* Harmondsworth, UK: Penguin.
— (1976). *Selected Poems.* Harmondsworth, UK: Penguin.

Chapter 3

American Poet-teachers and the Academy

Alan Golding

In 1829 Henry Wadsworth Longfellow, later the most popular and widely read poet of his age, became Professor of Modern Languages at Bowdoin College, moving on to Harvard in 1836 and staying till 1854. Ever since, American poets have frequently worked as professors – though not always professors of poetry – and ever since, they have argued about the relationship of poetry to the academy. In a 1972 interview, Allen Ginsberg asserts that "school is irrelevant to poetry. I mean school is something from the nineteenth century. Poetry has gone back to 15,000 BC" (Ginsberg 1974: 17). The position that the Columbia University graduate and Brooklyn College professor states in that first sentence, however, is one that American poets have argued over since Longfellow complained about his teaching assignments and Walt Whitman, one of American poetry's great didacts and innovators, published this poem in 1865 about walking out on a teacher figure:

> When I heard the learn'd astronomer,
> When the proofs, the figures, were ranged in columns before me,
> When I was shown the charts and diagrams, to add, divide, and
>   measure them,
> When I sitting heard the astronomer where he lectured with
>   much applause in the lecture-room,
> How soon unaccountable I became tired and sick,
> Till rising and gliding out I wander'd off by myself,

> In the mystical moist night-air, and from time to time,
> Look'd up in perfect silence at the stars. (Whitman 2002: 227)

The speaker of Walt Whitman's poem is not exactly walking out of class in disgust here, but he's close. And although that speaker calls his negative response to the astronomy lecture "unaccountable," it really isn't. The oppositions that structure the poem are familiar ones from the legacy of Romantic poetry in English, and from Whitman's precursor and contemporary Ralph Waldo Emerson: inside–outside, culture–nature, society–solitude, institutional setting–individual impulse, established learning–spontaneous action. Emerson, in essays such as "The American Scholar," "Self-Reliance," and "The Poet," argued against institutions and for what he called "creative reading as well as creative writing" – the earliest use of that latter term that I know of (Emerson 2001: 60). His American scholar was closer to the poet than the academic, embracing "the mind of the Past" and its literary expression without worshiping it, setting the independently intuitive self against the reification of "the book, the college, the school of art, the institution of any kind" (2001: 58–9).

In "Song of Myself," Whitman writes "He most honors my style who learns under it to destroy the teacher," for "I teach straying from me" and (unlike the astronomer) "I do not give lectures" (Whitman 2002: 73, 74, 64). If destroying the teacher anticipates popular New Age titles like Sheldon Kopp's *If You Meet the Buddha on the Road, Kill Him*, it also anticipates one recurrent component of American poets' attitudes toward learned authorities and institutions. A similar skepticism to that directed against the learned astronomer is enacted in a different, ironically deferential, rhetoric in Emily Dickinson's letters to Thomas Wentworth Higginson. Writing to Higginson, one of the most powerful literary arbiters of the age, to ask if he thought her poetry "breathed," Dickinson responded to what we must infer was Higginson's bafflement (his half of the correspondence has not survived) with the sly amusement of the "student" who knows better than the teacher. "You think my gait" spasmodic – "I am in danger – Sir," she joked, even as she asked "will you be my Preceptor?" and she signed herself "your scholar" during the 24 years of their subsequent correspondence and friendship (Dickinson 1986: 171, 174–5). Dickinson was very much an American scholar in the Emersonian mode, as Adrienne Rich picked up a century later in basing a poem of female and feminist independence, "I Am in Danger – Sir –," on Dickinson's letters.

In Whitman and Dickinson, the skepticism toward the teacher is couched in individual terms (though implicitly extended, in Dickinson's poetry and letters, to the whole system of patriarchal literary authority of her time). By the time of Ezra Pound – perhaps the first quintessential American avant-gardist in his polemics, his manifestos, his preoccupation with the principle that modern poets "make it new," and his own inauguration of a new mode of writing (in the *Cantos*) that used collage principles to construct what he called "a poem including history" – we can already see the experimental poet's skepticism extending to academic institutions. In a well-known 1913 poem, Pound made a "pact" with Whitman, citing himself not as the inaugurator but as a continuer of an emergent American tradition: "It was you that broke the new wood, / Now is a time for carving" (Pound 1952: 98). Pound thought of Whitman as an utterly negative aesthetic model and mostly a bad writer, however, and framed one critique with a striking comment: "Certainly the last author to be tried in a classroom" (Pound 1960: 192). Pound assumes here that aesthetic values – such as the attention to the careful shaping of an aesthetic object implied in "carving" – get passed on "in the classroom," that the classroom is, or is becoming, a primary site for the dissemination of new poetry. In tension with that assumption is Pound's equally powerful belief that the academy represents forms of intellectual and cultural orthodoxy utterly antithetical to the avant-garde imagination. This tension marks and structures the relationship of much innovative American writing to the institution that is one of its main sites of reception.

Pound's own formal teaching career lasted only a few months; in early 1908 he was fired from Wabash College for hosting a young woman overnight in his quarters, a symbolic moment in an early avant-gardist's relationship to the academy. However, he continued to think of himself as a teacher for much of his career, engaged in educating an audience in how to read and in curing the deficiencies of the "beaneries," his unflattering term for universities. His poem "The Jewel Stairs' Grievance," a translation from the Chinese poet Li Po, embodies the relationship between "newness" (that key term of Pound's and high modernist poetics) and teaching – the teaching *of* the new:

> The jewelled steps are already quite white with dew,
> It is so late that the dew soaks my gauze stockings,
> And I let down the crystal curtain,
> And watch the moon through the clear autumn.

> NOTE. – Jewel stairs, therefore a palace. Grievance, therefore there is something to complain of. Gauze stockings, therefore a court lady, not a servant who complains. Clear autumn, therefore he has no excuse on account of weather. Also she has come early, for the dew has not merely whitened the stairs, but has soaked her stockings. The poem is especially prized because she utters no direct reproach. (Pound 1957: 55)

The lesson involves how to read Pound's emergent modernism, and it occurs in the relationship between poem and note, between "primary" text and the pedagogical commentary on it – between poet and teacher. This note does not provide extra information about the poem's content, explain an allusion, or identify a source. It is not the kind of note we recognize from today's massive classroom anthologies. Rather, it offers instructions on how to read the parataxis (the use of juxtaposed elements without explicit connection) of Pound's modernism, containing the whole method of that modernism within a few short sentences. As modernist readers, we are to infer narrative, social context, and emotional tenor from concrete images. Pound's note fills in the logic that the paratactic poem suppresses, and concludes with a canonizing judgment: "The poem is especially prized because she utters no direct reproach." What are we to make of that passive verb? The poem is "prized" by whom? Doesn't "prized" really mean "praiseworthy"? Pound is praising here what T. S. Eliot calls "impersonality" in his influential essay "Tradition and the Individual Talent" – emotion communicated via compressed image rather than statement. Not incidentally, this praise also reflects a now-familiar gender dynamic within high modernism: in uttering no direct reproach, "she" remains "free from [the] emotional slither" (Pound 1968: 12) with which Pound commonly associated women and women's writing. In multiple ways, then, "The Jewel Stairs' Grievance" is a teaching parable, a lesson in how to read.

Pound's persistent writing of textbooks and guides, his generation of reading lists and of anthologies both disguised (*The ABC of Reading*) and full-fledged (*Confucius to Cummings*), reflects this sense of himself as poet-pedagogue. His pedagogic stance is inseparable from his literary avant-gardism and his commitment to the principle of "discovery" or "newness." This stance consisted simultaneously of a desire to teach and a suspicion of teaching institutions, contradictory impulses both to exclude and to instruct from his position as self-constructed "genius." Pound sets himself up as an academy of one, the self-styled "Ezuversity."

In *ABC of Reading* (first published 1934), evaluation or critical judgment constitutes for Pound a means to enlivening and streamlining the academic canon, producing a "drastic separation of the best" from the mass of material "that has overweighed all curricula" (Pound 1960: 13) in the previous 50 years of the Luddite bureaucracy that is American higher education. Formally, Pound's pedagogic method is one with his poetic method: parataxis. In other words, when extended to criticism or pedagogy, juxtaposition or parataxis, the structural method of Pound's poetry, becomes a method of evaluation, of the emergence of self-evident quality or superiority:

> Hang a painting by Carlo Dolci beside a Cosimo Tura. You cannot prevent Mr. Buggins from preferring the former, but you can very seriously impede his setting up a false tradition of teaching on the assumption that Tura has never existed, or that the qualities of the Tura are non-existent or outside the scope of the possible. (Pound 1960: 26)

This teaching experiment extends what Pound had called as early as 1911 his "New Method in Scholarship," "the method of Luminous Detail" (Pound 1975: 21). In "The Teacher's Mission," an essay from the same year as *ABC of Reading*, Pound connects his poetic and critical method with pedagogy even more explicitly: "All teaching of literature should be performed by the presentation and juxtaposition of specimens of writing and NOT by discussion of some other discusser's opinion *about* the general standing of a poet or author" (Pound 1968: 60).

While Pound was busy setting himself up in London (and later in Paris and Rapallo, Italy) as the antiacademic maverick teacher-poet, the university of Ezra, founding and disbanding short-lived but influential movements (Imagism, Vorticism) outside the academy, a rather more sedate group of poets, mostly professors or students at Vanderbilt University, were starting to meet in Nashville and formulate principles that would eventually shape how students read poetry for the next 50 years or so. This all-male group of a dozen or so writers started meeting to exchange and discuss their work around 1916 and continued into the 1920s. The best-known names associated with the group are John Crowe Ransom, professor of English at Vanderbilt University; Donald Davidson, a Ransom student who also joined the Vanderbilt faculty in 1920; and two precocious younger students, Allen Tate and Robert Penn Warren. (Laura Riding, then

Reichenthal, who published in *The Fugitive*, the magazine that the collective started as a publishing outlet in 1922 and from which they took their name, is the most famous anomaly, as she became a crucial figure for many writers associated with a later avant-garde movement, Language writing.) Though the poetic achievement of the major Fugitive figures was not insubstantial, and the poems of Ransom, Tate, and Warren are still anthologized, their primary influence came through the New Criticism, the critical method that they pioneered as poet-critics, editors, theorists, and teachers, and their influence on the reading of poetry cannot be overestimated. The key principle of New Criticism, the method of "close reading" that first and foremost paid attention to a poem's craft – prosody, diction, tone, form, structure – before questions of biography, history, or social context, originated in the meetings of the Fugitives, in which they exchanged their poems and discussed them from a technical point of view. The New Criticism, then, has its roots in the practical considerations of poets invested in improving their own work – but poets who subsequently saw in their academic affiliations an opportunity to generalize their developing poetic principles into more widespread critical ones.

The central categories, principles, and objects of analysis of New Criticism pervade essays and books by Tate, Ransom, Warren, Cleanth Brooks, William Empson, R. P. Blackmur and others: ambiguity, paradox, tension, irony, symbolism, structure, unity, allusion, the heresy of paraphrase and so forth are all part of a long-familiar critical lexicon. By the mid-1940s, New Criticism was so academically well-established as the "right" way to read poetry that it was shaping contemporary poetic production and publishing. In other words, emerging poets whose sense of the poem had been formed in an intellectual environment dominated by New Criticism and by the powerful model of T. S. Eliot (whose ideas of the objective correlative, poetic impersonality, and the power of tradition and whose promotion of the English metaphysical poets form part of the New Criticism's foundation) were, in circular fashion, tending to write poems that were susceptible to New Critical methods of reading. It was this literary and academic establishment against which the poets associated with the counter-academy of Black Mountain College reacted.

At Black Mountain, a school generated a poetry "school," though the movement was not named as such until the publication of Donald Allen's anthology *The New American Poetry* (1960). All faculty at the college were active practitioners in their respective arts and subjects, so that to study "English" at Black Mountain meant to study it from the writer's point of view – the goal, equally, of the creative writing movement that was still getting off the ground in the late 1940s. At various points in the period 1948 to 1956 (when the college closed), some of the major poets of the last 50 years attended Black Mountain as students, faculty, or both: Charles Olson, Robert Creeley, Robert Duncan, and Edward Dorn, along with Joel Oppenheimer, Jonathan Williams, and Hilda Morley (the last an unusual case in that she did not publish widely until some time after teaching at the college). Other writers who never attended the college in any capacity came to be associated with the name via their shared aesthetics, personal and literary relationships, and publication in little magazines like *Origin* (edited by Cid Corman) and *Black Mountain Review* (edited by Robert Creeley): Denise Levertov, Paul Blackburn, Larry Eigner, John Wieners. If these lists are predominantly male, we might realize that literary avant-gardes have historically been no more immune to gender-based exclusiveness than any other area of American culture, and that, especially under Olson's leadership, Black Mountain was a heavily masculinist environment.

Black Mountain was the first American academic institution to cultivate avant-garde activity in the arts and to produce its own avant-garde movement. How could a college be "avant-garde?" It helped that Black Mountain was not just any college. Financially self-sustaining (though constantly on the verge of the bankruptcy that eventually destroyed it), it was beholden to no mechanism of state funding, to no influential private donors, and to no board of trustees (beyond its own faculty). If avant-gardes aspire to cultural influence from an initially marginal position, the artists associated with Black Mountain were probably the first to ground that avant-garde influence in any kind of educational institution, and Olson was perhaps the first poet to theorize that influence in poems and in his own sense of himself as poet-teacher. On this point, a key poem is Olson's characteristically dense "The Praises." With this 1950 poem, Pound's coterie audience of initiates has moved into the academy, albeit into a marginal part of it. Here is the first full stanza:

> Observing
> that there are five solid figures, the Master
> (or so Aetius reports, in the *Placita*)
> concluded that
> the Sphere of the Universe arose from
> the dodecahedron (Olson 1987: 96)

"The Praises" in one of Olson's sources, Plutarch's *Morals*, are specifically those of the number five, a key number in Pythagorean thinking, but more generally they are directed here toward the principle of coterie knowledge and audience that Black Mountain College represented for Olson. The poem's diction is expository and even academic, the language of the pedant writing a poem-essay and aiming to teach. Olson establishes this mode early in the hypotaxis and dry diction of the first stanza, with its introduction of a "master" teacher, Pythagoras, and footnote-like claims to scholarly credibility ("or so Aetius reports, in the *Placita*"). The language continues to be that of the academic, with summarizing transitions and overt connectives marking stages in an argument: "So we have it"; "Here we must stop And ponder"; "we turn now to Ammonius" (pp. 97–8). The key feature of this special knowledge for Olson's purposes is that it "must remain enigmatic" and it "excepts . . . / those who are entirely brutish" (p. 99).

Many of the tropes and the stance of "The Praises" recur in the first volume of *The Maximus Poems*, which Olson was writing while teaching at Black Mountain College and in between drafting course descriptions, syllabi, reading lists, catalogue copy, memos to colleagues, letters to potential benefactors and visiting scholars – all the mundane writing tasks of the working academic. Apostrophe and the imperative mode run throughout *Maximus*, which Olson consistently addresses to an intellectual coterie similar to that of "The Praises": "the few of us there are/ who read" (Olson 1960: 24). In "Letter 3," "polis now/ is a few" (p. 11), but that few constitutes a potentially influential pedagogical minority: "so few/ have the polis/ in their eye/ . . . /So few need to, / to make the many share (to have it,/ too)" (pp. 28–9). As we move through the sequence, "Tyrian Businesses" (which began as a prose piece for a Black Mountain student) begins with the announcement of a lesson plan: "This is the exercise for this morning" (p. 35). "Letter 10" features a typically essayistic beginning, announcing its subjects, posing a topic question, and answering it for a thesis: "on John White/ on cod, ling, and poor-john,// on founding: was it puritanism,/ or was it fish? // . . . It was fishing was first" (p. 45). This self-conscious avant-gardist's early style, then, is marked by academic – or at least discursive – conventions, by the tropes that professors use.

Olson was a teacher, and in these poems he writes like one. In an unlikely conjunction, the forms of his institutional life are the forms of his avant-garde poetics. With "The Praises" in particular, we can address the apparent political contradictions of the committed democrat embracing elite or coterie knowledge by reading the poem in terms of an avant-garde pedagogy in two senses: Olson is laying out what form the pedagogy of an avant-garde might take, what kinds of influence it might aspire to, and is in turn teaching his Black Mountain audience how to *be*, how to behave as, an avant-garde. Thus Olson is defending the principles on which Black Mountain could be seen to rest and projecting his hopes for an improbable cultural influence. The poetry that Olson wrote at Black Mountain reflects the paradoxical impulse of some American avant-gardes towards institutionalization, as well as a certain faith in at least one kind of academy (though not in conventional English departments). Among other alternative poetries of the 1950s, even the different groups and workshops around Jack Spicer and Robert Duncan in San Francisco can be seen from a pedagogical point of view, the master with a small circle of students. (We might compare the Spicer and Duncan circles to Pound's model of the teacher in Canto 13, in which Confucius holds a walking tutorial with a handful of devotees.) But for all its ambition, the experimental work of the 1950s went largely unnoticed until the war of the anthologies.

The literary historical moment that came to be known as "the war of the anthologies" involved a lightning-rod opposition between two radically different collections, an opposition that came to shape readers' understanding of American poetry for decades afterwards. The texts in question were Donald Hall, Robert Pack, and Louis Simpson's *The New Poets of England and America* (first edition 1957, second edition 1962) and Donald Allen's *The New American Poetry 1945–1960* (1960). The 1957 *New Poets* gathered 52 poets, 36 American and 16 British, of 40 years old and under, presented in alphabetical order under the presumed rubric of a continuous English-language tradition. Regarding the American poets: a number of them were by the time of this anthology fairly well-established, had published books with visible university and commercial presses, and won significant prizes (in a number of cases, the Yale Younger Poets Prize, then the most prestigious prize available to a young poet and typically a launching pad for a successful career). Their work fulfills all the then-dominant mainstream criteria for poetry, those dictated by the New Criticism: the poems make conventional use of meter, rhyme, and stanza, and they are tonally and stylistically controlled, learned in their allusiveness to canonical texts and concepts, sophisticated and cultured, modestly personal in the lyric tradition while stopping short of significant self-revelation. These writers appeared under the imprimatur of no less a dignitary than Robert Frost, who concluded his introduction to the anthology with the claim that "a thousand, two thousand, colleges, town and gown together in the little town that they make, give us the best audiences for poetry ever found in all this world. I am in on the ambition that this book will get to them" (Hall, Pack, and Simpson 1957: 12). This claim that the academy constitutes the best – indeed, the best ever – audience for poetry is crucial for understanding the poetry wars, for Allen's *New American Poetry* sets itself deliberately against everything then associated with the term "academic."

The New American Poetry gathered fugitive, hard-to-get work from writers who in a number of cases had published only in obscure little magazines, followers not of Frost (nor of Auden and Eliot, the other two unstated masters of *The New Poets*) but of Pound and William Carlos Williams's more experimental modernism. Allen grouped them mostly according to specific writing communities (San Francisco, Boston, New York, Black Mountain College). Social context is explicit, with Allen commenting on the network of magazines and small presses that sustain his poets. And his concluding section, "Statements on Poetics," puts forward a range of poetics that directly conflict with the implicit norms of *New Poets*. The work in *The New American Poetry* is almost exclusively free verse, diverse in its visual layout, by turns revelatory, didactic, comic, intellectual, heavily influenced by the exploratory, breath-based, processual poetics articulated by Olson in his essay "Projective Verse," which leads off the "Statements on Poetics" section as Olson's poetry leads off the anthology. Olson's emphasis in that essay on the poetic act as open-ended process, rather than something resulting in a polished aesthetic product, captures the difference between the anthologies. But equally crucially, what connects Allen's poets is their "total rejection of all those qualities typical of academic verse" (Allen 1960: xi) – a rejection from some very learned poets, we should realize, not of learning *per se* but of institutionalized learning and of a particular poetics associated with the critical practices of the academy. In the "Statements on Poetics" section, Robert Creeley rejects "the great preoccupation with symbology and levels of image in poetry insisted upon by contemporary criticism" (Allen 1960: 410). Allen Ginsberg "hear[s] ghostly Academics in Limbo screeching about form" when "the trouble with these creeps is they wouldn't know Poetry if it came up and buggered them in broad daylight" (pp. 415, 417). James Schuyler pokes fun at "campus dry-heads" and promotes Duchampian Dada over the classical mythology of Robert

Graves's *The White Goddess* as a source for poetry (pp. 418–19). For LeRoi Jones (later Amiri Baraka), "the diluted formalism of the academy (the formal culture of the U.S.) is anaemic & fraught with incompetence & unreality" (p. 425). The anthology wars were partly an argument over the academy as the appropriate site for the consumption and production of poetry, and for Allen's poets the contemporary academy was utterly inimical to poetry.

Robert Lowell, seen by many as the most significant poet of the age, and a poet who gradually moved in the 1950s from writing tangled neo-metaphysical lyrics to a Williams-influenced, more vernacular poetry, put the opposition behind the anthology wars most memorably in 1960:

> Two poetries are now competing, a cooked and a raw. The cooked, marvelously expert, often seems laboriously concocted to be tasted and digested by a graduate seminar. The raw, huge blood-dripping gobbets of unseasoned experience are dished up for midnight listeners. There is a poetry that can only be studied, and a poetry that can only be declaimed, a poetry of pedantry and a poetry of scandal. (Lowell, quoted in Kunitz 1960)

We can realize the longevity of this admittedly simplified conflict in American poetry by seeing it as a version of the differences between Longfellow and Whitman, and of the distinction posed in Philip Rahv's well-known 1939 essay "Paleface and Redskin," an earlier version of the cooked and the raw in which the poles are represented by Henry James and Whitman respectively. By the time of the anthology wars, it was Williams vs. Eliot. Williams complained in his *Autobiography* that *The Waste Land* "gave the poem back to the academics" (Williams 1951: 146); Eliot stayed out of the argument, but Cleanth Brooks, one of Eliot's earliest apologists and finest New Critical readers, represented the opposition in finding much of Williams's poetry "quite inert" and worthy merely of "a blank uncomprehending stare" (Brooks 1965: xx).

By the 1962 second edition of *New Poets,* Robert Pack clearly realized what was at stake. In this edition the definite article is tactfully dropped: no longer *The New Poets,* implying a stereoscopic view of the whole field, but, more modestly, just (some) *New Poets.* Pack begins his introduction to the American section thus (in this edition the two poetries are divided by their common language, and Louis Simpson has dropped out, his own poetry evolving in a direction contrary to that of *New Poets*): "Dividing American poetry into two camps, the Academics and the Beats, has obscured the distinction between good and bad, honest and pretentious writing" (Hall and Pack 1962: 177). (While Pack may question the opposition, as he does Lowell's cooked–raw polarity, his anthology helped reinforce it. American poetry was sufficiently divided from 1957 to 1962 that not a single poet appears in both the Hall, Pack, and Simpson and the Allen anthologies, and only one, Denise Levertov, appears in both Allen and the 1962 edition of *New Poets*.) Pack is right to dismiss this distinction as a popular caricature, but he knows that *New Poets* is already coming to be associated with a stodgy academicism, with stereotypes of the ivory tower. Like Frost in the 1957 edition but at much greater length, he defends poetry's association with the academy, which he sets up as the site of poetry's survival and best audience:

> The problem of an audience – of a community of informed and open discussion and dissent, concerned and yet free from commercial or vested interest – is inseparable from the question of the vitality of any art. In our time, the university, rather than the literary cliques, the poetry societies, the incestuous pages of little magazines, is capable of nurturing and supporting such an audience. (Hall and Pack 1962: 182)

Only the university could provide a context for appropriate critical judgment, an audience that fulfilled New Critical ideals in its ability to be "both passionate and detached, responsive and yet willing to judge" (p. 182).

Both the insider's and outsider's stance toward pedagogy and its institutions presume an authority to teach that has historically been more easily available to white men than to women or to racial and ethnic minorities. If the poets of *The New American Poetry* (in which LeRoi Jones/Amiri Baraka was the only black poet out of the 44 included) located everything antipoetic in the literary academy, black poets offered a parallel critique of an institution whose dominant feature to them was its whiteness. Lacking access to academic authority, black poets – especially but not only those associated with the Black Arts movement – have generally felt less inclined to coopt that authority for themselves and more inclined to point out its built-in inequities and subvert it, treating the largely white poetic and academic establishments and their canons with varying degrees of critical irony. Langston Hughes's "Theme for English B" (written in 1949) is written in the voice of a 22-year-old black student at CCNY, "the only colored student in [the] class," as he responds to the assignment to *"go home and write/ a page tonight./ And let that page come out of you – / Then, it will be true."* The student questions the white teacher's glibly expressivist assumptions about writing "what is true," addressing the question of what we would now call essentialism: "So will my page be colored that I write?/ Being me, it will not be white." The student's page tries or hopes to subsume racial difference under the category of "American," but it concludes by acknowledging the power differential: "you're older – and white – / and somewhat more free" (Hughes 1994: 409–10). Later, Dudley Randall directs "Black Poet, White Critic" against a different site of white academic authority, one that would dismiss political topics in favor of an idea of poetry still widely extant in a white-dominated academy at the time of the poem's publication:

A critic advises
not to write on controversial subjects
like freedom or murder,
but to treat universal themes
and timeless symbols
like the white unicorn.

A white unicorn? (Randall 1968: 7)

One year after Randall's poem, Ishmael Reed wrote "Badman of the Guest Professor" while teaching at the University of Washington, where "they didn't like [him]" because he did not fulfill white stereotypes of the black male (athlete, rapist) and because he "wasn't teaching [their] kind of reading list" (Reed 1972: viii). Reed speaks not as Black Bart but as "black bard," a stage robber-poet out to hijack the white canon. (On the supposed deadness of that canon, and the violence it represents, see Reed's "This Poetry Anthology I'm Reading": "every page some marbled/ trash. old adjectives stand/ next to flagcovered coffins./ murderers mumbling in/ their sleep" (1972: 74).) After satiric dismissals of, among others, Eliot, Faulkner, and Fitzgerald, Reed shifts the basis of his academic critique from race to the related one of class:

dats why u didn't like my reading list – right?
it didn't include anyone on it dat u cd in
vite to a cocktail party & shoot a lot of bull – right?

so u want to take it out on my hide – right?

From the black poet's perspective, cultural evolution will render this professor extinct, a museum exhibit in "d plot . . . between u &/ charles darwin. u know, whitefolkese/ business" (Reed 1972: 81).

Poetry as academic, apolitical cocktail-party chatter: this is the satiric target of Lorenzo Thomas's "The Marvelous Land of Indefinitions." While Thomas, unlike Randall and Reed, mocks not the academy specifically but the New York uptown poetry reading circuit, both social locations share an apolitical formalism, an " 'in' crowd" that "in slavish style follows the ways of the world (European, Anglo-Saxon, White)," and a view of poetry as "the 51st. state/ . . . / Where everyone goes along/ Where poets gather to read poems/ And sip cocktails/ And talk har har har/ Chat har har har blah blah blah/ Talk har har har" – to talk poetry and to "evade" and "escape" the social inequities that the poem has set against the academic middle-class poetry circuit (Thomas 1979: 79–81). This social and intellectual ethos is part of what LeRoi Jones rejected in the poems of *The Dead Lecturer* and *Black Magic*, criticizing himself as "a slick/ colored boy" writer who is "no longer a credit/ to [his] race" and turning away from "all the pitifully intelligent citizens/ I've forced myself to love" (Jones 1969: 6).

Numerous poets in the 1957 and 1962 editions of *New Poets* were moving toward the more "open" forms that defined their subsequent work, even as their earlier, formally traditional, and often prize-winning work was being anthologized: Robert Bly, Robert Lowell, W. S. Merwin, Adrienne Rich, Louis Simpson, James Wright. These poets came to be favored in the creative writing workshops that proliferated from the late 1960s on – but not solely these poets. In fact poets from both sides of the anthology wars went on to enjoy considerable success, as measured by critical attention, prizes and awards, appearances in other widely used anthologies, and teaching positions (many in the burgeoning creative writing industry). Creative writing's long and complex history is well laid out in D. G. Myers's *The Elephants Teach* (1996). Suffice it to say here that if "creative writing" in the disciplinary form that we know it today began with the foundation of the Iowa Writers Workshop in 1941 (the first year that the phrase "writers workshop" was used in the university catalogue), closely followed by programs at Johns Hopkins University (1946), Stanford and the University of Denver (1947), and Cornell (1948), it nevertheless expanded dramatically with the infusion of funds into the academy in the late 1960s and early 1970s. Founded to counter the professionalization of literary study, with the utopian goal of uniting critical and creative work in the academy, it became the quintessential *form* of literary professionalism. If the academic poem of the 1950s and early 1960s was densely textured, tonally restrained, traditional in meter and form, replete with classical and mythological allusion and symbol, the academic poem of the next 20 years adopted certain values of the New American Poetry but without its ambition or sense of formal purpose: it was commonly a low-key, first-person mini-narrative in rather loose free verse, commonplace and transparent in diction, image-centered (fulfilling the classroom mantra "show, don't tell"), projecting an accessible personal voice and concluding in a mild understated epiphany. Creative writing programs and English departments moved further apart in this period as literary critics adopted a wide range of ideas from French post-structuralist theory – ideas that questioned the very notions of voice, subjectivity, authorship, imagination, and feeling that sustained the workshop poem or scenic lyric, as it was variously called.

The reception of the most serious poetic avant-garde of the last 30 years, then, Language writing, has occurred in a complex set of circumstances. Though Language writing has resisted the idea of brand-naming poets as "major" names, significant figures associated with the movement would include Lyn Hejinian, Barrett Watten, Ron Silliman, Charles Bernstein, Rae Armantrout, Bruce Andrews, Steve McCaffery, Carla Harryman, Bob Perelman, and Robert Grenier. Just as the New American Poetry reacted to the poetic norms of its own time, Language writing began partly (though by no means only) in reaction to the workshop lyric, and sometimes parodied mainstream products – as when Rae Armantrout, in "Traveling Through the Yard," reworks William Stafford's rather portentous "Travelling Through the Dark." The movement developed outside the academy, primarily in San Francisco and New York in the mid-1970s. However, many poets associated with it were becoming, independently, quite well read in the literary theory and philosophy circulating in the literary academy and discovering that that theory corroborated much of what they were already doing in their own work. As Lyn Hejinian puts it:

> what was striking to me in reading [French feminist theory] was that the kinds of language that many of these writers advocate seem very close to, if not identical with, what I think of as characteristic of many contemporary avant-garde texts – including an interest in syntactic disjunctures and realignments, in montage and pastiche as structural devices, in the fragmentation and explosion of subject, etc., as well as an antagonism to closed structures of meaning. (Hejinian 1985: 283)

Although very few of the writers associated with the quite large and diverse Language network were career academics in the movement's formative years, its antagonists disparaged the work as academic and theory-driven. This claim has little weight, however: as I've said, the Language writers (like the New Critics) came to their theoretical positions via their own poetic practice, independent and extra-academic reading, and the sort of community practices that have often sustained avant-gardes – small presses, their own magazines, talk and reading series. Only in mid-career did some of them take academic positions, and even then not usually as creative writing teachers.

Nonetheless, Robert Pack's 1962 remarks on the academic audience, which unsympathetic readers have usually dismissed as retrograde, have to be seen today in a light that he never intended, for now many poets associated with the more innovative wings of American poetry – the inheritors of Allen's New Americans – take the academy seriously as a site of poetic reception, just as Pack did. One flashpoint for subsequent debate over experimental writing's relationship to the academy has been the SUNY Buffalo Poetics Program, an academic doctoral program in innovative poetics. In 1990, Charles Bernstein, a key figure in the Language movement and coeditor of one of its main outlets, the magazine *L=A=N=G=U=A=G=E*, became professor of English at Buffalo, and in 1991 he cofounded the Poetics Program with Robert Creeley. Not that the program has been marked by uniformity – there is no Buffalo "school" with an identifiable poetics, even though there may be a recognizably Buffalonian range of commitments and sympathies (students do not go there to write dissertations on James Merrill). Indeed, six issues of the magazine *Apex of the M*, edited by young poets and critics connected with the program, took polemical issue with various forms of perceived Language-writing orthodoxy, promoting as an alternative a spiritually passionate avant-garde that the editors associated with the work of, for instance, Susan Howe and John Taggart. But the program, along with the move into academic positions of a number of Language writers since about 1990, still puts before us, quite starkly, a real question: can there be such a thing as a professional, or professionalized, avant-gardism? If the avant-garde is a way of thinking about art in relation to an oppositional cultural politics, a way of thinking and art-making that claims to critique and resist institutionalization, isn't it fundamentally incompatible with assimilation into the academy? That's always been the assumption. These questions are as old as the idea of the avant-garde itself, but the reception of Language writing poses them again in particularly pressing terms, because this is an avant-garde less committed to a thoroughly oppositional inside–outside model than earlier ones, and more willing to consider the implications of its own reception.

Bernstein in particular has become a kind of poster child for the contradictions of the poetic avant-garde's academic success. Critics often miss Language writing's capacity for ironizing its own reception, from Bob Perelman's "I/ seem to have lost my avant-garde card/ in the laundry" (1998: 11) to Hejinian's "they used to be the leaders of the avant-garde, but now they just want to be understood" (2002: 73). Nevertheless, Bernstein's career is of special interest because more than almost any of his peers (the other example would be Perelman), he has made his own institutional status a recurrent subject of his criticism and poetics. Since his appointment at Buffalo, Bernstein's poetry has frequently addressed the fact, process, and likelihood of its own cooption. He preserves the possibility that a professional avant-gardism is not a total oxymoron in three ways: by his critique of the conventions of academic style and logic and his performance of alternatives in his critical writing (in *Content's Dream*, *A Poetics*, and *My Way*); by the range of extra-academic literary activity that he has used his professional position to foster – the Electronic Poetry Center, Poetics listserv, small presses, magazines, reading series and talk series associated with the Buffalo program; and by making his own assimilation one of his central poetic and critical subjects.

For Bernstein, poetic self-reflexiveness is almost always reflection on po-biz, on the business of poetry. Thus "Emotions of Normal People" includes three paragraphs of advertising copy for the 1989 edition of *Poet's Market* (Bernstein 1994: 94–5). If this move incorporates the marketing context for poetry (instead of being incorporated by it), Bernstein writes his own assimilation into his work through his use of business or marketing language to make comic statements about poetics. With his wonderful ear for the rhetoric of hucksterism, Bernstein coopts critiques of Language writing's alleged careerism by adopting the voice of a literary carnival barker marketing poetic disjunction: " 'We're all serialists now,' said the barker for/ the Language Contortionist live act on the Net. 'Words/ bent and mangled beyond belief, syntax twisted to/ an inch of sense by our grammar-defying, double/ jointed linguabats, who speak out of both – all three – / sides of their mouths & through their heads too!' " (Bernstein 2001: 123). In "The Lives of the Toll Takers," mainstream poetry of the time is "the show-me business" (1994: 17), while Bernstein couches his own parody of poetry as business in terms that provocatively and uncomfortably make the link between avant-gardism and the capitalist obsession with new product:

> . . .   Our new
>   service orientation
>   mea
>
>   nt
> not only changing the way we wrote poems but also diversifying
> into new poetry services. Poetic
>   opportunities
>
>   however, do not fall into your lap, at least not
> very often. You've got to seek them out, and when you find them
>   you've got to have the knowhow to take advantage of them.
>   Keeping up with the new aesthetic environment is an ongoing
> process: you can't stand still. (Bernstein 1994: 22)

Bernstein argues that "the university's role is not to be the center of authority but a place that responds to, and aids, the poetic activity that is generated, by and large, far from its precincts" (1999: 251). That ideal of nonassimilative responsiveness may be more easily stated than achieved, however, in a context like Buffalo's where public money sustains the education of future professors of alternative poetics (many of whom have gone there from a "community" background). In a number of brief but trenchant essays over the last few years, the poet Susan Wheeler has commented on this tension, and especially on the brand-naming of experimental poetry. As she puts it, "radical poetics are so widely read and taught now that thousands of idiosyncratic assimilations and responses vie for our reading and discernment" (Wheeler 2004: 152), like products on the supermarket shelves. In Wheeler's essay "Poetry, Mattering?" the academy is merely another assimilative corner of the cultural marketplace: "What began as an assault from a fringe becomes more centralized, assimilated within the institution (the academy) that supports it. The fact of [Susan Howe's] interest in Emily Dickinson and Herman Melville sells them anew within this institution" (Wheeler 2000: 319). The market, the academy, professionalization, and teaching become crisply conflated in her pithy observation that experimental poets "find themselves a market share now resisted by students with proximity to their endowed chairs" (p. 322). In response Wheeler calls for "the ambition to find language combinations, structures, methods of composition, that remain *unassimilable* in the broad banality of the cultural market" (p. 324) – which sounds like nothing so much as Bernadette Mayer's injunction to "work your ass off to change the language & dont ever get famous" (Mayer 1986: 560), itself the conclusion to a list of teaching experiments. At the same time unassimilability, Wheeler well knows, is as much a fantasy as avant-garde outsideness once was, a metaphor or horizon, a motivating ideal rather than a possibility, so that it paradoxically operates by a form of "insideness." She praises, for instance, "the poet who hopes he can, in some small way, alter the path of the steamroller [of cultural objectification] by inserting the 'uselessness' of elegant form . . . into the lives of the . . . academic 'players' around him" (Wheeler 2000: 324). That's another way of putting what I mean by professional avant-gardism, the distant, quixotic possibility that Charles Bernstein's work and career puts before us as we continue to wrestle with the relationship of especially experimental poet-teachers to the academy.

References and Further Reading

Allen, Donald (ed.) (1960). *The New American Poetry 1945–1960*. New York: Grove.

Bernstein, Charles (1994). *Dark City*. Los Angeles: Sun and Moon.

— (1999). *My Way: Speeches and Poems*. Chicago: University of Chicago Press.

— (2001). *With Strings*. Chicago: University of Chicago Press.

Brooks, Cleanth (1965). *Modern Poetry and the Tradition*. New York: Oxford University Press.

Dickinson, Emily (1986). *Selected Letters*, ed. Thomas H. Johnson. Cambridge, MA: Belknap Press of Harvard University Press.

Emerson, Ralph Waldo (2001). *Emerson's Poetry and Prose*, ed. Joel Porte and Saundra Morris. New York: W. W. Norton.

Ginsberg, Allen (1974). *Gay Sunshine Interview*, with Allen Young. Bolinas, CA: Grey Fox.

Hall, Donald, and Robert Pack (eds.) (1962). *New Poets of England and America. Second Selection*. New York: World.

Hall, Donald, Robert Pack, and Louis Simpson (eds.) (1957). *The New Poets of England and America: An Anthology*. New York: Meridian.

Hejinian, Lyn (1985). "The Rejection of Closure." In Bob Perelman (ed.), *Writing/Talks*. Carbondale and Edwardsville: Southern Illinois University Press, pp. 270–91.

— (2002). *My Life*. Los Angeles: Green Integer.
Hughes, Langston (1994). *The Collected Poems of Langston Hughes*, ed. Arnold Rampersad. New York: Alfred A. Knopf.
Jones, LeRoi (1969). *Black Magic: Collected Poetry, 1961–1967*. Indianapolis: Bobbs-Merrill.
Kunitz, Stanley (1960). "The New Books," *Harper's Magazine*, 221: 100.
Mayer, Bernadette, and the Members of the St. Mark's Church Poetry Project Writing Workshop, 1971–5 (1986). "Experiments." In Ron Silliman (ed.), *In the American Tree: Language, Poetry, Realism*. Orono, ME: National Poetry Foundation, pp. 557–60.
Myers, D. G. (1996). *The Elephants Teach: Creative Writing Since 1880*. Englewood Cliffs, NJ: Prentice-Hall.
Olson, Charles (1960). *The Maximus Poems*. New York: Jargon/Corinth.
— (1987). *The Collected Poems of Charles Olson*, ed. George F. Butterick. Berkeley: University of California Press.
Perelman, Bob (1998). *The Future of Memory*. New York: Roof.
Pound, Ezra (1957). *Selected Poems of Ezra Pound*. New York: New Directions.
— (1960). *ABC of Reading*. New York: New Directions.
— (1968). *Literary Essays of Ezra Pound*, ed. with an introduction by T. S. Eliot. New York: New Directions.
— (1975). *Selected Prose 1909–1965*, ed. with an introduction by William Cookson. New York: New Directions.
Rahv, Philip (1939). "Paleface And Redskin," *Kenyon Review*, 1: 251–6.
Randall, Dudley (1968). *Cities Burning*. Detroit, MI: Broadside.
Reed, Ishmael (1972). *Conjure: Selected Poems 1963–70*. Amherst: University of Massachusetts Press.
Wheeler, Susan (2000). "Poetry, Mattering?" In Molly McQuade (ed.), *By Herself: Women Reclaim Poetry*. St. Paul, MN: Graywolf, pp. 317–27.
— (2004). "Reading, Raiding, and Anodyne Eclecticism: Word Without World," *The Antioch Review*, 62: 148–55.
Thomas, Lorenzo (1979). *Chances Are Few*. Berkeley, CA: Blue Wind.
Whitman, Walt (2002). *Leaves of Grass and Other Writings*, ed. Michael Moon. New York: W. W. Norton.
Williams, William Carlos (1951). *The Autobiography of William Carlos Williams*. New York: Random House.

Chapter 4

Feminism and the Female Poet

Lynn Keller and Cristanne Miller

Modernist poetry in the United States developed in large part in a context of feminist and socialist political activism. During the 1910s, Greenwich Village was the undisputed American center for the innovative arts. The Village was home to Alfred Stieglitz's 291 gallery and his magazine *Camera Work*, The Ferrer Modern School, meeting places of the Provincetown and the Washington Square Players, the feminist discussion club Heterodoxy, several literary and artistic salons, and the offices of *The Masses, Mother Earth, Woman Rebel, The Glebe, Trend, Rogue, Bruno's Weekly, The Chimaera, Others, The Little Review*, and other little magazines. Poets living in the Village during this early radical period included Hart Crane, Alfred Kreymborg, Mina Loy, Edna St Vincent Millay, Marianne Moore, Lola Ridge, Wallace Stevens, Genevieve Taggard, William Carlos Williams (briefly), and Elinor Wylie. This interactive community of writers, artists, and political radicals like Emma Goldman moved New York's modernism away from purely aesthetic concerns, foundationally linking social and gender politics with art. American modernism, in this regard, was radically different from European avant-garde movements and from ways it has been conventionally portrayed, as both antipolitical and politically conservative.

In Chicago women were very active in the innovative literary scene. There Harriet Monroe and Alice Corbin Henderson founded and edited *Poetry*, and Margaret Anderson and Jane Heap founded the *Little Review*, although after two years they moved it to New York. In

New York as well, during the 1910s and 1920s, many of the institutions supporting experimental arts and writing were founded or led by women. While not necessarily from a politically feminist posture, women ran galleries and studios, managed and directed theaters, and coedited or edited some of the era's most significant little magazines. In short, in an era still assuming male dominance in both aesthetic and business spheres, women confidently took on major economic, social, and aesthetic positions of leadership in the experimental arts.

The modernist poet whose work articulates the most thorough and broad-ranging congruence with early twentieth-century feminism is Marianne Moore. An active feminist, Moore lived with her mother, attended church regularly, had no bohemian inclinations, and was apparently celibate. Like most US modernist poets – male and female, black and white – Moore attended college and benefited from its support of nontraditional professional and life choices for women. During college, Moore lectured recalcitrant friends on women's legal and economic rights; after college, she campaigned for suffrage, marched in parades, and wrote suffrage essays for a local newspaper. Drawing on a history of women's leadership in reform movements like abolitionism and temperance, the women's movement in the United States fought for political, legal, and economic equality between the sexes through legislation and broad-based institutional change. While nineteenth-century campaigns for female suffrage were based on the concept of "natural rights" (woman's "special nature" as a nurturer justified her political and social parity with men), by 1910 women's associations were moving away from essentialized definitions of gender. Like most white feminists of the era, Moore believed optimistically in the possibilities of economic, political, and social reform; sought gender neutrality in appearance, aesthetics, and conceptions of human possibility; and took little interest in sexual liberation. Moore published reviews and essays as well as poetry, edited *The Dial* from 1925 to 1929, and eventually won every major poetry prize in the United States.

Moore's most openly feminist poems were published early in her career. In "Marriage" (first published 1921), Moore observes that "men have power/ and sometimes one is made to feel it" (Moore 2002: 301). "Roses Only" (first published 1917) warns women against their own complicity in their social and intellectual trivialization. The "petals" of physical beauty, she scolds, are not women's most significant characteristic; instead, logic tells all observers that women "must have brains." "Brilliance" – a property based on the use of personally and intellectually challenging "thorns" as well as the display of petals – is more interesting and longer lasting than beauty. The poem ends with the admission that thorns

> . . . are not proof against a worm, the elements, or mildew
> But what about the predatory hand? What is brilliance without
> co-ordination? Guarding the
> Infinitesimal pieces of your mind, compelling audience to
> The remark that it is better to be forgotten than to be
> remembered too violently,
> Your thorns are the best part of you. (Moore 2002: 229)

In implied response to centuries of *carpe diem* invitations to women to give themselves quickly to lovers before they lose the youthful bloom which alone makes them desirable, and implying that woman's only valuable characteristic is her ability to arouse sexual desire in men, Moore caustically asserts that predation is not preferable to loneliness. This poem urges brilliant independence rather than heterosexual dependence for women.

"Roses Only" serves as a poetic as well as a feminist manifesto. A poem with "thorns," qualities that resist easy appropriation, has greater value for Moore than one that is merely lovely. In redefining the basis of women's attractiveness Moore also redefines poetic beauty as brilliant resistance to "the predatory hand." Beauty inheres in the combination of complicated but felicitous formal qualities and strong – for Moore, often ethical – argument; as she says in "The Monkey Puzzle" (first published 1925), "This porcupine-quilled, complicated starkness –/ this is beauty – 'a certain proportion in the skeleton which gives the best results'" (Moore 1981: 80). Moore's poetry is characterized by complex syntax, syllabic stanzaic structures, rhymes on function words and unaccented syllables ("mildew" and "to" in "Roses Only"), repeated questions and negations, and a proclivity to explain through minute description rather than exposition. Such characteristics are the "thorns" of her modernist verse transmuted into "brilliance" through combination with the "skeleton" of her feminist logic.

Other women in New York similarly played multiple roles in shaping modernist literature. Lola Ridge founded the Ferrer Modern School journal, was associate editor of *Others,* and US editor of *Broom;* her volume *The Ghetto and Other Poems* (1918) called attention to the fluid boundaries between the experimentalist aesthetics of American literary modernism and the ferment of ideas in large immigrant communities like the Yiddish-speaking world of New York's Lower East Side. Edna St Vincent Millay, while more devoted to the use of traditional forms and feminine self-formulation than Moore, provided a clear sense of the breadth and popularity of poetry responding to the changing opportunities of women's lives. Millay loved to provoke especially male adulation through highly feminine dress, but her verse was frequently critical of heterosexual power structures. Dorothy Parker was similarly critical but eschewed any whiff of femininity, writing antiromantic verses of cynical wit. Mina Loy published radical poems on female sexuality and social positioning, edited a special issue of *Others*, and participated in writing two issues of a New York Dada little magazine, *The Blind Man*. As a part of the broader Harlem Renaissance, African-American women hosted salons, acted as literary editors of major black journals, and published poetry. Anne Spencer, Angelina Grimké, Helene Johnson, Georgia Douglas Johnson, Mae Cowdery, and other women wrote pastoral, cosmopolitan, ironic, and erotic verse, in formal and open styles, often explicitly rebelling against gender and heterosexist as well as racial norms.

Differences between Moore and Gertrude Stein are instructive for thinking about this era of feminism in its range of intersections with female poets. Stein became openly hostile to the women's movement and feminism during her years at Johns Hopkins medical school. Like Millay, Parker, and Loy, she showed no interest in public and institutional politics or reform. On the other hand, like Moore, Stein was committed to the ideology of gender neutrality and convinced that women's abilities equaled men's. In a 1927 poem/essay called "Patriarchal Poetry" (not published during her lifetime) she creates unfamiliar word sequences so as to subvert fixed hierarchies and assumptions of grammar, verse, punctuation and logic, instead proceeding by patterns of association, image, and sound. The repeated phrase "We to be" abuts "Their origin and their history patriarchal poetry," suggesting that poetry is embedded within the "origin" of its author and that some categories of author ("We") are not yet inscribed in historical or aesthetic discourse, hence are yet "to be." Patriarchal poetry makes absolute distinctions unquestioningly – "makes no mistake makes no mistake in estimating the value to be placed upon the best and most arranged of considerations." Yet in the final pages of her poem/essay, Stein optimistically asserts that "Patriarchal Poetry makes mistakes . . . might be withstood . . . reclaimed renamed replaced and gathered together . . . Patriarchal Poetry might be finished tomorrow" (Stein 1998a: 116, 124, 132, 133, 140–1, 146).

Stein's *Tender Buttons* (1914) puns frequently on conventions of femininity and on lesbian sexuality; its organizing structure of Objects, Food, and Rooms elevates conventionally female domestic realms to the level of poetic and philosophical seriousness. Individual poems express gender critique with high humor. "A Petticoat" reads "A light white, a disgrace, an ink spot, a rosy charm" (Stein 1998b: 22) – perhaps referring to the social "disgrace" of being a professional woman writer, the "charm" of menstruation, and the "charm" of blushing when two women interrupt their writing to strip down to petticoats. "In Between" contains the clause "A virgin a whole virgin is judged made" (p. 24) indicating that the concept of virginity is both constructed or "made" and "judged" to be of value to patriarchal society. As a whole, however, the sequence works against the coherent ordering of its many parts, encouraging the reader to entertain multiple strands of potential interpretive order simultaneously. In its unravelings, the poem asserts pleasure and value in lesbian love (those erotic "tender buttons") and a woman-centered life.

During the 1920s, lesbian homosexuality first took on clear popular definition in the United States and came under attack by a variety of culture establishments. The cumulative heterosexual insistence of cinema, popular literature, advertising, and fashion eroded the broad homosocial continuum women had previously enjoyed but also pushed many women toward a more consciously politicized sense of sexuality and personal politics. By emigrating to Paris in the first decade of the century, Stein – like other women writers over the next two decades – avoided this changing culture of assumption in her home country; the French didn't care about the behavior of expatriate American women, which freed Stein to ignore their (strict) gender conventions as well as the Victorianism of her childhood, and the adamant heterosexuality of American popular culture in the 1920s. In her poems as in her life, she celebrated lesbianism without proclaiming or politicizing it. Cigar-smoking, openly lesbian poet Amy Lowell instead remained in the United States, but was partially protected from public opinion by her wealth. Like many women of this era, Lowell rejected masculinist assumptions about women's abilities and aesthetics through her masculine dress, unconventional behavior, and influence on modernist publication (she edited three anthologies of Imagist poetry) as well as through her poetry.

Although Stein's most experimental period (1905–32) coincided with early modernist formal innovation, during the 1910s and 1920s she published relatively little verse in the magazines printing work by

Williams, Eliot, Pound, Moore, Stevens, and Loy. By the 1980s and 1990s, however, her work was heralded as at the forefront of literary and theoretical radical movements. Stein's work similarly anticipates later twentieth-century feminist politics more than it represents that of the majority of her contemporaries, although it participates in the sexual and lesbian verbal play common to writers such as H. D., Loy, Lowell, and Djuna Barnes. Particularly influential for later poetry is Stein's radically disjunctive collage, her loosening of the word from the moorings of signification, and her sense of language as concrete, a thing of palpable sound and visual space. Lorine Niedecker and Laura (Jackson) Riding similarly became more important to late twentieth-century readers and poets than they were to their contemporaries in the 1930s and 1940s. Moore's poems, in contrast, were celebrated by her contemporaries as exemplary of modernism's highest goals but have been generally ignored by late twentieth-century feminists and less influential on late twentieth-century poetry.

With the end of World War I and the winning of suffrage in 1920, a backlash developed in the USA against both feminism and reform politics. The new generation of women was more interested in a psychological and lifestyle feminism of individual privileges and sexual reform than in broadly based legal and institutional change or a homosocial women's culture. Consequently, women coming of age in the 1920s had a different sense of themselves from those coming of age earlier in the century. Although H. D. is of precisely the same generation as Moore, even attending Bryn Mawr College for one year while Moore was there, her feminism prefigures that dominating the 1920s. H. D. wrote more openly of her bisexuality in prose than poetry, but even her earliest poems reject gender stereotypes through redefinition of the female and feminine in the realms of psychology and aesthetics. H. D. positions her speakers in relation to men of authority, working out contrasting modes of female power and beauty – for example in "Eurydice," "Sea Gods," or "Demeter." Like Moore, H. D. redefines feminine beauty as a model for redefining aesthetic values. "Sea Rose" asserts that the "harsh" sea rose, "meager flower, thin,/ sparse of leaf" is "more precious / than a wet rose" because it has experienced the full passions of life, weathered the hardship and elevation of storms (H. D. 1983: 5). In "Sheltered Garden," a first-person speaker gasps "I have had enough" of "border-pinks, clove-pinks, wax-lilies"; because "beauty without strength,/ chokes out life," she wants "to find a new beauty/ in some terrible/ wind-tortured place" (1983: 19, 20, 21). Like Moore and Stein, H. D. constructs a poetic that manifests and sharpens her gender theorizing – in her early work, a poetic of "astringent," unrhymed, short lines, often rewriting myths or transforming traditional symbols of women's secondary, stunted, or ignored lives.

In the 1940s and 1950s, H. D. took the further significant step of launching feminist revisions of epic. While Moore, Stein, and Loy had all experimented with poem sequences, H. D. wrote a trilogy of long meditative poems that approach the epic in scale and ambition. Composed between 1942 and 1944 in response to experiencing the London Blitz, *Trilogy* explores H. D.'s belief that civilization can endure even war's catastrophic destruction through exploration of social and private consciousness modeled on female patterns of endurance and nurture. She uses ancient classical, Egyptian, and Christian myths to associate creative power with the feminine and to assert that such power may save human civilization, but only by developing new modes of relationship and value. At the end of Book II, a female figure identified as "Psyche"

> . . . carries a book but it is not
> the tome of the ancient wisdom,
> the pages, I imagine, are the blank pages
> of the unwritten volume of the new. (H. D. 1983: 570)

With *Helen in Egypt* (1961), H. D. produces a female-centered epic, claiming for women the grand poetic genre associated with sweeping history and national definition. Relocating the Helen of Homer's *Iliad,* H. D. rewrites the aftermath of the Trojan War as an exploration of female power. In a move influential for later women writers, she shifts epic's traditional focus on nationally defining events in military and public history to a spiritual/psychological focus – drawing at once on goddess worship, hermetic lore, and Freudian psychology, and asserting the necessity of continuing change. H. D. structures her epic visions around what she regards as feminine rather than female values, defining the feminine as a crucial, universally available, psychological resource.

With the Great Depression, much of the political energy of American women poets turned from feminism to labor and economic issues – as manifested in Genevieve Taggard's 1936 volume of proletarian poetry *Calling Western Union* and her work as contributing editor of *The New Masses.* Muriel Rukeyser exemplifies the poets of this period in her combination of lyric, narrative, and documentary elements.

The poem-sequence "The Book of the Dead" (1938) investigates a mining disaster in Gauley Bridge, West Virginia, where a subsidiary of Union Carbide hired men to drill through a mountain that contained between 97 and 99 percent pure silicon, without giving them any safety equipment. Quoting Congressional records, constructing "interview" statements, and writing both descriptive and lyric witness accounts of individual's lives and the process of a national investigation, Rukeyser uses modernist juxtaposition and collage to articulate her political commentary, pointedly including interviews with women and people of color in her narrative. As this poem suggests, Rukeyser's feminism (like that of many of her contemporaries in the 1930s and 1940s) is expressed indirectly, through rebellion against multiple forms of inhumanity rather than through explicit gender and sexual critique. Women, however, often appear in nonstereotypical ways in her poems and, during the decades of national gender conservatism following World War II, she published more openly feminist poems, like "Long Enough" (first published 1958); here the speaker comments "I am that woman who too long/ Under the web lay," a realization that leads her to begin "to wake/ And to say my own name" (Rukeyser 1978: 413).

Rukeyser's metaphorical expression of a need for feminist awakening is appropriate for the late 1950s: by that time, the social and psychological gains of early twentieth-century feminism had been largely erased, first through concern with national and international crises (the Depression, World War II), and then, in the immediate postwar years, through a highly conservative social climate. By the late 1930s the term *feminism* had come to be narrowly associated with the single issue of the Equal Rights Amendment to the US Constitution, and young women were rarely drawn to the cause. After the war, reaction against the power and freedom women had enjoyed as workers contributing to the war effort resulted in a national social agenda redefining women's place and roles as primarily domestic. The artistic climate, too, was conservative, with poetic practice dominated by T. S. Eliot and the Southern Agrarians (a group of traditionalist writers including John Crowe Ransom, Allen Tate, and Robert Penn Warren).

Given this context, it is not surprising that female poets at mid-century tended to write without an obvious feminist consciousness. Elizabeth Bishop, whose first volume *North & South* was well received in 1946, was not untypical in wanting to avoid being positioned – or, later, anthologized – as a woman poet. Despite having attended a prestigious woman's college, Vassar, and despite living as a lesbian,

Bishop wished simply to avoid the implication of second-class achievement often conveyed with the label "woman poet."

Gwendolyn Brooks was somewhat unusual for the period in the forthrightness with which she engaged social and gender issues, particularly with reference to African-American life. In her elaborately formalist *Annie Allen* (1949), the antiromantic mock-epic "The Anniad" narrated a young black girl's life in terms criticizing at once the color hierarchy within black America, the damaging gender roles and expectations fostered by Anglo-European romance, and society's treatment of black veterans. Despite the conservatism of the era, Brooks received a Pulitzer Prize for this volume – the first African-American writer to be so honored. Throughout her writing career, Brooks took on topics of controversy: She wrote on the ethics and social politics of abortion in "The Mother"; in a sonnet sequence, she protested the racism practiced against African-American soldiers during and following World War II; and several poems represent the heroism of early civil rights workers, school desegregation, the effects of impoverishment, and the persecution of black people.

"A Bronzeville Mother Loiters in Mississippi. Meanwhile, a Mississippi Mother Burns Bacon" reveals ways in which Brooks links racial issues with analysis of gender norms. The wife of the white man responsible for Emmett Till's death finds herself having to think about the links between social expectation and control of white women and white patriarchy's anxieties about black men. After the murder the woman imagines "It was necessary/ To be more beautiful than ever. . . . As if he considered, Had she been worth it?/ Had *she* been worth the blood, the cramped cries, the little stuttering bravado,/ The gradual dulling of those Negro eyes." Growing increasingly alienated from her husband, the supposed romantic hero, she identifies cross-racially with Till's own mother, linking her husband's violence against their mischievous child to his violence against the young black boy. At the poem's end, she cannot isolate her husband's insistent sexual desire for her from the "Decapitated exclamation points" in Till's mother's eyes, recognizing her complicity in the construction of a myth of white female purity theoretically justifying racist violence as well as her hatred of it (Brooks 1987: 335, 335–6, 339).

Following the 1967 Fisk University Writer's Conference featuring several writers prominent in the Black Arts Movement, Brooks began to write poetry both of looser, unrhymed forms and of greater militancy. By 2000 when she died, Brooks had published over 20 volumes of poetry, taking on the most charged social and political issues of a half century in a variety of forms, from the repeated alliteration, dense rhymes, and jazzy rhythms of her early work to the sparer directness of her late poems.

In its formalism, if not its social engagement, Brooks's early verse was typical of American poetry at mid-century, which had come to be characterized by careful ironies, neatly woven image patterns, formal regularity, and an impersonal stance. By the late 1950s several groups of poets who found these conventions oppressive responded by exploring alternate traditions, looking for innovative models in the visual arts, and propounding theories of nonregular poetic form. While some women seeking a less conservative aesthetic environment were drawn to these alternatives, the innovative movements of the late 1950s and 1960s were led and dominated by men. (Tellingly, Donald Allen's groundbreaking anthology of this *New American Poetry* [1960] contained work by only four women poets among 40 men.) Each group had at least one token recognized woman – for instance, Denise Levertov among the Black Mountain writers, Diane di Prima among the Beats, Barbara Guest in the New York School – and these women certainly wrote with a keen consciousness of gender. In contrast to their modernist predecessors, however, these women did not take leading roles in the journals or small presses associated with the New American writing.

The small numbers of women in the avant-garde writing communities of the 1950s and 1960s suggest the pressure on women to conform to established models in aesthetic as well as political and social spheres. By mid-century, feminism – as a set of ideas as well as a movement – had slipped into invisibility. Middle-class female oppression had acquired an equally invisible form, which Betty Friedan exposed in 1963 as the "feminine mystique." Increasingly educated, affluent, and isolated in the suburbs, white middle-class women were relegated to domestic roles of wife and mother; the availability of time-saving conveniences such as refrigerators, vacuum cleaners, and electric mixers only increased the private, nameless anguish of supposedly ideal lives that felt restricted and empty. Women who entered the paid workforce were excluded from higher paying jobs and positions of responsibility, and received lower pay than their male counterparts.

Sylvia Plath's work and career demonstrate the toll the feminine mystique often took on ambitious women of that era. As a young woman of multiple talents and great drive (as well as depressive tendencies), Plath was selected for a prestigious position with

Mademoiselle magazine, graduated *summa cum laude* from Smith College, and won a Fulbright to study at Cambridge University. Her aspiration was to combine the erotic and domestic fulfillment promised by the feminine mystique with success as a writer. When she married English poet Ted Hughes in 1956, Plath imagined herself embarking on a life in which both of their careers and their family life could flourish. However, the effort of simultaneously supporting Hughes's career (even typing his manuscripts), advancing her own, and raising two small children, took a great toll on her physical and mental health; after Hughes left her for another woman, Plath was unable to survive a bitterly cold and lonely winter in London and took her own life in 1963. The conflict she experienced between domestic and poetic roles is poignantly evoked in "Stings," one of a series of late poems that use the social organization of bees and bee-keeping as metaphoric structures for self-exploration:

> I stand in a column
>
> Of winged, unmiraculous women,
> Honey-drudgers.
> I am no drudge
> Though for years I have eaten dust
> And dried plates with my dense hair.
>
> And seen my strangeness evaporate,
> Blue dew from dangerous skin.
> Will they hate me,
> These women who only scurry,
> Whose news is the open cherry, the open clover?

Lacking any sense of female solidarity, the speaker triumphs at the end as the singular exception, the queen, who has escaped domestic entombment (the wax house) through the searing record of her poetry and through a death that might have been only figurative but in Plath's case proved literal. She proclaims, ". . . but I/ Have a self to recover, a queen . . .":

> Now she is flying
> More terrible than she ever was, red
> Scar in the sky, red comet
> Over the engine that killed her –
> The mausoleum, the wax house. (Plath 1965: 61–2)

"The blood jet is poetry,/ There is no stopping it," one of her last poems ("Kindness") declares (Plath 1965: 82). Plath's posthumously published *Ariel,* which contains many of the poems that poured forth in the last months of her life, is regarded as a founding volume of confessional writing because of its frank expressions of rage – especially against her father, her husband, and patriarchal society more generally (famously, in "Daddy," "Lady Lazarus," "Fever 103") – and because of its revelations, sometimes half-comic and sometimes stunningly austere, of self-hatred, ambivalence about motherhood, internalized misogyny, depression, and death-wish.

The other female poet famous for developing "confessional writing," Anne Sexton, focused even more explicitly on her own bouts with madness, and on the female body and sexual desire. Although her achievements – for instance, in the bold revisions of fairy tales presented in *Transformations* (1971) – are quite distinct from Plath's, her suicide in 1978 meant that their lives provided a similar example of the costs of female creative ambition, an example that was disheartening, if not terrifying, to young women who aspired to be poets.

Fortunately, the rise of the women's movement in the late 1960s and the 1970s – the "second wave" of twentieth-century US feminism – fostered models of female poetic achievement alternative both to the decorous downplaying of gender seen in work like Bishop's (though feminist critics since have revealed extensive, if coded, concern with lesbian sexuality, gender roles, and gender oppression in her poetry) and to the self-destructive energies displayed in the explicitly female poetry of Plath and Sexton. One key model has been Adrienne Rich, who began her career, in the conservative late 1940s, as the dutiful daughter of her poetic fathers but developed rapidly into an outspoken feminist activist, essayist, and poet, adapting poetic tradition to reflect women's perspectives and to suit her radical politics. W. H. Auden, who selected Rich's elegantly restrained debut volume for the Yale Younger Poets Prize in 1951, was not entirely inaccurate when he patronizingly praised its poems as if they were proper young women: the poems, he said in his foreword to the book, are "neatly and modestly dressed, speak quietly but do not mumble, respect their elders but are not cowed by them, and do not tell fibs." Rich's startling subsequent evolution, growing from her early involvement in civil rights and antiwar movements, helped guide some key shifts in American feminism and feminist poetry over half a century. In 1956 Rich began situating her poems within public history by dating each one, as her poetry began to reflect the understanding, crucial to second-wave feminism, that the personal is the political. Renouncing formalism as "asbestos gloves" that had protected her from confronting the intensity of her feelings, she began to employ free verse in looser and more fragmented forms as she wrote directly about experiencing herself as a woman.

While Rich's poems now exposed the anger and frustration she felt as a wife and mother of three small children, struggling to find the time, energy, and potentially subversive imaginative freedom necessary for artistic creation, her stance was never confessional. Instead, Rich used her poetry to analyze social and institutional structures shaping her experience and that of women of earlier times or other races and social classes. Each volume – to date she has published nearly 20 collections, as well as four books of prose nonfiction – courageously revealed a new stage in her political thinking. Thus, Jungian androgyny which provides a crucial resource for female empowerment in *Diving Into the Wreck: Poems 1971–72* is explicitly refuted in *The Dream of a Common Language: Poems 1974–77*:

> There are words I cannot choose again:
> *humanism androgyny*
>
> Such words have no shame in them, no diffidence
> before the raging stoic grandmothers:
>
> their glint is too shallow, like a dye
> that does not permeate
>
> the fibers of actual life
> as we live it, now; ("Natural Resources," Rich 1978: 66)

That collection, which reflects Rich's concurrent interest in criticizing compulsory heterosexuality and highlighting the "lesbian continuum" of female bonding, contains "Twenty-one Love Poems," a powerful series of explicitly lesbian love poems; these revise the male-centered tradition of the sonnet sequence, substituting ideas of personal choice and societal context for the traditional notions of fated or doomed romantic love. Such revisions of genre conventions and such ambitious entries into the still predominantly male terrain of longer poetic works were undertaken by increasing numbers of women writers in the 1970s and 1980s.

The evolution of Rich's work through critiques of militarism and patriarchal institutions surrounding marriage and family to an interest in lesbian separatism, and her poetry's increasing sensitivity to the divergent racial and economic situations of women around the globe, suggest some of the contemporaneous upheavals within American feminism. Second-wave feminism was full of internal division; feminist activists differed passionately on their willingness to work with men, on their priorities for social change, on lifestyles and sexual identities, on the intersections of class or race and gender. Because the late 1960s and 1970s were years of nationalist activism for many racial and ethnic minorities, feminists of color – victims of gender oppression within their racial communities and of racial discrimination outside them – often found themselves in a conflicted relation to the white-dominated feminist movement. Similar ambivalence was experienced by many white working-class women who had never known the luxury of identifying primarily as housewives and mothers, and by some single or lesbian women for whom the ideals of the feminist mystique were equally inaccessible. Women of color who joined the women's movement were accused of betraying their racial community, yet the nationalist movements such as the Black Power movement were often focused on rebuilding manhood. Black Arts poet Sonia Sanchez points to the double oppression faced by black women in a poem for jazz singer Billie Holiday, Lady Day, published in 1969:

> if someone
> had loved u like u
> shud have been loved
> aint no tellen what
> kinds of songs
> u wud have swung
> against this country's wite mind.
> . . .
> if some blk/man
> had reallee
> made u feel
> permanentlee warm.
> ain't no tellen
> where the jazz of yo/songs.
> wud have led us. ("for our lady," Sanchez 1970: 41)

Sanchez's transcription of black vernacular and her celebration of songs directed (with a suggestion of violence in the punning "swung") against white culture and ideology position this poem within the Black Aesthetic, but her pointing to a failure on the part of black men speaks to what Alice Walker would call a "womanist" agenda. Adrienne Rich – whose partnership with Jamaican-born writer Michelle Cliff presumably intensified her awareness of racial injustice – was among those white feminists who built bridges with feminists of color; in 1974 she accepted the National Book Award for *Diving Into the Wreck* with African-American poet/novelists Alice Walker and Audre Lorde in the name of all women who are silenced.

"Poetry is not a luxury," Lorde (1984) asserted in one of her best-known essays. That notion was one held in common by the feminist poets of the 1970s and 1980s, despite the political and aesthetic differences that otherwise divided them. It was shared, too, by their growing audiences, who read poetry in the proliferating women's coffeehouses and bookstores; who purchased emerging feminist literary journals such as *Sinister Wisdom, 13th Moon, Conditions*, books published by feminist presses, and such groundbreaking anthologies as Florence Howe and Ellen Bass's *No More Masks!* (1973, its title from a Rukeyser poem); who listened to poems at political rallies; who quoted from them at women's consciousness-raising groups. If the personal is the political, then poetry reflecting on one's personal situation may be key to political insight; or as Lorde put it, speaking of poetry as illumination, "The quality of light by which we scrutinize our lives has direct bearing upon the product which we live, and upon the changes which we hope to bring about through those lives" (Lorde 1984: 36). Some feminist poets advanced women's liberation by exploring such taboo subjects as menstruation, female eroticism, childbirth, incest, or rape. Others reconstructed lost histories – whether of individual women, of matriarchal societies, or, especially for ethnic minorities, of partially lost traditions. The last is evident, for instance, in Audre Lorde's invocation of West African religion and art in *Black Unicorn* (1978), in Lucille Clifton's repositioning of biblical figures in Caribbean contexts and patois, or in Gloria Anzaldúa's linguistically mixed reclamation of the Aztlan heritage in *Borderlands/La Frontera* (1987). Some used poetry to build bonds among working-class women, or among working-class lesbians, as did Irena Klepfisz and Judy Grahn. Grahn's focus on "the common woman" in combination with her interest in the origins of gay culture led her to revisionary mythmaking on an epic scale in the first two books of a projected quartet, *A Chronicle of Queens* – a work partly inspired by HD's *Helen in Egypt*.

By the mid-1980s, feminism had so changed public consciousness and academic curricula that women's writing had gained sufficient respect – or at least marketability – to be separately anthologized even by such "establishment" publishers as Norton, and the category of feminist poetry was clearly established. But the cost of such recognition was an apparent homogenization. What was identified as feminist poetry – writing that aimed to alter society's images of women, to enact an empowering claiming of voice, and to strengthen bonding among women – presented a coherent accessible voice narrating female experience in terms that conveyed authenticity and sincerity. Many recognized feminist poets (a capacious category that would include Paula Gunn Allen, Alta, Olga Broumas, Sandra Cisneros, Toi Derricotte, nikki giovanni, Susan Griffen, Joy Harjo, Carolyn Kizer, Robin Morgan, Alicia Ostriker, Marge Piercy, Diane Wakoski, Margaret Walker, and many more) eschewed traditional formalism and bent the conventions of received genres, yet their feminism was inscribed primarily through new content and themes or through revisionary perspectives on old (androcentric) ones. There existed, however, women poets of far less visibility who considered formal and linguistic experimentation as central to their feminist project.

Doubting that either the introduction of female content or the claiming by women poets of previously male subject positions would be sufficient to produce fundamental change, these poets were asking, as Rae Armantrout did in "Feminist Poetics and the Meaning of Clarity," "What is the relation of readability to convention? How might conventions of legibility enforce social codes? Does so-called experimental writing seek a new view of the self? Would such a view be liberating?" (Armantrout 1992: 16). Female poets who were violating convention-bound intelligibility gained reinforcement and some fresh conceptual frameworks from the influx, beginning about 1980, of French feminist theory by Luce Irigaray, Hélène Cixous, Julia Kristeva, and Monique Wittig and of European post-structuralism, to which some French feminist thought was indebted. Kristeva's linkage of poetry with the semiotic, for instance, or Cixous's provocative theorizations of an antiessentialist *écriture feminine* encouraged nonlinear modes of writing that rejected traditional forms of unity and closure as they explored polymorphous female pleasure and the plurality of subject positions seen as constituting the feminine.

This understanding of poetic practice ran counter to the dominant feminist consensus on the need for accessibility and for narration of women's stories, as did the outsider poets' interest in modernist traditions of radical formal innovation. Kathleen Fraser has recalled her "uncomfortable feelings of marginality vis-à-vis the women's writing community" (Fraser 2000: 33) in the 1970s, as she wondered:

> Why was there no specifically acknowledged tradition of modernist women's poetry continuing out of H. D., Stein, Dorothy Richardson, Woolf, Mina Loy, Djuna Barnes, Laura Riding, Lorine Niedecker, and Marianne Moore as there clearly was for men working out of the Pound-Williams-Olson tradition or the Stevens-Auden lineage? Why had most of the great women modernists been dropped cold from reading lists, anthologies, and university curricula? And why were most feminist and traditional critics failing to develop any interest in contemporary women poets working to bring structural and syntactic innovation into current poetic practice? (Fraser 2000: 34)

Some women who were interested in both feminism and linguistic innovation, such as Armantrout, Lyn Hejinian, and Carla Harryman, found sufficient support within the community of avant-garde poets beginning to gain recognition as "Language writers." Others who were not integrated into the Language group sought specifically women's intellectual communities in which the relation of language to the construction and expression of gender would be the primary concern. In 1983 Fraser, joining forces with Frances Jaffer, Beverly Dahlen, Rachel Blau DuPlessis and others, founded the journal *HOW(ever)* which brought together feminist poets and scholars to put forward in an explicitly female context some new choices in women's poetry, choices often developing from prior achievements of female modernists.

In the two decades since the mid-1980s, the choices available in feminist writing have continued to expand, even if the force of feminism as a political movement has weakened in the years of "postfeminism" or, some claim, "postpostfeminism." That *HOW(ever)*, which lasted for six volumes, was reborn in 1999 as an electronic journal, *HOW2*, suggests the continuing vitality of women's poetic interventions into dominant discourses as well as the transformations those interventions are undergoing to keep pace with the times. In recent years, as many "mainstream" poets have grown restless within the confines of the personal lyric and begun exploring strategies of disruption derived from experimentalist texts, and as the Language avant-garde has gained prestige, poetic practice has become more eclectic and feminist writers have gained easier access to more varied aesthetics. Young feminists now, often looking to the models offered by their immediate female precursors, are bringing together resources gleaned from significant female poets who have not been identified primarily as feminist writers – among them Jorie Graham, Maxine Kumin, Mary Oliver, Rita Dove, Louise Glück – as well as the divergent examples offered by more obviously feminist poets. These would include, to offer just a few suggestive examples, Susan Howe's elliptical histories that have exploded the resources of page space and typography, the over-the-top formalist artifice through which Marilyn Hacker represents her transnational gay coterie, the anticolonial multilingualism of Theresa Hak Kyung Cha's *Dictee* or, in an Afro-Caribbean context, of Nourbese Philips, the fractal forms and inventive punctuation of Alice Fulton, the vernacular verve of June Jordan, the generative chance operations of Joan Retallack.

Harryette Mullen – who delights in being "licked all over by the English tongue" (Mullen 2002: 57) but remains keenly aware of the historical anguish, particularly for African Americans, of "inklish" (p. 51) – can exemplify this liberating eclecticism. Mullen began her career writing personal lyrics influenced by the Black Aesthetic. Since then, however, she has given fresh twists to her highly political project by drawing upon a diverse array of prior voices and linguistic strategies. Her recent books play not only with multiple word games – puns and homonyms, anagrams, twisted sayings, shifted letters – and samplings of various discursive conventions and vocabularies, but also with the text-generating procedures of Oulipo (the French movement of the 1960s interested in the systematic elaboration of arbitrary, often mathematical, methods for generating texts) and Steinian manipulations of syntax. The several lineages behind *Trimmings* (1991) are suggested by the different aesthetics of the poets who composed the cover blurbs, Bernadette Mayer, Charles Bernstein, and Gwendolyn Brooks. It seems fitting to close this chapter with a section that reworks Stein's "A Petticoat," from *Trimmings* – a series depicting articles of women's clothing in language that highlights the social constraints on women, the violence so frequently directed against them, and the intertwining of demeaning racial and sexual stereotypes. Mullen reads Stein as alluding to "Olympia," Manet's provocative painting of a reclining white nude and a black woman:

> A light white disgraceful sugar looks pink, wears an air,
> pale compared to shadow standing by. To plump recliner,
> naked truth lies. Behind her shadow wears her color, arms
> full of flowers. A rosy charm is pink. And she is ink. The
> mistress wears no petticoat or leaves. The other in shadow,
> a large, pink dress. (Mullen 1991: 15)

In this compressed piece, "mistress" suggests the legacy of slavery that continues to shadow black identity; identification of skin color via comparison (pink next to sugar, "white" skin acquires whiteness only when compared to dark skin) points to the constructedness of race; and the white woman's "rosy charm" overshadowing the "other" signals how dominant standards of feminine beauty and sex appeal have excluded women of color. "Naked truth" may lie, but the duplicity – more precisely, the polysemous layering – of Steinian word play is here adapted to reveal truths about the complex interplay of gender and racial identity.

Where the twentieth century began with focused drives led by white middle-class women to overcome the naturalized gender distinctions of the Victorian era, to enact legislation giving women suffrage and other rights already accorded men, and to assert female sexual desire, the century ended with feminist agendas, both political and aesthetic, whose diversity resists categorization. Mullen's passage, however, reflexively highlights the ongoing challenges faced by feminist poets of rendering "she" in "ink"; of disrupting societal norms; of inscribing the historically particularized truths of the struggles that have surrounded feminine appearance, female stereotypes, the female body; of at once questioning and realizing the possibilities of women's language.

References and Further Reading

Allen, Donald M. (ed.) (1960). *The New American Poetry*. New York, Grove.

Armantrout, Rae (1992). "Feminist Poetics and the Meaning of Clarity," *Sagetrieb* 11(3): 7–16.

Bishop, Elizabeth (1983). *The Complete Poems, 1927–1979*. New York: Farrar, Straus, Giroux.

Brooks, Gwendolyn (1987). *Blacks*. Chicago: The David Company.

DuPlessis, Rachel Blau (2001). *Genders, Races, and Religious Cultures in Modern American Poetry, 1908–1934*. New York: Cambridge University Press.

Fraser, Kathleen (2000). *Translating the Unspeakable: Poetry and Innovative Necessity*. Tuscaloosa: University of Alabama Press.

Frost, Elisabeth A. (2003). *The Feminist Avant-garde in American Poetry*. Iowa City: University of Iowa Press.

H. D. (1961). *Helen in Egypt*. New York: New Directions.

— (1983). *Collected Poems, 1912–1944*, ed. Louis L. Martz. New York: New Directions.

Herndl, Diane Price and Warhol, Robyn W. (1997). *Feminisms: An Anthology of Literary Theory and Criticism*, 2nd edn. New Brunswick, NJ: Rutgers University Press.

Hogue, Cynthia (1995). *Scheming Women: Poetry, Privilege, and the Politics of Subjectivity*. Albany, NY: SUNY Press.

Howe, Florence and Bass, Ellen (1973). *No More Masks! An Anthology of Poems by Women*. Garden City: Doubleday.

Keller, Lynn (1997). *Forms of Expansion: Recent Long Poems by Women*. Chicago: University of Chicago Press.

Keller, Lynn and Miller, Cristanne (eds.) (1994). *Feminist Measures: Soundings in Poetry and Theory* Ann Arbor: University of Michigan Press.

Kinnahan, Linda A. (2003). *Lyric Interventions: Feminism, Experimental Poetry, and Contemporary Discourse*. Iowa City: University of Iowa Press.

Lorde, Audre (1984). "Poetry is Not a Luxury." In *Sister Outsider: Essays and Speeches*. Freedom, CA: Crossing, pp. 36–9.

Marek, Jayne (1995). *Women Editing Modernism: "Little" Magazines & Literary History*. Louisville: University of Kentucky Press.

Miller, Cristanne (forthcoming 2005). *Placing Modernism and the Poetry of Women: Marianne Moore, Mina Loy, and Else Lasker-Schüler. Gender and Literary Community in New York and Berlin*. Ann Arbor: University of Michigan Press.

Miller, Nina (1999). *Making Love Modern: The Intimate Public Worlds of New York's Literary Women*. New York: Oxford University Press.

Moore, Marianne (1981). *Complete Poems*. New York: Viking.

— (2002). *Becoming Marianne Moore: The Early Poems, 1907–1924*, ed. Robin G. Schulze. Berkeley: University of California Press.

Mullen, Harryette (1991). *Trimmings*. New York: Tender Buttons.

— (2002). *Sleeping with the Dictionary*. Berkeley: University of California Press.

Plath, Sylvia (1965). *Ariel*. New York: Harper & Row.

Rich, Adrienne (1951). *A Change of World*, with a foreword by W. H. Auden. New Haven, CT: Yale University Press.

— (1978). *The Dream of a Common Language: Poems 1974–1977*. New York: Norton.

Ridge, Lola (1918). *The Ghetto and Other Poems*. New York: W. B. Huebsch. Available online at <http://www.writing.upenn.edu/~afilreis/88/ghetto.html>.

Rukeyser, Muriel (1978). *Collected Poems*. New York: McGraw Hill.

Stein, Gertrude (1998a). *Writings, 1903–1932*, ed. Harriet Chessman and Catharine R. Stimpson. New York: Library of America.

— (1998b). *Tender Buttons*. Los Angeles: Sun & Moon Press.

Sanchez, Sonia (1970). *We a BaddDDD People*. Detroit: Broadside Press.

Sexton, Anne (1971). *Transformations*. Boston: Houghton Mifflin.

Vickery, Ann (2000). *Leaving Lines of Gender: A Feminist Genealogy of Language Writing*. Hanover, NH: Wesleyan University Press.

Chapter 5

Queer Cities

Maria Damon

Minoritized people without political power can often still have a great representational presence in public life, or, on the other hand, they can be anonymous, invisible to mainstream sensibility. The queer – or "gay and lesbian," "homosexual," "sapphic," "invert," "unvert," "pansy," or simply and more expansively "nonnormative" – presence in major American cities, and in mainstream US American poetry, has been steady; but widespread recognition of it as such, and the political and aesthetic meaning of this presence, has changed over the course of the twentieth century. When queer presence is politicized, as happened in the late 1960s under the double aegis of the gay liberation and feminist movements, visibility in poetry and in public life becomes more pointed, more purposeful, and potentially – at least at the level of public discourse – more complex. This chapter treats developments and significant poets from before as well as during that "era of liberation," aiming to show how identities were shaped and constituted by participation in queer urban activities, spaces, and mindsets – in other words, cultures and cultural practices. The primary urban spaces in which queer subjectivities and poetics took (continually mutable) shape were New York, the San Francisco Bay Area and Paris, though Boston, Tangier, Berlin, Los Angeles, Key West, Provincetown, and other urban or resort centers played important subtending roles; many of the poets discussed below found communities in more than one urban center over the course of their careers. Emphasis on major metropolitan centers doesn't deny the role played by multiple minor sites in which an underground "queer" culture produced writers; but often these writers had to migrate to larger cities in order to fully flourish among peers.

The United States boasts a proud legacy of queer poetry's centrality to national identity, starting with Emerson's recognition of Walt Whitman as the answer to the former's call for a representative national poet in his essay "The Poet," despite Emerson's chagrin that Whitman used, without permission, a personal letter from the former congratulating him on this status as a blurb for his *Leaves of Grass*. Whitman certainly saw himself as such a representative poet, and the States themselves as undergirded by a homoerotic love between men running as a "half-hid warp" (Whitman 1898) through the history and spatial expanse of the country; this love, in Whitman's eyes, legitimized American democracy and guaranteed its authenticity as based on emotion rather than merely rational Enlightenment ideals – emotion, moreover, that, excluding the heterosexual imperative to reproduce, he saw as uncorrupted and noninstrumentalist. Queer sensibility, articulated through poetry and poetics, was the bedrock of the USA's textually "imagined community," to use Benedict Anderson's apt phrase. One can discern a not-very-submerged tradition of the "queer national epic" reaching from *Leaves of Grass* through Hart Crane's "The Bridge," Gertrude Stein's *The Making of Americans*, multiple Ginsberg extravaganzas such as "Wichita Vortex Sutra" and "Howl," Adrienne Rich's "Atlas of a Difficult World," Robert Duncan's ongoing, open-ended Passages series, especially those contained in *Groundwork* I and II (wherein national politics plays a central thematic role), Tony Kushner's play *Angels in America*. Another, less central but sometimes overlapping, queer national aesthetic could be said to accrue to the legacy of the Greek lyric poet Sappho via Emily Dickinson: that of hermeticism scripted in spare, fragmentary, sometimes gnomic phrasings: Jack Spicer, Marilyn Hacker, John Ashbery, Marianne Moore, Elizabeth Bishop, John Wieners, Crane and Rich; dissimilar as these poets are from each other – as different as the differences within the potentially homogenizing phrase "queer American poetry," one can nonetheless tentatively posit a family resemblance between the styles and affective modalities invoked by the foregoing lists of names. Even these lists are misleadingly narrow in their scope of queer poetry and the spaces associated with them: both New York and San Francisco, as well as some of the other cities menioned earlier, are island and/or peninsular cultures typified by hybridity, ethnoracial as well as stylistic and linguistic mixing, transience across borders of all kinds, and multiplicity of contact that complicates and destabilizes concepts of purity in poetic form or genealogy.

Moreover, as John D'Emilio has pointed out, contemporary understanding of modern homosexual identity is so closely intertwined with the rise of urban culture that one cannot talk of the latter without invoking the former as directly causal. Drawing on Marxian historiography as well the specifics of gay US history, D'Emilio shows how the rise of industrial capitalism during the so-called "age of revolution" entailed massive migration by individuals (rather than families) to centers of industry (usually cities), where the trade of labor for wages instead of goods made it possible for people to survive individually, without reliance on an extended family to produce food, shelter, and clothing through small-scale agriculture, communitarian building projects, and home-based textile production. Freed from the constraints of having to participate in family life to be assured of the bare necessities, individuals who may have felt same-sex desire but had not been in a position to develop a life around it were now enabled to do so with more autonomy. Thus the rise in individualism went hand in hand with both a demographic shift to city life and a shift in the understanding of nonnormative desires or sexual practices as innate and essential to the "abnormal personality" rather than simply a set of discrete if aberrant activities (D'Emilio 1983). Part of this shift to the individual as the center of activity, both interior and exterior, was an accompanying development and refinement of lyric poetry as the favored mode for expressing individual subjectivity. Emphasis on the self and its expression through supple uses of lyric verse gained popular ascendancy over forms like the epic, the popular ballad, or tightly constrained court poetry, representing a complementary genre to the novel, whose populous expansiveness and multivocality made it in some ways an industrial genre. Thus one can discern a nexus that links – though not exclusively or simply – the emergence of queer identity, the rise of urban centers, and a poetic trend toward lyric to the vast economic movements of Western history. The United States came into being as part of this economic expansion, and quickly developed major urban centers for the proliferation and management of capital, government, and culture, though its puritanical legacy made it slower to recognize, tolerate, or assimilate queer communities into its various national projects.

Paris

The early part of the twentieth century was thus a difficult time for the queer US denizen. Consequently, one looks to expatriate communities of artists, bohemians, and the demimonde that surround such communities for concentrated poetic flourishing and cutting-edge vanguard experimentalism. From 1900 to just before World War II, Paris was the site of a community of "sapphic modernist" American poets and writers, including Gertrude Stein, Djuna Barnes, Natalie Barney, H. D. (Hilda Doolittle – though she is not exclusively associated with Paris but rather with a series of European capitals), Sylvia Beach, and their friends and lovers. In addition to sharing and supporting each other's writing projects, the group held frequent salon gatherings where topics such as same-sex eroticism among women, women's rights, and the philosophical, social, and civic underpinnings and repercussions of feminist or queer prowoman activism were actively debated. The city was, if not ready to pass legislation on their behalf, certainly tolerant of such bohemian gatherings. These women regarded Paris as their playground and workshop; though Stein called a group of expatriate US male writers in Paris a "lost generation," the evidence suggests that this community of women discovered themselves here.

Some scholarship on this community, notably Shari Benstock's book *Women of the Left Bank* (1987) and the film *Paris Was a Woman*, document and celebrate its existence, while others analyze its politics, addressing some of the women's attraction to Mussolini-style fascism. Many evinced, if not outright subscription to fascist ideologies, striking naïveté about the direction and consequences of the emergence of European strongmen and their ability to meld the interests of the state into those of business and the military, and the subsequent genocide and/or enslavement of target populations. Gertrude Stein is perhaps the most noted of these cases of strong queer identity blended with a myopic and naïve view of world politics even as her own world – that of European Jewry – was falling apart around her. Protected by a friend in the Vichy government during World War II, she and her partner Alice B. Toklas spent the war in the village of Belley frightened but ultimately unharmed by their many brushes with German or French soldiers. Stein expresses her preference for the Old World over the New specifically in terms of its acceptance of singularity and "queerness":

> It takes time to make queer people . . . Custom, passion, and a feel for mother earth are needed to breed vital singularity in any man, and alas, how poor we [Americans] are in all these three.
>
> Brother singulars, we are misplaced in a generation that knows not Joseph. We flee before the disapproval of our cousins, the courageous condescension of our friends who gallantly sometimes agree to walk the streets with us, from all them who never any way can understand why such ways and not the others are so dear to us, we fly to the kindly comfort of an older world accustomed to take all manner of strange forms into its bosom . . . (Stein 1934: 21)

Stein may also be speaking of writers or Jews: later in the book she speaks of the "queer feeling," the shame that comes from having literary ambitions that are not encouraged by one's surroundings, and from persisting in writing what others do not understand. The evocation of Joseph of the many-colored coat suggests the flamboyant Otherness associated with queer culture. That Stein felt more comfortable in France than in the United States even during Europe's darkest hour speaks to the degree to which she identified as someone needing the Old World's more accommodating and permissive attitude toward sexual difference. By emphasizing the "peaceful and exciting" aspects of French culture, *Paris France* (1940) pleads for the specialness of France's role in fostering creativity for the twentieth century, and warns of the horrors of a second European war so soon after the first. Though composed in Majorca during a flight from the hardships of World War I, the intensely erotic and experimental *Lifting Belly* (now commonly interpreted as a reference to female same-sex erotic play) and *Tender Buttons* (French argot for nipples) could not have been written without the support system of queers and vanguard artists of Stein's Paris.

The phrase "Paris Was a Woman" provocatively suggests that cities are gendered, sexualized, or otherwise embodied in imaginative writing. Certainly, many poets and writers have written of their cities as lovers, or have mapped out their particular communities, tracing less-traveled circuits against the backdrop of a familiar street-plan, subway system, or other familiar cartographic material. Djuna Barnes, a writer associated with both Paris and New York, produced satires about queer women's bohemia in both cities. *The Book of Repulsive Women* corporealizes, in "8 rhythms and 5 drawings," Manhattan streets and neighborhoods as a woman's body to suggest an erotic, if abjectly repellant, mapping of travail/travel across a female terrain during same-sex lovemaking. The "rhythms" describe women's bodies under titles like "From Fifth Avenue Up," and "From Third Avenue On," and "Seen from the 'L'" – the elevated subway. These could map out not only the contours of lesbian neighborhoods, but of anatomical regions: "L" forms a crotch, as well as indicating lips, labia, and so forth. Throughout the jingly though syntactically and lexically complex verses, women emit "cries" both "high [and] hard" and "short sharp modern/ babylonic" – the bestial sounds of sexual excitation induced by a lover's "rhythm"ic ministrations (Barnes [1915] 1989). *Ladies' Almanack* is a witty send-up *à clef* of the circle of lesbians and feminists around Natalie Barney ("Dame Evangeline Musset" spreading the gospel of woman-to-woman love); one episode has the entire posse – the Misses Nip and Tuck, Patience Scalpel, Doll Furious and Musset herself hunting Bounding Bess around Paris to brand her "i' the Bottom, Flank, or Buttocks-boss" (Barnes [1928] 1992: 31–2).

Some decades later, during late 1958–9, a seedy, nameless hotel at 9 rue Gît le Coeur in Paris nicknamed the "Beat Hotel" occupied an important if short-lived place in US queer literary culture as the birthplace of the "cut-up," generally attributed to the collaborative team of William S. Burroughs and British visual artist Brion Gysin. This technique, which consisted of cutting up and rearranging arbitrarily either extant text or text produced by the cutter-uppers, intended to break down authorial control and concomitant oppositions such as self/other, subject/object, will/chance. The theory was that wrenching phrases and words out of their quotidian syntactic regimen would liberate the mind and also cultural (including sexual) practices from the totalitarian rule of convention; the effect and affect was disoriented, mutilated, liberated. One could hypothesize a link between queer sexual experience/identity in oppressive circumstances and the simultaneously dissociative and liberating effect of cut-up. Many Beat productions echoed aesthetic and consciousness experiments by earlier avant-garde writers, including Stein. Most of the writers – all male – associated with this short period and concentrated site – among them Allen Ginsberg, Jack Kerouac, Gregory Corso, Harold Norse, James Baldwin – had stronger and more long-lived ties to other cities, especially New York and San Francisco. An even briefer stint in Tangier was likewise constellated around Burroughs, as well as the queer couple Paul and Jane Bowles. Not protracted expatriate affairs, these visits were rather quasi-pilgrimages to sites to which queer men had an historic relationship.

New York

George Chauncey's magisterial *Gay New York* is unmatched for its richness of description and analysis of queer urban male culture in the first half of the twentieth century. Chauncey identifies Greenwich Village, Times Square, and Harlem as centers of both literary and gay activity for men and women, stressing the degree to which the Harlem Renaissance's cultural flowering was produced by a group of gay men, out to each other but not to their parents, families, or larger community. Anxiety about exposure became more acute as they and their institutions (publications, theater houses, galleries, cultural societies, etc.) gained recognition; according to Chauncey, even during what he identifies as the "pansy craze" of the 1920s, where large drag balls and gay-themed nightclub acts provided entertainment for straight spectators as well as queer participants and/or audience, it was easier for working-class than educated or upwardly mobile queer culture to express itself uninhibitedly, as the social repercussions for transgressing norms were considered less devastating for those without public profiles (Chauncey 1994). The queer-identified men of the Harlem Renaissance included Claude McKay, Countee Cullen, Alain Locke, Wallace Thurman, Bruce Nugent, and, it is both rumored and denied, Langston Hughes (queer but not gay?); as well as Carl Van Vechten, a white patron of many Harlem cultural productions, booster of all things modern (close friend of Stein and Toklas as well), and author of the novel *Nigger Heaven*, which W. E. B. Du Bois condemned for its voyeuristic, racist Negrophilia.

If gay or homoerotic themes are not explicit in the texts of the period (and sometimes, in novels at least, they were), one might ask, what is the purpose of "outing" writers who may or may not have wanted to keep their sexual practices secret or separate from their literary output? This is where notions of queer or gay textuality, texts as performances, themes that may address homoerotics obliquely, or style and affect, come into play. With regard to the earlier half of the twentieth century, these questions have been addressed most thoroughly in recent critical work on Hart Crane, a famously gay writer whose life in New York and brief but productive writing career coincided with the relatively unconcealed public gaiety of the 1920s: the two books published during his lifetime, *White Buildings* and *The Bridge*, appeared in 1926 and 1930 respectively. Both volumes detail in tortured chaotic syntax and rich Church-of-Latterday-Symbolists imagery the excitement and transcendent energy of New York City, finding in its cityscapes, its labyrinthine claustrophobic depths and vertiginous heights, both vastly expansive and intimate scales for the experience and never-fully-successful articulation of modernity at an almost spiritually fevered pitch. Crane's city is obliquely (queerly?) queer; Thomas Yingling and others have named Crane's thickly wrought diction and abrasively ornate style as an instance of "homotextuality." Moreover, Crane's attraction to the maritime themes and imagery has been associated not only with New York's status as a harbor city but with his attraction to sailors, who comprised a notable element in the teeming transient population that characterized this destination for immigrants and other seafarers, escapees from small homophobic rural towns and cities in the center of the country (Crane was himself one of these, having fled Cleveland for Greenwich Village at the age of 17), and northwardly migrating African Americans. Crane did not seek out fellow literati for sexual liaisons; the relationship most celebrated in his verse, particularly "Voyages I–VI," was a short-lived one with Danish mariner Emil Oppfer. The affair stimulated Crane's creativity; the epic "Bridge," most commonly read as an allegorical mapping of the spatial dimensions of the Brooklyn Bridge onto the temporal history and geographical expanse of the USA, is suffused with meaning partly because the bridge was a primary site of Crane's and Oppfer's amatory promenades. Likewise,

> Under thy shadow by the piers I waited;
> Only in darkness is thy shadow clear.
> The City's fiery parcels all undone,
> Already the snow submerges an iron year . . . (Crane 1966: 46)

an unusual autobiographical interjection in "To Brooklyn Bridge," suggests a scenario of cruising for anonymous sex. The "City"'s shadow side, its lively, illicit, underground cultures, emerge most safely and beautifully by night; in an almost contemplative mien, the personal can venture forth without fear of reprisal. Such a personal and geographical signal would have been clear to other gay men and members of New York's varied demimondes, while still general and "poetic" enough to pass to the uninitiated as standard nocturnal reverie. The difficulty of Crane's verse has itself been considered not only a kind of double-valenced gesture of revelatory concealment, a circumlocutory confession symptomatic of illicit desires, but also a reflection of the inherent difficulty of transposing overwhelming perceptions and emotional states into communicable language – the common lyric/urban problem of reconciling interiority with sociability. Such readings, while they risk anti-intellectualism by pathologizing stylistic density, have the value of politicizing style. A less pejorative reading of the phenomenon of difficulty, but one which retains something of the politics of identity and style, proposes that Crane's highly pitched, gnomic language and over-the-top imagery shares something with the celebratory aspects of camp or drag – an exaggeration that evinces mastery, skill, respect for one's medium, and a delight in the sensuous effects of extreme artifice. Additionally, "The Bridge"'s canonical status as a paean to the technological sublime is usefully complemented by an understanding that "bridging" itself is constitutive of gay experience, in that queer identity was commonly termed "third sex," "neither one nor the other," or even the current prefix "trans" (transsexual, transgender, "trannie") to indicate a crossing-over, a creative and generative joining of culturally constructed binaries across chasms of difference. The search for opportunities for nonnormative sexual activity often sent the urban queer subject into parts of an otherwise tightly boundaried city where he or she (usually he) would be under less surveillance than elsewhere, not only because of the anonymity involved in being far from one's own neighborhood, but because less judgmental mores prevailed in certain enclaves – the white queer might find some refuge in black, working-class sections of Harlem, where speakeasies and clubs were less uptight about maintaining a certain clientele, and attitudes toward the nonnormative were more lenient and accepting. Thus the queer poet is himself a bridge, a point of negotiation between different sites, sensibilities, and states of citizenship.

Though Crane appeared to operate independent of a queer poetic community (if not a queer community *tout court*), later queer poets of New York came into their own as a self-conscious, self-identified coterie, most notably in the form of the emergence of the "New York School" in the 1950s and 1960s. D'Emilio's account of the purges of the 1930s and 1940s, culminating in the "psychiatric interview" initiated to screen out homosexuals from armed service during World War II (but, tellingly, not acted upon aggressively until the Korean War because the need for manpower in the earlier war outweighed the protocol of banning homosexuals from the military), describes how the very practices intended to discourage homosexuality encouraged the growing self-consciousness of gay people as a community under the sign of "deviant" – and unjustly minoritized – sexuality.

Paradoxically this enabled the constitution, if not the visibility as yet, of communities based on intentional bonds between gay folk. Beyond merely being proximal in living quarters or favored haunts, these communities were artistic and cultural, and despite the sharper repression of queer visibility that marked the 1950s (a bar could be closed down for even serving a drink to someone who appeared to be gay or Otherly sexed/gendered), they laid the groundwork for continued visibility and viability of collaboration, institution-building, and ongoing cultural production that was queer in spirit if not in letter, in sensibility if not in official or exclusive outdom. And they were never *exclusively* gay; here, queerness can truly be said to be an aesthetic and philosophical sensibility more than a sexual identity.

The so-called New York School arose around the world of visual art, studio, gallery, and museum culture – especially abstract expressionism, its direct descendants and siblings – as well as informal hangouts like bars and cafés, though the term describes writers rather than artists. As the name indicates, these writers were and are deeply identified with the city. Frank O'Hara, John Ashbery, Kenneth Koch, Kenward Elmslie, Barbara Guest are poets usually associated with the "first generation New York School"; subsequent "second-generation" poets are Ted Berrigan, Alice Notley, Ron Padgett, Joe Brainard, Bernadette Mayer, David Shapiro, James Schuyler, Steven Malmude, Anne Waldman, Eileen Myles, among others. Now a third generation, some say, comprises 30-somethings like Jordan Davis, Anselm and Edmund Berrigan, Drew Gardner, Katie Degentesh, Brendan Lorber, and countless others, with each successive generation becoming less identified with "queer" affect, content, and vernacular. While there were important aesthetic differences, both the New York School and its adjacent movement, the more publicity-hounded Beat scene (including Ginsberg, LeRoi Jones/Amiri Baraka, Corso, Burroughs, Joan Volmer Burroughs, and Kerouac) thrived on artistic friendships, collaborations, free-wheeling experimentation with art and life conducted in a ludic spirit of adventurous intimacy.

Frank O'Hara is perhaps the most iconically New Yorky of all New York poets. The term "New York School" is itself a loose, unofficial catch-all rubric for the poets who adopted his breathless, conversational, verging-on-trivial paeans to the everyday minutiae of urban social life: dinner or chance encounters with friends, gallery and bar news, street sights garnered en route to the subway en route to casual but thrilling assignations, passing notations on the weather, political events, and others' lives. Buoyant randomness, charming self-deflation, wit, and cosmopolitan delight – in short, a sophisticated campiness and lighthearted irreverence – suffuse this affective mode that blends casual observation with whimsy and poignant hints at an emotional "inner" life glimpsed like a view into a lit floor-level apartment living room as one hurries by: enough to give the poem an auratic glow of warmth and life, but not enough to overwhelm or draw the reader in to the poet's psychoemotional interior. O'Hara is perhaps the poet who most obviously embodies the concept of the queer city: the critical aura surrounding him merges him so perfectly with the 1950s Manhattan scene that the titles of the secondary literature tell the story: *City Poet: The Life of Frank O'Hara, Standing Still and Walking in New York, To Be True to a City*. His poetry maps queer/Bohemian New York, from the Cedar Tavern to the Café San Remo Bar to the "john door in the 5 Spot" against which he leans, hanging breathlessly on Billie Holiday's and Mal Waldron's whispery piano notes ("The Day Lady Died," O'Hara 1995: 325). Hazel Smith's *Hyperscapes in the Poetry of Frank O'Hara* (2002) merges these themes – textuality, queerness, urban geography – under the rubric of the "hyperscape," a coinage suggesting a level of rarified excess and breadth (spread-thinness, as it were) verging on the postmodern; it has often, in fact, been postulated that O'Hara straddles the limen between modernism and postmodernism. Although one could claim this about many poets, it seems especially apt for O'Hara who, on the one hand, eschewed both the heavy-handed interiority and the archaic formality of much mainstream poetry, but on the other hand, repudiated the brazen postmodernism of explicitly commercial pop art.

Lunch Poems, the small, sparkling paperback that comprised City Lights's Pocket Book #19, exemplifies as both material object and poetic text O'Hara's elegant insouciance. The bright blue and orange, slim little square fits very hiply – unsquarely – and sexily into a tight back pocket, especially when one sashays from one's office to lunch in a crowded urban scene, with a friend or solo, stopping at a typewriter store to type out a spontaneous poem or two on the display Olivetti. After all, as O'Hara observes about formal verse technique in "Personism: A Manifesto," one wants to buy a pair of pants that fits "tight enough so everyone will want to go to bed with you" (O'Hara 1995: 498–9). ("Personism" foreshadows the centrality of performativity to queer theory four decades later: this particularly playful "ism" was born, O'Hara writes, when the poet realized he could just as well pick up the phone and call a friend as write a poem.) A self-confident campiness that collapses sexuality and textuality (embodying Walt

Whitman's admonition from a previous century: "This is no book/ Who touches this touches a man" [Whitman 1975: 513]) pervades the work, as does a sense of free movement through the city. In "Poem (Lana Turner has collapsed!)," a screaming headline caught by the poet's glance as he "trot[s] along" a traffic-snarled street bickering with a friend about the weather ("I" say snow and rain, "you" say hail) occasions a highly queenly soliloquy concluded by a sister-to-sister remonstration that anticipates, in spite of itself, the celebrity culture that postmodernists would promote, and that O'Hara himself deplored:

> I have been to lots of parties
> and acted perfectly disgraceful
> but I never actually collapsed
> oh Lana Turner we love you get up (O'Hara 1964: 72)

The joyful audacity of calling this text a poem matches its high energy level and the spontaneity with which it was apparently written (on the Staten Island Ferry en route to a poetry reading where it had its debut).

"Poem en forme de Saw" contrasts mainstream American poetry, values, and imagined landscape with O'Hara's own queer urban(e) poetics – gregarious, homosocial, unorthodox – in a tour de force that confronts the heteronormative, machismo poetics-cum-public-persona of the quasi-rustic Robert Frost, who had become the USA's highest-profile poet with his recitation at Kennedy's presidential inauguration. O'Hara plays off Frost, the poet of self-reliance ("good fences make good neighbors"), American individualism, and private property ("whose woods these are I think I know"), against the poem's "lyric I," who, veering line by line between this gruff persona and its campy doppelganger, imagines emulating Frost but just can't handle the "board"-dom of Frost's old-saw predictably back-and-forth poetics or the solitary life it advocates:

> I wanted to be alone
> which is why I went to the [saw]mill in the first place
> now I'm alone and hate it
> I don't want to just make boards for the rest of my life . . .

O'Hara understands the paradoxical nature of poetic celebrity whereby a misanthrope can become a national hero, and attributes some cynical savvy to Frost on this score:

> I think I may scamper off to Winnipeg to see Raymond
> but what'll happen to the mill
> I see the cobwebs collecting already
> . . .
> if I stay right here I will eventually get into the newspapers
> like Robert Frost
> willow trees, willow trees . . . (O'Hara 1964: 60)

O'Hara constantly undercuts Frost's familiar images – willows and birches, tree-cutting accidents, reclusive narrators – both visually (formally, the lines alternate between short and long, not only concretely suggesting serrations, but the short lines literally "undercut" the long) and affectively, by intercutting the grand soliloquy of solitude with sociable gay argot and restless desires for cultured male company. New York is clearly a far more significant metropolis than "Winnipeg"; perhaps O'Hara chose the smaller, outpost city for its campy name, which not only combines two female names but suggests campy animal noises (whinnying) and a pun (peg) that provides a male sexual organ *and* a wooden ornament to hang your hat on. Scampering, nipping, and whinnying, in turn, suggest a sublime send-up of "Stopping by Woods on a Snowy Evening": "My little horse must think it *queer*/ To stop without a farmhouse near" (italics, obviously, added). Even the horse, O'Hara suggests (what exactly is going on between horse and man, come to think of it?) has more sociability and common sense than the pretentiously contemplative Frost-persona. The poem's final lines, "alone as a tree bumping another tree in a storm/ that's not really being alone, is it, signed The Saw," indicates the speaker as the tool itself, using its sharp teeth to castrate the frosty father – with words referencing a subaltern vernacular. One could say that the doubling in this poem typifies gay experience before the closet became the sole metaphor for gay life: life was a dualistic performance of masked peekaboo rather than stultifying claustrophobic self-denial. A fluid identity could be negotiated with dignity, finesse, even pleasure.

San Francisco

Just as New York has been a center of commerce and culture, the San Francisco Bay Area has, since the Gold Rush, welcomed mavericks, free-thinkers, and nonconformists. A haven for mostly beneficent utopian experiments, the region values leisure, pleasure, anarchopacifistic democracy, the intermingling of various progressive cultures, and experimentation with domestic, affective, and sexual arrangements that span the gamut. Even the state's name was a gender-bending myth: in a popular Spanish romance of the early sixteenth century, Queen Calafía's band of women warriors lived on the island of California. San Francisco's rise as a "gay mecca" originated in the post-World War II discharge of thousands of dislocated, uprooted soldiers from the military bases in Oakland and San Francisco into the general population of the Bay Area, and it was a natural fit. As in Manhattan, but arguably more concentratedly, queer culture rubbed shoulders (at least) with overlapping countercultures in the classic homosocial/homosexual continuum outlined by Eve Sedgwick (1985). These subcultures were, notably, the great Bohemian/beat scene of North Beach in the 1950s, the political activist communities, and the maritime underworlds. The first gay community center in the country opened in San Francisco in 1966; the city's gay community and progressive cultural politics have reached international renown. It was a Bay Area psychiatrist who encouraged Allen Ginsberg to drop out of the advertising world to pursue the life of an openly homosexual poet, and it was there that he and other Beats encountered Eastern philosophies that challenged the stark moralistic dualities of 1950s America. "Nakedness" and "candor" characterized Ginsberg's ethos of raw confessionalism, enabling the verbal deluges of his masterpieces, "Howl" and "Kaddish," as well as other poems contained in eponymous chapbooks – both, like *Lunch Poems,* were City Lights Pocket Books. The legendary recitation of "Howl" at the "big queer reading" marking the Six Gallery opening in 1955 and its subsequent publication, confiscation, and censorship trial in San Francisco thrust into national awareness and literary history a small book that Ginsberg himself had initially imagined destined for a clandestine "lavender press" limited edition for private circulation. The offending lines? "Who let themselves be fucked in the ass by saintly motorcyclists and screamed with joy,/ who blew and were blown by those human seraphim, the sailors, caresses of Atlantic and Caribbean love . . ." (Ginsberg 1956: 12).

The Bay Area has been home to active literary and queer alternative institution-building since before the public inauguration of the "Gay Liberation Movement" in 1969. Unlike Hart Crane's 1920s, which, despite the "pansy craze" and the proliferation of gay bars and drag balls, lacked visible literary venues for its queer population other than those of the Harlem Renaissance (and those were not explicitly queer), San Francisco from the 1950s on witnessed first the "mimeo revolution," then the "xerox revolution," then the "small press revolution" and now the desktop publishing and zine revolutions. The New York School developed similar institutions, most notably, in the 1970s, the St. Mark's-in-the-Bouwerie Poetry Project, which ran classes, workshops, reading series, a journal, and a nationally circulated newsletter; these publishing revolutions affected the whole country. But the Bay Area's special role in developing a vanguard poetics of sexual and formal openness is manifest in the plethora of quality queer-oriented presses that flourished from mid-century to the present, among them Grey Fox, Manroot, Panjandrum, Gay Sunshine, Shameless Hussy, Sand Dollar, Enkidu Surrogate, HerBooks, and Aunt Lute.

San Francisco's sense of itself as a "gay town," and gay poets' sense of ownership and belonging in the area, are manifested early in the city's gay history, and strongly. 1950s poet Jack Spicer's fierce sense of loyalty to the Bay Area was such that he felt tremendously uncomfortable with the idea that his work might circulate beyond the region. Robert Duncan, like Spicer a key member of the lively literary and artistic communities now known as the Berkeley and San Francisco Renaissances, published in 1957 "This Place Rumor'd to Have Been Sodom," an elegy eerily foretelling the ravages of the AIDS epidemic and the resultant destruction of the bathhouses and other venerable sites of gay underground culture ("Certainly these ashes might have been pleasures"). He ascribes to San Francisco the weighty aura of an ancient city both destroyed and blessed by "the hand of the Lord that moves." This figure – the ruined city – allows Duncan to connect the area's past – the catastrophic 1906 earthquake and fire – with its present as a gay magnet, imagining that, like Blake's Jerusalem, earthly paradise can be rebuilt by strong poetic vision and "arrows (eros) of desire." What keeps this desert alive is friendship – the homoerotic continuum that echoes Walt Whitman's assertion that it is the "half-hid warp" of "manly love" that guarantees authentic democracy:

> The devout have laid out gardens in the desert
> How tenderly they must attend these friendships
> Or all is lost. All *is* lost.
> Only the faithful hold this place green. (Duncan 1993: 59)

The language of pilgrimage pervades the poem, as does the typology whereby an earthly city incarnates a spiritual ideal (Rome, Jerusalem, Sodom, San Francisco); moreover, despite the poem's hieratic stateliness, the use of "rumor" as a creditable historical record and cultural practice resonates with O'Hara's use of camp and gossip as alternative communicative styles, and with Ginsberg's concept of the "Whispered Transmission," where erotic couplings link generations ("[Neal Cassady] slept with [Gavin Arthur, a San Francisco astrologer and sexologist] who slept with [Edward Carpenter] who slept with Whitman, and . . . I slept with [Cassady], so . . .") (Ginsberg 1973: 16) as well as by a legacy of poetic inspiration (etymologically, inbreathing: a whispered transmission is aurally inhaled as erotic sound, as in the synesthesiac epigraph to *"Kaddish" and Other Poems* [1961], "Taste my mouth in your ear"). The notion of an embodied poetics, common to both Duncan and Ginsberg, derives directly from Whitman's radical prosodic dictum that a poetic line imitate a man's natural breath.

These poets, aware of their "half-hid" queer genealogy, did their best to educate younger poets. Stan Persky, one of the latter, affirmed to John D'Emilio that "[Duncan, Spicer and Robin Blaser] not only kept alive a public homosexual presence in their work, but kept alive a tradition, teaching us about Rimbaud, Crane, and Lorca . . . There was a conscious searching out, in fraternity, of homosexual writers" (D'Emilio 1983: 180). While a *fin de millénium,* looser concept of queerness might include writers like Kathy Acker, Dodie Bellamy, David Rattray, Alden Van Buskirk, Bob Kaufman, Jack Kerouac, and other "high-risk" heteros with unorthodox public sexualities or strong ties to queer communities or aesthetics, this language of "keeping alive" (echoing so closely the Duncan poem) a "homosexual tradition" underscores the urgency of the task of cultural and social survival for a community under siege in the McCarthy–Eisenhower 1950s, and even the early 1960s. These writers were not nostalgic conservatives; their commitment to the past served a political present. (Spicer had been active in the Mattachine Society, the first "homophile" political group in the country to advocate for the decriminalization and the depathologizing of homosexuality.) These poets were formal innovators; even 50 years later some of them remain underrecognized, their reputations thriving on the fringes as cult figures or poet's poets, or not at all. Ginsberg is the exception but, curiously, the critical literature on his work is just starting to reflect the theoretical or historiographic rigor one might expect in analyses of important work. Other significant participants in this lively era – writers, publishers, artists – included John Wieners, Jack Spicer, Robin Blaser, Madeline Gleason, Helen Adam, James Broughton, Stan Persky, George Stanley, Donald Allen, Joe Dunn, Nemi Frost and Joanne Kyger, Russell FitzGerald, David Meltzer, Lenore Kandel, George Hitchcock, Robert LaVigne, Richard

Brautigan, Bob Kaufman, Michael McClure, and Philip Lamantia. Not all of the writers in this partial list were/are gay-identified, but many publicly advocated sexual experimentation and lived alternative domestic arrangements well before the "sexual revolution" of the late 1960s. Later gender activist and/or queer/gay poets include Susan Griffin, Pat Parker, Gloria Anzaldúa and Cherrie Moraga, Ntozake Shange, Mitsuye Yamada, Paul Mariah, Alta, Judy Grahn, Paula Gunn Allen, Adrienne Rich (in the latter part of her career), Bruce Boone, Thom Gunn, kari edwards.

Duncan's Whitmanian sense that friendship forms the core of a sustainable poetics is emphasized by Spicer's *Collected Books*, a body of work comprising an argument for community despite its frequent thematizing of queer loneliness and unfulfillable desire. Starting with *After Lorca*, a series of translations and appropriations accompanied by (posthumous) letters to and from the Spanish poet, Spicer envisions a global community of queer renegade poets that crosses not only geopolitical but temporal and mortal boundaries – a signal instance of "bridging" that would have done Hart Crane proud. Stephen Jonas, a queer Boston poet equally on the fringes of society, echoed this time/space travel and complex inheritance in his poetic salute to Spicer, "Cante Jondo for Soul Brother Jack Spicer, His Beloved California & Andalusia of Lorca" (Jonas 1994: 160). *Admonitions* comprises letters to friends that spell out an aesthetic/ethics of community: "[My earlier poems] are one night stands, . . . as meaningless as sex in a Turkish bath . . . Poems should echo and re-echo against each other . . . They cannot live alone any more than we can." (Spicer 1975: 61). Though he problematizes rather than merely affirms his queer themes, Spicer's use of poetic seriality as metonym for homosocial community echoes albeit ambivalently, the national imaginary of Whitman's vision, proof positive that queer concerns have made for important formal innovations in twentieth-century US poetry: Stein's and Barnes's erotic syntaxis, Crane's baroque imaginary, O'Hara's campily choreographed lines, Ginsberg's naked surrealist obligatos, and Duncan's Romanticism.

References and Further Reading

Barnes, Djuna ([1915] 1989). *The Book of Repulsive Women: 8 Rhythms and 5 Drawings*. Los Angeles: Sun & Moon (no page numbers).

— ([1928] 1992). *Ladies Almanack*. Elmwood Park, IL: Dalkey Archive.

Benstock, Shari (1987). *Women of the Left Bank*. Austin, TX: University of Texas Press.

Cándida Smith, Richard (1993). *Utopia and Dissent: Art, Poetry, and Politics in California*. Berkeley: University of California Press.

Chauncey, George (1994). *Gay New York: Gender, Urban Culture, and the Making of the Gay Male World 1890–1940*. New York: Basic Books.

Crane, Hart (1966). *Complete Poems and Selected Letters and Prose*. Garden City: Anchor.

Davidson, Michael (1986). *The San Francisco Renaissance: American Poetry at Mid-Century*. Berkeley: University of California Press.

D'Emilio, John (1983). *Sexual Politics, Sexual Communities: The Making of a Homosexual Minority in the United States, 1940–1970*. Chicago: University of Chicago Press.

Duncan, Robert (1944). "The Homosexual in Society," *Politics*, 1(7): 209–11.

— (1993). *Selected Poems*, ed. Robert Bertolf. New York: New Directions.

Ferlinghetti, Lawrence and Peters, Nancy J. (1980). *Literary San Francisco*. New York and San Francisco: Harper & Row and City Lights.

Ginsberg, Allen (1956). *Howl and Other Poems*. San Francisco: City Lights.

— (1961). *"Kaddish" and Other Poems, 1958–60*. San Francisco: City Lights.

— (1973). *Gay Sunshine Interview*, with Allen Young. Bolinas, CA: Grey Fox.

Jonas, Stephen (1994). *Selected Poems*, ed. Joseph Torra. Hoboken, NJ: Talisman House.

Killian, Kevin and Ellingham, Lew (1998). *Poet, Be Like God: Jack Spicer and the San Francisco Renaissance*. Middletown CT: Wesleyan University Press.

O'Hara, Frank (1964). *Lunch Poems*. San Francisco: City Lights.

— (1995). *The Collected Poems of Frank O'Hara*, ed. Donald Allen. Berkeley: University of California Press.

Sedgwick, Eve Kosofsky (1985). *Between Men: English Literature and Male Homosocial Desire*. New York: Columbia University Press.

Smith, Hazel (2002). *Hyperscapes in the Poetry of Frank O'Hara: Difference/Homosexuality/Topography*. Liverpool, UK: Liverpool University Press.

Souhami, Diana (2004). *Wild Girls: Natalie Barney and Romaine Brooks*. London: Weidenfeld and Nicolson.

Spicer, Jack (1975). *The Collected Books of Jack Spicer*, ed. Robin Blaser. Santa Barbara, CA: Black Sparrow.

Stein, Gertrude (1934). *The Making of Americans*. New York: Harcourt Brace.

— (1940). *Paris, France*. New York: Liveright.

— (1990). *The Autobiography of Alice B. Toklas*. New York: Vintage.

-- (1997). *Tender Buttons*. New York: Dover.

Stryker, Susan and Van Buskirk, Jim (1996). *Gay by the Bay: A History of Queer Culture in the San Francisco Bay Area*. San Francisco: Chronicle.

Whitman, Walt (1898). "Democratic Vistas." In *The Complete Prose*. Boston: Small Maynard (no page numbers).

— (1975). *The Complete Poems*. Harmondsworth, UK: Penguin.

Yingling, Thomas (1990). *Hart Crane and the Homosexual Text*. Chicago: University of Chicago Press.

Chapter 6

Twentieth-century Poetry and the New York Art World

Brian M. Reed

On February 17, 1913, an art exhibition opened in the Sixty-ninth Regiment Armory in New York City. Its organizers, the Association of American Painters and Sculptors, intended the show to be a patriotic celebration, proof positive that the United States had not only industrial and political might but also artistic genius. To this end, the Association quixotically decided to make the exhibition comparative, that is, an opportunity to view US civilization cheek-by-jowl with its European rivals.

The plan backfired. The Association's agents dispatched to Europe brought back 70 years of some of the most adventurous art in Western history, from the colorful swirls of the Impressionists to the jagged jumbles of Pablo Picasso's Cubist canvases. Very few American gallery-goers had ever seen the like. Although there had been trans-Atlantic interchange for decades, it had been almost exclusively one way, the United States exporting its best talent to Paris, Rome, and London. Prior to 1913, the art produced in the United States itself tended to be straightforwardly realist, seeking innovation not through bold formal experiment – Monet's clouds of color, Cézanne's slab-strokes of paint, Picasso's gray-brown intersecting planes – but through the introduction of new kinds of content. The Ash Can School, for example, attained notoriety early in the twentieth century by portraying down-and-out urban dwellers, everyday city scenes, and other subject matters previously considered too coarse for serious painters. Such an aesthetic project looked rather tame when its results were

Figure 6.1 Marcel Duchamp, *Nude Descending a Staircase No. 2*. Photograph the Philadelphia Museum of Art/Art Resource, NY.

hung alongside works such as Marcel Duchamp's *Nude Descending a Staircase No. 2*, which depicts a "nude descending" via a wild, toppling assemblage of irregular geometrical shapes (see Figure 6.1).

The Armory Show lasted less than a month. It closed on March 15, 1913. The press it received, however, was prodigious, and Duchamp in particular quickly became a byword for the curious craziness that had appeared to have dominated European art since the 1850s. *Nude Descending* was described in print as "an explosion in a shingle factory" – and much worse. The exhibition's fame was compounded by its subsequent stops in Chicago and Boston. Before the end, close to three hundred thousand Americans had a chance to view first-hand its scandalous oddities and, in the process, receive a speeded-up education in modern European art.

For many, it was a case of information overload. Too much, too soon. The Armory Show's runaway popularity did not overnight produce a drastic shift in American artistic taste. Indeed, the bulk of American art from 1913–45 remained staunchly within the realist tradition. The Armory Show did, however, provoke a few artists and intellectuals to reassess what art is and could be. It also made it possible for innovative European artists to find a small but appreciative audience in the United States. In short, it made thinkable the establishment of an art scene in New York that could foster work on a par with that coming out of London, Paris, Berlin, and Rome.

And this new arts scene thrived. Now-famous US artists such as Stuart Davis, Georgia O'Keefe, Joseph Stella, and Alfred Stieglitz developed an avant-garde tradition that could plausibly be set alongside its European analogs. Moreover, numerous immigrants and other long-term foreign residents – among them Duchamp, Arshile Gorky, and Roberto Matta – served as conduits for the latest news from the Old World. When Hitler's armies devastated the Continent and set back European economies by decades, New York was ready and willing to succeed Paris as the preeminent site for the production, consumption, and study of avant-garde art. During the 1950s and 1960s, figures such as Jackson Pollock, Robert Rauschenberg, and Andy Warhol at last won for US art the prestige that the Association of American Painters and Sculptors had prematurely believed was the nation's due back in 1913.

By now, readers can be forgiven for asking why this story appears in a volume dedicated to twentieth-century poetry. There are several answers. First, the New York art world, as it took shape over the course of the twentieth century, provided several generations of writers with ever-new aesthetic provocations. If *this* is art, poets asked themselves again and again, perhaps I might call *this* poetry. The art world also provided a vibrant, cosmopolitan community that gave writers the confidence to explore the furthest limits of their imagination. Finally, the varied experiments that visual artists undertook in their efforts to catch up to and surpass European models provided poets with an archive of examples to draw upon in their own processes of composition.

The end result is a distinctive challenging body of writing that departs fundamentally from the first-person lyric that has been the English-language poetic norm since Keats and Wordsworth. Poets working in proximity and in response to the New York art world have dared to explore other ways of thinking about verse than as a heightened utterance meant to convey profound, often intimately personal, truths from speaker to audience. Such innovative poetry deserves attention as a risky but ultimately rewarding exploration of how to rethink the most basic aspects of the art form. Anyone trying to define the nature and function of "the poetic" in the twenty-first century will have to grapple with the extraordinary precedents set by the likes of Mina Loy, William Carlos Williams, John Cage, Jackson Mac Low, and Susan Howe.

This chapter begins by looking at poets' efforts to determine where (and whether) to draw the line between "poetry" and everything else. It then takes up a more specifically formal concern, the proposition that there are no rules to guide how a poet proceeds while writing a poem. Finally, the chapter recounts how poets came to conceive of their medium as innately theatrical, a multimedia performance that involves much more than words on the page. Throughout, the argument follows a roughly chronological order. The goal is not comprehensiveness. There are many other poets – and many more artists – who could make appearances here. Rather, the goal is to introduce a fascinating but often confusing body of verse in order to prepare readers to investigate further its origins, development, and diverse achievements.

I

In April 1917, the recently formed Society of Independent Artists put on an exhibition intended to rival the scandalous success of the Armory Show. They had grounds for such aspirations. The notorious Duchamp, living in New York since 1915, was one of the society's 20 founders. Moreover, having concluded that the lesson of the Armory Show was "anything goes," they did not want aesthetic judgment limiting in advance which or what kinds of work they would put on display. The Independents pledged to include two works by anyone who could afford the society's six dollar dues. In addition, the artworks would be displayed in alphabetical order of artists' names, beginning with a randomly determined letter.

Duchamp decided to test the Independents' resolve. He took a men's urinal, signed it "R. Mutt," and submitted it to the 1917 show. In effect, he asked the Independents whether they truly believed that taste was irrelevant. Were they willing to call a piece of plumbing a work of art? Were they willing to put up with the inevitable toilet humor? Duchamp knew his fellow society members. He was a worldly Frenchman living among puritanical Americans. The urinal did not make it into the exhibition. Duchamp then had fun resigning from the Independents in protest over the unfair treatment of the enigmatic R. Mutt.

The story of Duchamp's urinal is one of the most frequently retold episodes in modern art history. One can draw many morals from it. First, it concisely indicates that, whatever populist or inclusive rhetoric Americans might have been using during the Progressive Era, there were certain subjects, above all sex, that remained excluded from frank public discussion. The body's "plumbing" was just too vulgar for polite public mention. More profoundly, Duchamp's urinal posed the problem of the boundary between art and nonart. Where and when does one make a distinction? The urinal, as a mass manufactured item, also phrased this question in a uniquely vexing manner. Painting and sculpture traditionally offer us representations of things. A painting serves as a window on a scene, and a sculpture provides a scale model or replica of one. A urinal, however, represents nothing. It is what it is, an object made in a factory, a ceramic and metal lump with no special craft value and no expressive content.

Though rejected by the Independents – and therefore presumably ruled "nonart" as well – Duchamp's urinal presaged a century-long war against any definition of art that excludes anything or anyone. In 1910s New York, the shorthand dismissive name given to this "antiart" stance was "Dada," a label borrowed from a contemporary French and German movement in the arts renowned for its defiantly unmeaning writings and its antisocial behavior. In retrospect, though, New York Dada was anything but a fad imported from abroad. Its "antiart" turns out to have been not destructive but extraordinarily creative, inaugurating a giddy expansion of artistic possibility.

Duchamp's mockery of US sexual mores was typical of the New York Dada moment. His in-your-face presentation of matters sexual had many literary analogues. Indeed, another colorful European expatriate, the Baroness Elsa von Freytag-Loringhoven, wrote verse that put human "plumbing" on display even more gleefully than Duchamp. The speaker of her lyric "A Dozen Cocktails – Please" ponders whether she is more in the mood for oral sex or masturbation. Although initially favoring her "lusting palate," she concedes that both sex acts have their attractions:

No spinsterlollypop for me – yes – we have
No bananas – I got lusting palate – I
Always eat them – – – – – –
They have dandy celluloid tubes – all sizes –
Tinted diabolically as a baboon's hind-complexion.
A man's a –
Piffle! Will-o'-th'-wisp! What's the dread
Matter with the up-to-date-American-
Home-comforts? Bum insufficient for the
Should-be wellgroomed upsy! (Hass et al. 2000: 99)

The speaker goes on in this vein, eventually opting, it seems, for self-pleasure over a one-night stand, since "Home-comforts" are more clean and convenient for a "wellgroomed upsy" than putting up with the "Piffle" of a mere man. Throughout, the poem employs an excitable, exclamation-point-strewn, self-interrupting free verse. Freytag-Loringhoven's style of writing makes her speaker's arousal and enthusiasm palpable; nothing could be further from the maidenly decorum expected of a turn-of-the-century "poetess."

The British-born poet Mina Loy, a close friend of Duchamp's, provoked a scandal of her own in April 1917 – the same month as the urinal incident – by publishing verse even more basely animalistic in its sensuality than Freytag Loringhoven's. Her long poem "Songs to Joannes" opens:

Spawn   of   Fantasies
Silting the appraisable
Pig Cupid   his rosy snout
Rooting erotic garbage
"Once upon a time"
Pulls a week   white star-topped
Among wild oats   sown in mucous-membrane (Loy 1996: 53)

Spawn, silt, membrane, pig, mucous – hardly pleasant words to associate with "Cupid." The few traces of old-style love poetry here, such as the references to roses and stars, are submerged in "garbage" and clichés ("Once upon a time," sowing "wild oats"). Loy writes in a deliberately ugly, awkward manner that parallels the blunt vulgarity of her reduction of Eros to "Rooting erotic garbage." She implicitly acknowledges that forward expressions of female sexual desire remain unwelcome and threatening in a 1910s US literary scene dominated by men. She refuses, though, to camouflage or dilute her subject matter. She glories in her stance as an "antipoet." Loy's insight here – that definitions of "beauty" and "poetry" tend to exclude writings that treat topics uncomfortable to those in power – and Loy's strategy – the zestful indulgence in the ugly, the outré, the abject, even the disgusting – have proved remarkably prescient. They have been recycled innumerable times in the decades since by such edgy poets as Bruce Andrews, Allen Ginsberg, John Giorno, and Patti Smith.

II

There have been other, perhaps harder to grasp but no less important, outcomes of the 1910s "what is art?" debate, above all a variety of creative responses to the proposition that art has no fundamental duty to represent anything. Like Duchamp's urinal, it can just *be*, an object presented to us so that we then contemplate it as a thing in a gallery, not as an occasion to imagine an absent scene or action. If in the 1910s New York Dadaists and their colleagues sought to expand the range of what counts as poetry, other and later poets began to challenge the very essence of the art form.

The first iteration of this dissent from conventional representation stressed the expressive freedom of the artist. A painting, visual artists began to contend, can do many other things than provide window-like access to another reality. In fact, its value can lie in its removal from, its "abstraction" from, straightforward realism. Poets were quick to perceive the value that this argument might have for verse, too. One of the first to do so – E. E. Cummings – was a natural bridge figure, skilled both as a painter and a writer. He frequently delights in impeding readers' ready visualization of what he describes:

> twi-
>   is -Light bird
> ful
> -ly dar
> kness eats
>
> a distance (Cummings 1998: 113)

Here, Cummings aggressively fragments words ("twi- . . . -Light," "ful/ -ly," "dar/ kness"). He also badly wrenches grammar. The verb "is" occurs in the middle of the word "twilight." The noun "darkness" functions ambivalently as the objective complement of "twilight" and the subject of the clause "darkness eats a distance." With effort, though, one can discern Cummings's subject matter. He is talking about dusk falling and listening to birdsong. This kind of pastoral topic is as old as English-language poetry, but he makes it newly unusual, makes it interesting again, by scrambling his language.

The thesis that poetry need not represent the world led some writers to attempt more radical experiments. They tried to produce poems that, like Duchamp's urinal, would be autonomous objects, that is, purely textual, stand-alone creations. William Carlos Williams, a poet who lived in New York during the height of the Dada craze and was also an avid collector of modern art, was among the first US writers to attempt to write poems that were simply "things" instead of vehicles for their thoughts and feelings:

> The red paper box
> hinged with cloth
>
> is lined
> inside and out
> with imitation
> leather (Williams 1970: 123)

Williams here sounds as if he is depicting something that exists in the external world. But can one actually picture this "box"? It is made of multiple clashing materials, paper, cloth, and "imitation/ leather." Can one truthfully call it a "paper box" if it consists of stuff other than "paper"? It is also strangely described as "lined/ inside and out" with the fake leather. A lining, however, is almost always something that appears on the *inside* of a thing. Who would imagine a box "lined with goose down" as being *covered* as opposed to *filled* with feathers? Moreover, if it is "lined" outside with "imitation/ leather," isn't the *faux*-leather properly speaking the "red" part, not the "paper"? Williams, like Cummings, makes it difficult to envision what he is talking about. This obstructiveness serves a different purpose, however. He seems to want us to stop thinking about the world external to the poem and focus on *the poem itself*. It, after all, has "lines." It has "boxes," too, that is, stanzas. And "hinges," that is, line breaks. It is "lined/ inside and out" as well, insofar as a poem on the page has no interior or exterior: it is a flat (hence depthless) assemblage of words grouped in left-to-right rows. If a poem ceases to refer to things other than itself, "The red paper box" intimates, then it can still comment endlessly and inventively on its own origins, appearance, and purpose.

The most ambitious of pre-World War II New York-based painters, like Arthur Dove in *Golden Storm* went much further in their quest to create autonomous art. They ceased offering even the ghost of representation in their work. They preferred instead to undertake free abstract explorations of shape, color, texture, and other fundamental, formal aspects of their trade. Poets of the era, however, generally avoided such dizzying extremes of unconstrained play. There were a few exercises in pure sound, such as Freytag-Loringhoven's "Klink – Hratzvenga" ("Idrich mitzdonja – astatootch/ Ninj – iffe kniek" [Hass et al. 2000: 100]). But these remained exceptions, not the norm. The period's most prominent writer to pursue a total break between writing and representation – Gertrude Stein – lived not in New York but Paris. Not until Nazis marched down the Champs-Élysées did US-based writers begin to rival her boldness. And when they did so, they followed less her example than that set by mid-century New York visual artists intent on revolutionizing age-old rules governing the making of art.

III

Duchamp's urinal might be his best-known puckish, pie-in-the-face statement, but during his career he made many other discomfiting gestures. Another of these, *3 Standard Stoppages* (1913), touches on issues that would come to the fore in the New York art world, and latterly its poetry scene, in the immediate post-World War II years (see Figure 6.2). Duchamp told people that he created the piece by dropping three strings a meter long onto a canvas from a ladder at a height of one meter. He then glued each where it fell. In essence, he proposed that random gestures could make art. This idea was as shocking, in its own way, as his R. Mutt "sculpture." Shakespeare, after all, did not pull words out of a hat. Michelangelo did not throw paint at chapel walls.

Duchamp's urinal kicked off one conversation. It made people ask what is art. *3 Standard Stoppages* initiated a different discussion. It made people ask how art comes into being. The former question was definitional, the latter procedural. And the post-World War II New York School – of art *and* poetry – was not terribly worried about

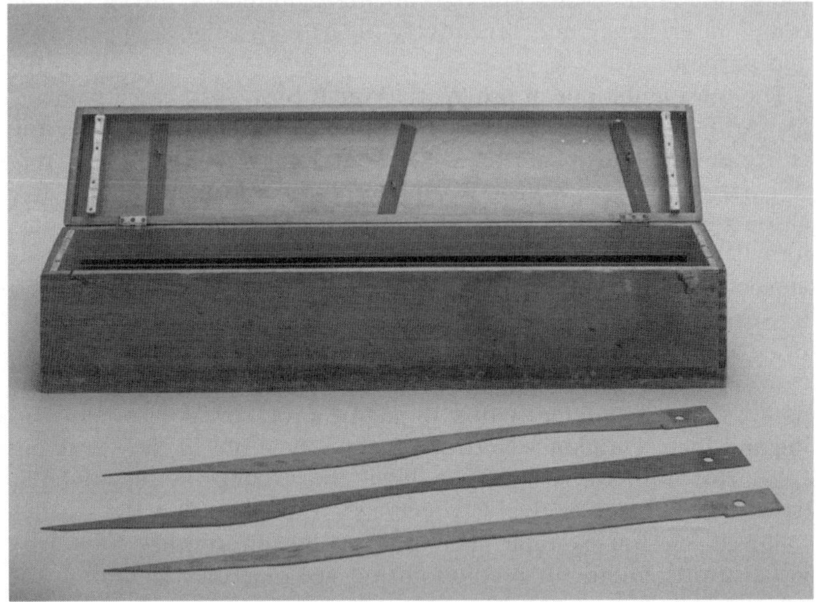

Figure 6.2 Marcel Duchamp, *3 Standard Stoppages*. Digital image © The Museum of Modern Art/licensed by SCALA/Art Resource, NY.

definitions. The first half of the century had pretty decisively demonstrated that people will gamely accept anything as art if an artist insists loud enough. Rather, the New York School question concerned process. How do I, as an artist, *go on*, how do I take paint, wood, stone, notes, or words and turn them into something worthwhile?

The thesis that art could be made randomly instead of through careful deliberation first entered the New York arts scene via French Surrealism. Many of the artist-refugees during the World War II years acquainted US painters and sculptors with the experiments that André Breton, Salvador Dalí, Joan Miró and others had been conducting since the early 1920s with "automatism." The Surrealists, drawing on Freud, held that accident, coincidence, mistakes, hallucinations, and other interruptions of logical, rational behavior were moments when one's deeper self, lurking subterranean-fashion beneath the veneer of the conscious ego, made itself felt. This argument prompted US painters to experiment with the improvisatory application of paint to canvas. They sought to act out their innermost selves through big, bold, spontaneous strokes, unmixed brash color, thick variable

Figure 6.3 Joan Mitchell (1926–1992), *Hemlock*, 1956. Oil on canvas, overall 91 × 80 in (231.1 × 203.2 cm). Whitney Museum of American Art, New York; purchase with funds from the friends of the Whitney Museum of American Art 58.20. Reproduced with permission of the Estate of Joan Mitchell.

smearing, and complete disregard for polish or finish. Joan Mitchell's *Hemlock* is a good sample of this American offshoot of Surrealism, usually called Abstract Expressionism (see Figure 6.3). The canvas is crowded with gestures, not images, and there is no one part or shape that stands out as more important than any other. By 1960, this emotive manner of painting was instantly recognizable as New York's signature style. And a few Abstract Expressionists – Jackson Pollock, Willem de Kooning, and Mark Rothko among them – achieved international fame.

The poet most associated with Abstract Expressionism, Frank O'Hara, not only worked at the New York Museum of Modern Art but also befriended a bewildering number of 1950s and 1960s visual artists. He collaborated with them, hung out in their studies, and praised them in his verse. He also adopted a correspondingly improvisatory style, dashing off poems in the middle of conversations, while on the telephone, or during his lunch hour. Like a New York School canvas, an O'Hara poem is often brash, immediate, and high-energy:

> It is 12:10 in New York and I am wondering
> if I will finish this in time to meet Norman for lunch
> ah lunch! I think I am going crazy
> what with my terrible hangover and the weekend coming up . . .
> I wish I were staying in town and working on my poems
> at Joan's studio for a new book by Grove Press
> which they will probably not print
> but it is good to be several floors up in the dead of night
> wondering whether you are any good or not
> and the only decision you can make is that you did it
>
> (O'Hara 1971: 328)

In verse of this kind, quality ("whether you are any good or not") is an after-the-fact concern. One does not worry whether others will find it acceptable ("a new book . . . which they will probably not print"). What truly matters is capturing the here-and-now ("It is 12:10 in New York") and celebrating its wonders ("ah lunch!"). For the palpable traces of the artist's hand in Abstract Expressionism – its record of moment-by-moment decisions where to push, smear, slather, spill, and layer paint – O'Hara substitutes cheerful documentation of his every thought, desire, and action. Readers are brought so close to the experience of "being O'Hara" that there is no opportunity for the whole to come into view, for us to perceive which of the topics glancingly touched upon should take precedence. O'Hara's raw reeling verse has subsequently proved widely influential. His exuberant tours of urban life have inspired not only a "second generation" of New York School poets (among them Ted Berrigan, Alice Notley, and Anne Waldman) but also a third (Tim Dlugos, Eileen Myles) and, arguably, a fourth and fifth.

IV

The Surrealist approach to chance – the proposition that accident allows a closer approach to an artist's inner being than carefully planned out and controlled self-expression – represents only one response to the idea that art can be made randomly. Indeed, Duchamp's chief mid-twentieth-century acolyte, the composer John Cage, criticized Surrealism for treating chance instrumentally, that is, as a special means for them to gain access to the unconscious. He argued that this goal-oriented thinking prevents Surrealists from appreciating that *all* art is fundamentally chance-dependent, a product of artists arbitrarily choosing to adhere to rules that either they or someone else invents. A poet writing a sonnet commits to following a particular set of procedures, but, for Cage, those rules carry no more and no less weight than Duchamp's rules about dropping a string from a ladder. In 1951, seeking to put this principle into practice, Cage composed one of his most famous works, *The Music of Changes*, by using coin-flips to determine what notes a pianist should play. He thereby dispensed with the most basic musicological rules governing harmony and rhythm. He also made it impossible to interpret the piece as "expressing" anything, conscious or unconscious.

The poet John Ashbery, a friend of Frank O'Hara's, happened to attend a performance of *Music of Changes* on New Year's Day 1952. At the time, Ashbery was going through an extended period of writer's block. Cage's music struck him as a revelation (Shoptaw 1994: 21). In his verse he thereafter began to explore outrageous, random-seeming leaps in and between statements and phrases:

> "The skin is broken. The hotel breakfast china
> Poking ahead to the last week in August, not really
> Very much at all, found the land where you began . . ."
> The hills smouldered up blue that day, again

> You walk five feet along the shore, and you duck
> As a common heresy sweeps over. We can botanize
> About this for centuries, and the little dazey
> Blooms again in the cities. (Ashbery 1977: 38)

Here Ashbery moves from quotation to indirect discourse; rotates between second, first, and third person; and leaps from discussing "skin" to "hotel breakfast china" to "hills" to "heresy." Such a whirl induces readerly disorientation. What is there to hold onto? A few of the images are evocative: the "hills" that "smouldered up blue," the oddly impersonal announcement of wounded flesh ("The skin is broken"). One gains a sense of memory, nostalgia, and loss ("where you began," "again/ You walk"), on the one hand, and rebirth ("the little dazey/ Blooms again"), on the other. There is a hinted intimacy between "you" and the speaker that suggests but does not define a relationship. Ashbery provides atmosphere, tone, and the rudiments of character, action, and moral while exploiting jarring transitions and *non sequiturs* to keep a reader guessing. He gives us many of the themes and devices common in English-language verse from Spenser to Tennyson, albeit made newly skewed, strange, and absorbing.

Although this aesthetic incorporates certain Cagean insights, Cage himself would undoubtedly consider Ashbery's versecraft still overly reliant, Surrealist-fashion, on intuition and whimsy when deciding what should follow what. Cage's own poetry sought to discover what happens when chance truly overrules personal preference. When working on "Empty Words," for example, he followed arbitrary but strict procedures for extracting and reassembling letters, words, and punctuation from Henry David Thoreau's *Journals*. He could not have foreseen passages such as the following:

> oi for osurprisingy ter spect y-s of
> wildclouds deooa Di from the
> ocolorsadby h allb eblei ingselfi foot
>
> low c squealschimney
> require high theaparta or dust to the
> thenarrowed sound (Cage 1979: 34)

The word-scramble here is indeed "osurprisingy." Some run-on words – "wildclouds" and "squealschimney" – are almost mini-poems, curious kennings that set the imagination spinning. Other clumps teasingly invite analytic decomposition. Should "thenarrowed" be understood as "the narrowed" or "then arrowed"? Is "ocolorsadby" a compressed ode to departure, "O [the fall] colors, [I am] sad, [good]by[e]"? Some of the other words – "ingselfi" and "theaparta" – look vaguely Anglo-Saxon. Some look foreign. "Di" could be an ecclesiastical abbreviation for "domini" or "dei"; "h allb" suggests the German "halb," meaning "half." Then there are the concrete bits of English, "dust," "sound," "foot," any of which could be read as participating in a subterranean self-reflexive statement on "Empty Words" itself, which gives us pulverized fragments ("dust"), mere "sound," not the original integral body of Thoreau's writing. Such interpretations might sound strained – isn't this just random babble? – but Cage wants his readers to manipulate his "empty words," sound them aloud, explore the possibilities sparked by their collisions and mergers. Knowing the curves in *3 Standard Stoppages* were arrived at by chance in no way prevents viewers from taking visual pleasure in them; knowing the equivalent of coin-flips produced "oi for osurprisingy" does not prevent us from delighting in its sound and word play.

V

In the 1960s, New York visual artists began to grapple with the potentially embarrassing egocentrism of Abstract Expressionism. Recall, for a moment, the social upheavals in the United States in the 1960s: the assassinations of John F. Kennedy, Martin Luther King, Jr., Malcolm X, and Robert F. Kennedy; the anti-Vietnam War protest movement; the widespread radicalization of university students; the explosive race riots in New York, Detroit, Los Angeles, and elsewhere. In such a tumultuous time, could painters credibly claim that the most important possible subject matter was their inner turmoil, as translated into whorls and splashes? Many New York artists began to worry about their complicity in a government bent on wars abroad and oppression at home, worries which in turn prompted a series of dramatic changes in their art.

One of these 1960s developments was a move toward serial production. Donald Judd, Carl André, Sol Le Witt, and others began to rethink whether making art involves the production of a unique object. Judd, for one, began to make sculptures that consist of multiple, precisely spaced, metallic boxes that fill a predetermined amount of space. André used tiles to cover a certain sector of a floor. Le Witt made lattice-structures of white cubes. Such "proceduralist" art imitated the modularity and repetitiousness of the assembly line. Like Duchamp's urinal, it also provoked a category error, in this case making a gallery-goer think factory-thoughts. A museum is thereby exposed as an extension of, not a refuge from, the "military-industrial complex" of American capitalism. An artist acknowledges that he or she is a laborer like any other, and therefore subject to the dictates of a capricious, unforgiving capitalist labor market, not a lollygagger sharing passing ecstasies and complaining of purely private traumas.

Some 1960s poets saw opportunities to transpose these methods into verse. Jackson Mac Low, for example, experimented variously with proceduralism. "Insect Assassins" from *Stanzas for Iris Lezak* is fairly typical. The poem's title serves as a seed-phrase for generating its text:

> Injects *no survive.* Efforts control the
> Animal *survive. Survive.* Animal *survive. Survive.* Injects *no survive.*
>
> In nasty spitting eye cost. This
> Assassin spitting spitting assassin spitting spitting in nasty spitting
>
> Insectivorous nutriment species encounter Charles to
> Are species species are species species insectivorous nutriment
> species (Mac Low 1986: 94)

Since the title has two words, each stanza has two lines. Each of these lines, in turn, consists of a string of words whose initial letters spell out "insect" and "assassin" (e.g., **I**njects ***no*** *survive.* **E**fforts **c**ontrol **t**he). Moreover, within a single stanza, every occurrence of a given letter in the seed-phrase must also employ the same word in its expanded form. Every "s" in the first stanza above becomes "*survive,*" in the second becomes "spitting," in the third "species," and so forth. Though Mac Low gives no indication of a source text, he has almost certainly chosen his words, according to a rigid predetermined algorithm, from an article on killer bugs. The use of italics and the periods that appear after "*survive*" and "cost" suggest that he is remaining strictly faithful to the specifics of whatever he sees on the page.

Part of the effectiveness of "Insect Assassins" is the poem's swerve from nature lyrics past. Instead of romanticizing the natural world, Mac Low treats the topic of "insects" with the demystifying literalness of a professional entomologist. Like the scientific method, his manner of writing is highly portable, applicable to whatever problem/ whatever texts come one's way. The insects themselves, too, come across as resolutely rational pragmatists. We hear about decisive actions ("spitting") and about clinging to life ("*survive,*" "nutriment"). In addition, there appear to be threats ("control"), from those who would consume the insect assassins ("insectivorous"). Like Judd refusing to allow museum visitors to escape the depressing effects of industrial capitalism, Mac Low turns the nature lyric into a demonstration that in nature, too, one finds violence, warfare, and a kill-or-be-killed (eat or be eaten!) mentality. Art, Judd and Mac Low inform us, will no longer provide pleasing illusions.

Strict proceduralism of the kind found in *Stanzas for Iris Lezak* is relatively rare in US poetry. More common is a partial adoption of proceduralist methods that then stand in tension with a poet's intimations of leakage and waste. This is hardly surprising. The New York art world itself fairly quickly pulled back from what came to seem too extreme a series of dehumanizing gestures. Eva Hesse's *Repetition 19 III*, for instance, consists of 19 bucket-like forms made of fiberglass, polyester, and resin. But these forms sag in various ways, as if from the pull of gravity or as if melting in the heat. The forms are strangely organic, too. They could be modeled on jellyfish, or the cilia of a sea worm. Here, the repetition of modular units is less factory-numbing than Freudian-uncanny. Hesse points to what Judd, André, and Le Witt ignored in their fantasy of identifying artist-as-creator with factory-laborer-as-serial-producer: mortality, corporeality, exhaustion, in short, everything that distinguishes people from robots.

One can find frequent parallels to Hesse's dissent from proceduralism in the poetry of Susan Howe, who began her career as a New York installation artist but started writing verse in the early 1970s. Most prominent are recurrent ragged arrays of words, partial words, and numbers that restage Hesse's implied opposition between, on the one hand, reason and rectitude and, on the other, the disruptions of entropy:

sh dispel iris sh snow sward wide ha

forest 1 a boundary mimic a land sh

whit thing : target cadence marked on

O about both or don't INDICATION Americ

sh woof subdued toward foliage free sh (Howe 1996: 122)

The rectangular shape and careful spacing recall the proceduralist preference for grids, matrices, and rectilinearity, but the words themselves do not display orderliness on a semantic level. There are hints of a scene: "forest," "land," "foliage," "snow," "wide," "boundary." She gives us scattered sounds ("ha," "woof," "sh") and barest indication of action ("subdued," "target," "dispel"). Howe gives us language either in decay or on its way to intelligibility – certainly not a clear picture or argument. She also implicates herself in this half-way space between pattern (geometry) and chaos (nonsense). Repeating "sh" four times, she interjects her own initials (**S**usan **H**owe). Selfhood, Howe suggests, emerges neither through rational self-fashioning nor through indulgence in subconscious irrationality but through their vexed, productive interplay.

VI

Duchamp's *3 Standard Stoppages* inaugurated a century of challenges to "symmetry" and "organic form," in other words, the injunction that good art exhibits harmony in its selection, disposition, and assembly of parts. Visual artists and poets came to see that, quite simply, anything could follow anything. The work's lessons do not end there, however. The arch-trickster Duchamp, it turns out, lied about how he made *3 Standard Stoppages*. Instead of dropping strings from a ladder, he in fact threaded them through a canvas on both ends. The results are gentle curves, not the random squiggles that drops would have produced. Duchamp's fib was easily disproved. All one had to do was look at the piece carefully and observe its construction. For 80 years, though, artists and scholars failed to do so. Instead, they told and retold Duchamp's story. They remained focused not on a made object but on an event, or more precisely, on the idea of an event (Shearer and Gould 1999).

Not until 1960 or so did this aspect of Duchamp's legacy – the dispensability of the physical artwork – capture the imagination of the New York art world. Allan Kaprow, in part inspired by John Cage, started staging Happenings, one-off, improvised, collaborative theater pieces. Soon a group of young artists began a series of inquiries into "performance art" as a genre in its own right. The Fluxus circle – which included George Brecht, Dick Higgins, Alison Knowles, and Jackson Mac Low – interrogated the minima involved in a performance, such things as script, stage, gesture, props, sound, and audience. Each performance piece contributed to a collective process of empirically testing their chosen medium's boundaries and possibilities.

One outgrowth of Fluxus experimentation was the "event score," a set of fanciful written directions that might or might not be things a person could do in the course of a performance. In some cases, as in Mac Low's *The Pronouns*, these scores become almost indistinguishable from poetry: "He makes himself comfortable/ matches parcels.// Then he makes glass boil/ while having political material get in/ & coming by.// Soon after he's giving gold cushions or seeming to do so" (Mac Low 1986: 182). Surely, when performed, the particular, verbal idiosyncrasies of *The Pronouns* would be made unavailable to an audience. A more extreme example: many of Yoko Ono's event scores could be performed without anyone (other than the performer) even noticing, as in "Snow Piece," which instructs a reader to imagine "snow . . . falling" on someone and to cease "when you think the person is covered by snow" (Ono 1998). Ono accentuated the generic indeterminacy of such pieces by both publishing them as poetry and hanging them in galleries as visual art. Artists affiliated with Fluxus began to teach that "performance" is a genre-of-genres, one that potentially includes within its purview poetry, music, painting, in short, all the arts. This realization hit the New York art scene like a thunderclap, and it helps explain the prominence and ubiquity of performance art from the 1970s onwards in almost every account of the New York art scene. A figure like Laurie Anderson, for example, can plausibly call herself a poet, a composer, a video artist, and an actress because the larger heading of "performance" that governs her work licenses her (and her critics) to compare her to the practitioners of its assorted subheadings.

The suspicion that poetry and visual art are both somehow fundamentally performative has also had a subtle, albeit thoroughgoing, effect on the kinds and quality of work produced in and around the New York art world. What if the proper way to understand Duchamp's urinal, for instance, is not as a pseudo-sculpture but as a prop in a theatrical event? After all, we the audience encounter it "on stage" (in a museum) when that museum decides it is appropriate to "show" it. A work such as *3 Standard Stoppages* was "performed" for the first time when Duchamp related the story to someone else; indeed,

I could be said to "rehearse" it again in these pages. Such metaphors make us aware that an artwork is an inordinately complex phenomenon, a combination of gestures, actions, perceptions, discussions, and audience reactions.

What bearing does this have on poetry? I would like to close this chapter by suggesting that it shifts the interest in writing away from conveying content, personal or merely informational, to facilitating a charged performative encounter between reader and text. A book such as Clark Coolidge's *The Maintains* exemplifies this shift. On first glance it can look like a long random string of words arbitrarily lineated:

> rope east also card an east
> due sea decay the ocean
> first full in state vase
> both tarp bias
> part point a group worse
> part any hence sex
> as lawn pen pump chop swell
> stub roof (Coolidge 1974: 62)

Clark gives a reader no narrative, no scene, no speaker, not even stable syntax. There are, though, a few observable patterns. The words, for instance, are predominantly one syllable in length. In lines such as "as lawn pen pump chop swell" the language plods as a consequence. Words begin to take on an imponderable heft, a tangible resistance, as one struggles through the thuds and bumps: "first full in state vase/ both tarp bias/ part point a group. . . ." The rampant consonance – in these lines, all those f's, p's, and b's – makes such word clusters physically difficult to utter. Coolidge also relies chiefly on nouns, many of them quite concrete ("rope," "tarp," "lawn," "pump"). He directs our attention to the thingness of the words on the page, their tangible, mysterious presence.

The Maintains proposes that poetry, at base, has little to do with paraphrasable meaning, emotional profundity, or grand concepts. It involves an active process of attending to a sequence of stonily self-sufficient words. Coolidge believes art to be obdurately *other*, the creation of something unique that has never existed before. Encountering such radical otherness on its, not our, terms requires that readers open themselves vulnerably, nonprejudicially, to the dauntingly unfamiliar. From this point of view, writing a poem is ultimately as much an ethical as an aesthetic act, a staging of an event wherein the audience puts itself, and its sense of the world, vertiginously at risk.

A book such as *The Maintains* could not have been written a century earlier. Like the poetry discussed in the rest of this chapter, it makes use of freedoms, models, and insights originating in and around the New York art world in the wake of the Armory Show. Coleridge, Dickinson, Emerson – even Pound and Eliot – would have found its precedents obscure, its purport hermetic, and its intent unfathomable. Yet its message concerns an ethics of difference, and a presumption of art's role as a space of ethical encounter, that could not be more timely at the turn of the twenty-first century, in a time of holy wars, racial division, and class resentment. One could do much worse, in trying to figure out the future of US poetry, than begin by studying the New York art world and pondering what its artists have taught, and might continue to teach, the nation's poets.

References and Further Reading

Ashbery, John (1977). *Houseboat Days*. New York: Penguin.

Cage, John (1979). *Empty Words*. Middletown, CT: Wesleyan University Press.

Coolidge, Clark (1974). *The Maintains*. Oakland, CA: This Press.

Cummings, E. E. (1998). *AnOther E.E. Cummings*, ed. Richard Kostelanetz. New York: Liveright.

De Duve, Thierry (1998). *Kant After Duchamp*. Cambridge, MA: MIT Press.

Hass, Robert, Hollander, John, Kizer, Carolyn, Mackey, Nathaniel, and Perloff, Marjorie (eds.) (2000). *American Poetry: The Twentieth Century, Volume 1: Henry Adams to Dorothy Parker*. New York: Library of America.

Howe, Susan (1996). *Frame Structures: Early Poems 1974–1979*. New York: New Directions.

Kotz, Liz (2001). "Post-Cagean Aesthetics and the 'Event' Score," *October*, 95: 55–89.

Loy, Mina (1996). *The Lost Lunar Baedeker: Poems*, ed. Roger L. Conover. New York: Farrar Strauss Giroux.

Mac Low, Jackson (1986). *Representative Works: 1938–1985*. New York: Roof Press.

O'Hara, Frank (1971). *The Collected Poems*, ed. Donald Hall. Berkeley, CA: University of California Press.

Ono, Yoko (1998). *Grapefruit: A Book of Instructions and Drawings*. New York: Simon & Schuster (no pagination).

Perloff, Marjorie (2002). *21st Century Modernism: The "New" Poetics.* Oxford: Blackwell.

Shearer, Rhonda Roland and Gould, Stephen Jay (1999). "Hidden in Plain Sight: Duchamp's *3 Standard Stoppages,* More Truly a 'Stoppage' (an Invisible Mending) Than We Ever Realized," *Tout-Fait,* 1. <http://www.toutfait.com/>.

Shoptaw, John (1994). *On the Outside Looking Out: John Ashbery's Poetry.* Cambridge, MA: Harvard University Press.

Williams, William Carlos (1970). *Imaginations.* New York: New Directions.

Chapter 7

The Blue Century: Brief Notes on Twentieth-century African-American Poetry

Rowan Ricardo Phillips

Paul Laurence Dunbar

Twentieth-century African-American poetry actually began in the last decade of the nineteenth century with the work of Paul Laurence Dunbar. While the poets and poems of the Harlem Renaissance can also stake a strong claim to this designation – due in large part to the dawn of the jazz age and a new consumer market for the black artist mainly by white patrons in the swelling urban centers of America – I would argue instead that it was the quiet turbulence of Dunbar's poems that form the start of twentieth-century African-American poetry. With *Oak and Ivy* (1893), *Majors and Minors* (1895), and *Lyrics of Lowly Life* (1896), Dunbar, born in Dayton, Ohio, created a poetics of duality. The titles alone of Dunbar's first two volumes of verse offer a manner by which to conceive of Dunbar's poetry as being riddled by a two-sided subjectivity, a play of needful contrasts: one and the other, this and that, not as canceling conceits but rather complementary parts of a whole; oak trees and ivy may form a forest, majors and minors produce emotional tones in the musical progressions of scales, chords, and melodies. But then what of the third title? "Lyrics of lowly life" as a phrase not only eschews the simplistic balance of the first two titles, but it gives the sense of a weariness, indeed a fatigue that may be – given the words of the title – of a moral ("lowly life") or aesthetic ("lyrics") nature.

The bifurcated sensibility evident in the first two titles – a twinning that implies a separation of familiar entities – is the first major mode of African-American poetry in the twentieth century. Dunbar's poems were of two minds. There was the poet of the traditional English lyric, such as in "Ere Sleep Comes Down to Soothe the Weary Eyes":

> Ere sleep comes down to soothe the weary eyes,
>   Which all the day with ceaseless care have sought
> The magic gold which from the seeker flies; (Dunbar 1993: 3)

But then there was the more lauded Dunbar: the poet of African-American rural speech, a dialect where the central personae would often have a sentimental eye on a simpler time (which would, given the chronology of the poems, inevitably be the antebellum period). For example, Dunbar's "When de Co'n Pone's Hot" (Dunbar 1993: 57) utilizes the line "When yo' mammy says de blessin' /An' de co'n pone's hot" both as refrain and as calming respite from destabilizing moments ("When de worl' jes' stahts a-spinnin'"). Corn meal was commonly referred to as "corn pone" in Southern dialects and served as a primary staple for African Americans during the antebellum era, Reconstruction, and after. For the sake of taking in more of the performative aspects of Dunbar's use of dialect (precisely, how it sounds and looks on the page) here is a small excerpt from the poem.

> Dey is times in life when Nature
>   Seems to slip a cog an' go,
> Jes' a-rattlin' down creation,
>   Lak an ocean's overflow;
> When de worl' jes' stahts a-spinnin'
>   Lak a picaninny's top,
> An' yo' cup o' joy is brimmin'
>   'Twell it seems about to slop,
> An' you feel jes' lak a racah,
>   Dat is trainin' fu' to trot – (Dunbar 1993: 57)

Dunbar is a figure we should understand first and foremost as troubled by having ambitions for one particular type of poetry (the traditional lyric) but receiving great audience response for another type of poetry (the rural dialect). His tribute poems, such as "Fredrick Douglass," "Douglass," "Robert Gould Shaw," and "The Colored Soldiers," give a sense of the level of the poet's ambition: he sought to have his poetry enter the public register of national memory, as would a great monument or edifice. The success of his dialect poems leaves us with a sense that poems like "We Wear the Mask" and, later, "Sympathy" (in which Dunbar penned the phrase, "I know why the caged bird sings!") speak to the plight of the poet himself. Before long Dunbar discovered himself to be hemmed in by his blackness, and his response – how many options could he have had? – was this formal and tonal discursiveness on the plight of being heard but not being heard that has left Dunbar as a great mystery to critics and admirers alike. To read Dunbar now is like looking at a bas-relief. His is a drama of background and foreground; and to read one poem in search of Dunbar never suffices, for his crux was, like Lowell's, of a plurality of poems wrought by thirst and dissatisfaction. As I write this I recognize how this should be the case for every poet, that one poem does not capture the poet. But it was never dramatized in African-American poetry with such clarity and poignancy before Paul Laurence Dunbar. And in this sense, despite wading in the waters of the end of the nineteenth century, Dunbar is the originary moment, his crux the archetypal conundrum, of twentieth-century African-American poetry. As W. E. B. DuBois wrote so famously in 1903, "the problem of the Twentieth Century is the problem of the color-line." And for Dunbar, that line was real and terrible: a suffocating border by which his sense of two poetries sat separate, and forever irreconcilable.

"The Weary Blues"

DuBois, in that same text, *The Souls of Black Folk*, introduced each chapter with a bar of musical notation as a sign of the roots from which African-American writing and thought developed, but also tantalizingly as a trope of the untranslatable and emergent relationship between music and the written word. Since poems create and manage their distinctive cadence through rhythm, meter, punctuation, and the juggling and jarring of consonants and vowels by means of assonance and alliteration, music in this sense has long been regarded as a dynamic internal to a poem. In other words, a poem is made by music and that music consists of words clustering the space on a page. While I am hesitant to turn to particular and inherent differences in an African-American poem from another type of poem, it is nevertheless impossible to ignore the strong and seemingly unshakeable correlation between music and African-American poetry. Music in these instances often emerges as the symptom of, or cure for, a poetic situation. If a lyric poem is generally understood to begin at a moment of disequilibrium in the speaker's sense of the world, and further if poetry can be considered a form of altered speech or altered reckoning, then it is African-American poetry's powerfully successful tendency to revel in music's transformative qualities as a catalyst for poetry that makes for such a unique example of American literary art. Therefore, though there are many varieties of African-American poetry that I could discuss in the space provided, I will instead choose to focus upon music – in particular the blues – and the manner in which music distinguishes itself as a sustentative context by which to understand the evolving impetus behind African-American poetry in the twentieth century.

There are three foundations upon which my understanding of the blues rests: that it began as oral art, that it veers almost compulsively toward repetition, and that it seeks an empathetic though not sympathetic audience – in other words, the blues functions best with a (silently) implicit audience because no matter the problem the blues is not a call for help but rather an itemization of the problem itself. It is a desire embedded within the blues to articulate a problem without servicing it, a crux Ralph Ellison, author of *Invisible Man,* labeled as "tragicomic." While there are poems that expertly emulate the formal aspects of the blues, the *relationship* between the two genres, poetry and music, is best identified in one poem in particular, "The Weary Blues" by Langston Hughes, that circumscribes the blues, literally writing around the blues in order to make a narrative of the effect of the blues upon the speaker, and hence upon the poem itself. The speaker of the poem is situated as a member of the audience enthralled by music so captivating that it becomes the very reason for the poem.

> Droning a drowsy syncopated tune,
> Rocking back and forth to a mellow croon,
>   I heard a Negro play.
> Down on Lenox Avenue the other night
> By the pale dull pallor of an old gas light
>   He did a lazy sway . . .
>   He did a lazy sway . . .
> To the tune o' those Weary Blues.
> With his ebony hands on each ivory key
> He made that poor piano moan with melody.
>   O Blues!
> Swaying to and fro on his rickety stool

He played that sad raggy tune like a musical fool.
  Sweet Blues!
Coming from a black man's soul.
  O Blues!
In a deep song voice with a melancholy tone
I heard that Negro sing, that old piano moan–
  "Ain't got nobody in all this world,
  Ain't got nobody but ma self.
  I's gwine to quit ma frownin'
  And put ma troubles on the shelf."

Thump, thump, thump, went his foot on the floor.
He played a few chords then he sang some more–
  "I got the Weary Blues
  And I can't be satisfied.
  Got the Weary Blues
  And can't be satisfied –
  I ain't happy no mo'
  And I wish that I had died."
And far into the night he crooned that tune.
The stars went out and so did the moon.
The singer stopped playing and went to bed
While the Weary Blues echoed through his head.
He slept like a rock or a man that's dead. (Hughes 1995: 50)

Notice how the poem organizes the experience it describes. Though the poem seeks, at first glance, to say "I saw this, it happened like so," we discover that there is no turn after this occurs in the poem. The typical curve of a poem of this sort – and here I mean those poems that seek to reimagine significant experience – adds the element of "and therefore I did so" or "and thus I am like so." For example, John Keats gives his reader a sense of what happened to him after first reading Chapman's translation of Homer; and Elizabeth Bishop, after coming face to face with the venerable hook-bearded fish she caught, lets the fish go. Yet "The Weary Blues" stops far short of giving a sense of the altered life or action of the speaker. In fact, "I" only appears twice in order to locate the passive relationship between the speaker of the poem and the blues singer. What, then, is the objective of the start of the poem where the speaker seems more active ("droning" and "rocking back and forth") though lulled by the context of listening to the music? By starting in such a manner the poem seems to indicate that the poem will discover the transformative effect on the speaker of the poem by being in contact with the blues singer. Yet the active nature of the speaker fades into description, leaving the singer supposedly to his environment. Precisely at the moment in the poem where experience is expected to be condensed into insight or invocation – poems, after all, supposedly delight and instruct – is where one is left with an image of the musician, and only the musician, at a moment of rest; the musician in the rare and sublime moment of not-being-the-musician. Hughes here is deferring pleasure within the poem: a blues-like sacrifice for the sake of an aspiring kinship with the power of a cultural (and racial) icon.

Hughes's poem is a hopeful poem, though not hopeful for a simplistic change in social fortune. Instead the poem is hopeful that it can make art, as the blues singer makes art; the poem aspires to affect the emotions and sensibilities of a person outside of the poem in the way that the blues singer has done to him. Sympathy is not the main emotional register here. The poem behaves as it does in the hopes of establishing an empathy with the blues that it, as of yet, does not possess. Hence the end of the poem should be read as a type of subjunctive mood in which the poet wants to speak of something as though it plainly exists but the parameters of that possibility still chafe with doubt. Simply put: ask yourself, how does the speaker of the poem know of the scene that occurs in the final three lines of the poem?

> The singer stopped playing and went to bed
> While the Weary Blues echoed through his head.
> He slept like a rock or a man that's dead.

The English Romantics in particular stretched beautifully for this type of sublimity, this omniscience. But the very process of doing so was also rendered as content in the movement of the poem. Poems like Coleridge's "Frost at Midnight" made explicit the desire for the poetic voice to seize this type of omniscience as the self joins with the world outside of itself. It is an attempt at a poetics, a theory behind the making of the poem. But "The Weary Blues" is a poem that depends on a sense of narrative realism in which the interruption of the events by song is the only phenomenon that subdues a desire within the poem to describe as concisely as possible what it observes.

A cursory approach to reading this poem, as we have been encouraged to read many African-American poems, would ask new readers to regard the manner in which the poem provides a space for the blues singer to speak for himself, in his own words, and to regard the community-building aspects of a poem based, such as this one, on the blues. The Langston Hughes poem "Jazz Band in a Parisian Cabaret" is a poem far more in keeping with this type of thesis than is "The Weary Blues." "Jazz Band" contains a number of speaking characters, emphasized even further by the various languages at play in the poem. The concept is that jazz can bring people together as a common denominator of human interest. The poem's ending

> Can I go home wid yuh, sweetie?
> Sure. (Hughes 1995: 60)

is a monosyllabic response to the question, "Can I join you at your home?" and is spoken by an unidentified character in the poem, but the spacing of the line with the other indented lines leads one to believe that it is more background noise and different from the main speaker in the poem. This is a poem that allows its described participants to, if you will, take the poem over.

"The Weary Blues" defers pleasure in music for the sake of what I earlier referred to as an "aspiring kinship" – but it aspires for the *power* of the icon, not for a kinship *with* the icon itself. The poem does not provide a space for the blues singer's words in order to enliven our sense of the blues singer. The poem, after all, closes with the blues singer being spoken for and described in private by an outside voice. The two characters, we should never forget, are strangers and the candid vision of one offered by the other has not been garnered by familiarity but rather by poetic ambition. The concluding vision is an entreaty for privacy for the sake, at all costs, of poetic vision. One must remember that the blues singer is not provided a space in "The Weary Blues" to speak; he is permitted a stage on which to perform. The dynamic between the speaker of the poem and the blues singer is that of audience to performer, and that does not change. What does change is the power of the speaker of the poem: passive description gives way to the sublimity of what, in the end, may only be temporary omniscience.

I have added "temporary" to "omniscience" here in order to emphasize the subdued sense of hope and threat in the poem. Again, the most readily available reading of the poem is that it seeks to give a voice and stage to those who have generally been outsiders to the topics and themes of American poetry. This is one of the great interventions of the poetry of the Harlem Renaissance: it provided portraits of (urban) African-American popular art. Yet as we have seen, the voice of the blues singer is only the voice of performance (are people the same on stage as they are off?) and, consequently, the conclusion of the poem is deceptively a homage to the ability of poetic vision to see beyond its given locale (a locale clearly put forth as setting in line four of the poem, "Down on Lenox Avenue"). In this sense, "The Weary Blues" is a type of experiment in poetry in which the poet seeks to incorporate the thus far untamed and mystified subject of the blues. Hughes is approaching the blues in a moment before genre; there is no body of work in 1923 known as the blues poem to the extent that, in 1973, there so clearly was. He is, to dig up a phrase, in the wilds of literary history. Consequently, the task here for the poet is to make the wild, or Dionysian, coalesce with the calm and meditative – what would be traditional poetics – or the Apollonian.

Hughes starts the poem with a rhymed couplet in iambic pentameter, reminiscent of the heroic couplet most strongly identified with Alexander Pope and John Dryden. But the third line severs the traditionalism of that initial couplet: "I heard a Negro play." It is the introduction of the performer and of the blues that makes the poem veer from its original structure. We should also compare the poeticized diction of the couplet – "Droning," "drowning," "syncopated tune," "back and forth," "mellow croon" – with the plain succinctness of the intruding third line: "I heard a Negro play." From that moment on, until the final five lines of the poem, "The Weary Blues" is an intertexture of two types of poetry and the objective is to find a poetics by which both can function as one. This is a supremely ambitious poem whose task is to answer poetic ambition, not to give voice to another. The voice seeks to *incorporate* the voice of another within its own. The hope is that the would-be *ars poetica* succeeds; the threat, felt as it is in process of becoming, is that it may not. But this is where lyric poems find their balance and emotive power. Hughes is here working through a poem with an immense bravery behind a poetics that strays from the easy path of sentimentality for its perceived subject, the blues singer, to the fraught and tenacious possibility that the poet and the poet's ambition here are the subject. The last five lines of the poem are a taste of poetic inspiration (from the Latin "breathing in") in which the poet has, in the end, literally breathed in the blues, swallowing whole the perceived subject into the body of a poem, scored by ambition and brought forth by a music external to its first two intertwined metrical lines. The word "weary" in "The Weary Blues" is as much about the effort of the poet to incorporate what is not the poet's as it is about the worldly fatigue of the maestro of the blues.

Hughes's problem here with the blues is an archetypal circumstance for the poet in regard to music. He finds that he cannot at this point consolidate without interruption the formal properties of the blues with those more traditionally aligned with the poet. To transcribe inherently oral material, which is what Hughes is doing with the sung parts of the poem, is likewise a momentary turn of the poet into stenographer. Structurally, this problem is dramatized by the use of couplets – rhymed and, in the beginning, metrical, these couplets are rather self-consciously made – to emphasize the distinction between the two patterns. This is why, though the poet has the last word in the poem, the poem ends when the blues singer stops playing and leaves. The poet is modeling a problem of poetic influence in formal terms. As Hughes portrays the singer in a deep sleep, it is the singer's soundlessness, and thus the poet's inability to continue the poem, that in the end brings up the possibility of the singer's destruction. For in the end, the poet has little access to the private life of the singer save by way of the blues singer's enthralling performance and the poet's inspired momentary poetic vision. The end of the performance reveals a need on the part of the poet, which is represented as a private horror, an anxiety over the end of poetry itself. Music transcends language and can transcend place and identity. We believe that we appreciate and even "understand" music despite either the absence of lyrics or of lyrics we can understand. Can poetry hold up to such a standard? For African-American poetry, which was to become more and more intertwined with African-American music as the twentieth century progressed, the presence of music was to become the great challenging question: if music can reach and affect so many and produce what Wordsworth called in his definition of the lyric poem "a spontaneous overflow of powerful emotions," then what would be the role of poetry? Is poetry in the process of being replaced? And, in this vein, is "The Weary Blues" a response?

Blues and Jazz in Poetry

"The Weary Blues" is a staggering example of the effect that music can have on the design of a poem. While many poems have been, in terms of their content, about music, no poems before "The Weary Blues" dramatized the context under which African-American poetry and African-American music fought for the same stage. Hughes's poem is a coded poetics: a tale of poetic antagonism that does not rob the reader or steal from the critic its surface impression of being a tribute to the blues and blues performers. And yet, like all poems that withstand our considerable attention and probing, "The Weary Blues" embeds a story within a story. Poets, especially, are often intrigued by the story within the story in a poem: the narrative of what the poem intends by changing from one type of stanza to another, from one voice to another, how a poem ends where it began. Thus the manner by which poets after "The Weary Blues" have sought to address or circumvent the circumstances and "problems" contextualized by African-American music and poetry are various and telling.

Hughes's contemporary, and one of the most underappreciated poets of the past century, Sterling A. Brown, used humor in some instances to play with the assumption that African Americans have a more innate relationship to the blues. In his poem "Slim Greer" the protagonist, Slim, is a playful character who constantly finds his way in and out of trouble. Slim is in Arkansas and is passing for white. Passing is a situation in which people of color who do not appear to possess features common to the stereotypical conception of a racial type either do not reveal their racial identity or state explicitly that they are of another racial designation, in order to avoid the hardships of segregation and discrimination. Though Slim is a very dark man he is able, strangely, to pass. Brown is writing here in the tragicomic mode common both to the blues and its distant cousin, the ballad.

> How he in Arkansas
> Passed for white,
> An' he no lighter
> Than a dark midnight.
>
> Found a nice white woman
> At a dance,
> Thought he was from Spain
> Or else from France; (Brown 1996: 77)

Only one person has a doubt regarding Slim's racial identity, and that person – despite Slim's "midnight dark" complexion – is suspicious rather than certain. One subsequent day the suspicious "Hill Billy," a character in the poem who was also competing for the affection of the aforementioned woman, pays this same woman a visit and finds Slim there already and "comfy." It is when Slim decides to play the piano that all of the Hill Billy's suspicions end:

Heard Slim's music –
An' then, hot damn!
Shouted sharp – "Nigger!"
An' Slim said, "Ma'am?" (Brown 1996: 78)

Music in this instance speaks more to the way in which others have chosen to identify African Americans than to how music plays a part in the life of Slim Greer. In this context one may see the way in which music can define an individual (in this case racially) rather than the individual choosing to be defined.

"Slim Greer" is a ballad and accordingly observes the tendency of ballads to create a heroic and/or tragic figure. Music in African-American poetry has also been the template upon which heroism, at times a tragic heroism, makes its mark. For example, Robert Hayden's "Homage to the Empress of the Blues" (Hayden 1985: 32) strikes a subtle note for the situations under which performers and musicians share their love for musical expression. The structure of the four-stanza poem is cause-and-effect – because this happened, this happened – and it is deployed stanzaically, the first and third stanzas (starting "Because there was a man somewhere . . ." and "Because grey laths began somewhere to show from underneath") serving as causes, and the second and fourth ("She came out on the stage in a yard of pearls . . ." and "She came out on the stage in ostrich feathers . . .") serving as the effects. What is striking about the poem is that the causes are not clearly correlative to the resultant fact – that Bessie Smith, famed "Empress of the Blues," sang. Yet the poem alludes to the sense that the dangers explicit in the first and third stanzas are implicit in the power of the performance of Bessie Smith. Their suffering, spelled out in the first stanza, is answered by the beauty and elegance of the singing woman; their apprehension, identified in the third stanza, of leaving their safe-though-not-so-safe interior world of a blues tavern, is pardoned by the beauty and elegance of the singing woman. The poem does not center on a transformative power of Bessie Smith and her blues; rather, "Homage to the Empress of the Blues" takes the perspective of the enraptured member of the audience, who takes Bessie Smith's relevance as an emergent act of artistry amidst and arisen from within hard life. Consequently, Hayden here provides a definition of the blues through this poem. The blues manages somehow to make a collective out of individual suffering, and through the formation of this collective finds resolution by means of coping as opposed to resolving. The blues does not suggest cures; the blues is its own cure.

The manner by which the blues seeks to inspire a resiliency of the individual finds root often in repetition. Langston Hughes used what is typically referred to as a blues stanza for the voice of the blues singer. This stanza has in it a repetitive engine.

> I got the Weary Blues
> And I can't be satisfied.
> Got the Weary Blues
> And can't be satisfied –
> I ain't happy no mo'
> And I wish that I had died.

The idea behind repetition is that it is a mnemonic device: it aids in remembering something. Why would someone want to remember that they have the blues? Because the blues is an anodyne for a troubled soul. In "Deep Song" by Gayl Jones, we find a poem that forgoes the blues stanza and focuses on repetition. By doing so the poem is imbued with a sense of resilience weighted down by weariness.

> The blues calling my name.
> She is singing a deep song.
> She is singing a deep song.

and further along in the poem

> I care about you.
> I care.
> I care about you.
> I care. (Harper and Walton 2000: 338)

This is an example of a formal aspect of African-American music, the resonance of repetition in the blues, being reproduced by a poem. The compulsion to repeat, both in this poem and generally in the blues, leads to clear (though not unproblematic) statement. Therefore, the repetition observed is actually incremental: a building up of material for effect. If the effect here is to say, "I love you," the poem acts as a dramatization of what one goes through regardless of (or despite) saying those three words. The general simplicity of the poem and muted epiphany of its end provide a mysterious quality that is technical as much as it is situational. Repetition here implies contemplation, which is the structural dynamic by which the blues is an attempt to work through problematic situations – though it should be noted that because its poetic effect is more linear than stanzaic, the poem echoes the structures of jazz more than it does the blues.

Inside the Music

I have attempted to present a few of what I consider to be the more provocative contexts within which African-American poets have contextualized the blues and jazz. There are many more contexts and even more poets who have recreated or responded to the great challenge that music is for the writer. The poems created from these contexts have touched, for instance, the formal precision of the ancient Japanese form of the haiku. Etheridge Knight asserts with the last haiku of his poem entitled "Haiku" that

> Making jazz swing in
> seventeen syllables AIN'T
> no square poet's job. (Harper and Walton 2000: 224)

And the experimentalist nature of Nathaniel Mackey's poetics has given us poems rich in musical dreamscapes that in their arabesque syntax occupy a space somewhere between refinement and tantrum. With Jimi Hendrix in mind, Mackey's "Black Snake Visitation" repeats lines that invoke both the dedication to practice and the torque of madness that both poet and musician typically occupy:

> *been rehearsing,*
> *lizardquick*
> *tongues like*
>
> *they were licking*
> *the sky.* (Harper and Walton 2000: 336)

There is a sense in the poems by Yusef Komunyakaa of the modern urban man increasingly isolated from his surroundings and from himself, spared only somewhat by music present or by the memory of music. In his "Untitled Blues" the poem turns quickly, unexpectedly, from observing a photo of a poor black boy to a subjunctive-laden invocation of the calming effects of music.

> Sure, I could say everything's copacetic,
> listen to a Buddy Bolden cornet
> cry from one of those coffin-
> shaped houses called
> shotgun. (Komunyakaa 2001: 94)

Music here does not interrupt a stream of thought to provide clarity or poignancy. Instead music here is an option weighed and discarded by the speaker. Thus, not only does Komunyakaa present the speaker of the poem as being a devotee of music, but he also presents us with an aspect of authorial control that serves as the poem's antecedent scenario. In other words, the speaker of the poem is so comfortable with music that he can offer a tune as the immediate response to poignant memory and then dismiss it. This is a small and yet significant reimagining of the role of jazz and blues in the work of poets.

Finally, I would like to briefly discuss Michael S. Harper's use of the dramatic monologue as it pertains to jazz and blues performers of the past. If "The Weary Blues" produces a poetic amanuensis for the experiences of the blues singer, the dramatic monologues of Michael S. Harper are the responsive opposite. They provide a context and situations by which blues and jazz performers reveal an inner life and complex psychologies either before or in the midst of creating their music.

While poetry previously attempted to celebrate these musicians by means of encomium or replication, Harper's dramatic monologues delve into the antecedent scenarios of music's creation by giving a depth and interiority to musicians. Poems like "A Narrative of the Life and Times of John Coltrane: Played by Himself" answer the poetic problem outlined in "The Weary Blues" by turning the situation of poetry inside-out: the musician is now the poet, and the poet – the one writing, or "playing" the poem – is the musician. The first stanza reveals some of the pain that Coltrane suffered from during performance. The poem's central concern is the life out of the view of the public; how that life mediates and speaks of its own existence; and, finally, how the public parts of the persona – these songs that the audience comes to inhabit as its own – situate themselves in the circumstantial and private characteristics of the individual who has created them. As a dramatic monologue the poem includes a strange feature: it simultaneously intensifies the connection and the distance between the musician and the reader. The poem's setting is between shows, with Coltrane in transit, and the detailing of location, means of transit, bodily ache and mental fatigue is set within the crucible of *practice* instead of performance. The implication here is that the circumstances that constitute the public persona of the musician are circumspect and fractional. The emphasis of the poem on pain and practice as spoken by Coltrane reclassifies the jazz poem as a medium by which the subject/musician may consider a sensible present for the self without the interruption of audience, which unavoidably brings with it an emphasis on performance. Hence, "A Narrative of the Life and Times of John Coltrane: Played by Himself" is able to culminate and anchor its intent on the individual self's potential for useful change within its sensible present. The poem's elliptical expressiveness ends with a rumination on weariness as it admixes with desire. "Naima" is the name of Coltrane's ex-wife and also of one of his self-confessed favorite songs, but the desire most immediate here at the poem's end is a desire to break from addiction – an addiction to heroin; as well as, perhaps, an addiction to routine:

> And then, on a train to Philly,
> I sang "Naima" locking the door
> without exit no matter what song
> I sang; with remonstrations on the ceiling
> of that same room I practiced in
> on my back when too tired to stand,
> I broke loose from crystalline habits
> I thought would bring me that sound. (Harper 2000: 188)

Harper's poems prove to be an original turn in subject and tone. They also seduce with an instructive gravity. The poem is not subordinate to biography, instead these types of poems radiate in their ability to do what neither a reproduction of the music or a biography could do: they make aspects of the life repeatable, if only momentarily. The reader becomes John Coltrane. The poem is the thought made by the reader, as Coltrane, as the poem is read. One thus approaches an empathetic sensibility instead of a sympathetic one. And thus, the twentieth century seems farther and farther away from the theme of sentimentality with which the nineteenth century closed. Rich dramatic monologues like "A Narrative of the Life and Times of John Coltrane: Played by Himself" are also the poetic successors of "The Weary Blues" – and as such we should be thankful for that peculiar habit poets have of speaking *as* someone else instead of *for* someone else.

References and Further Reading

Benston, Kimberly W. (2000). *Performing Blackness: Enactments of African-American Modernism*. London and New York: Routledge, 2000.

Brooks, Gwendolyn (1991). *Blacks*. Chicago: Third World Press.

Brown, Sterling A. (1996). *The Collected Poems of Sterling A. Brown*, ed. Michael S. Harper. Evanston, IL: TriQuarterly Books.

Dove, Rita (1993). *Selected Poems*. New York: Vintage.

Dunbar, Paul Laurence (1993). *The Collected Poetry of Paul Laurence Dunbar*. Charlottesville: University of Virginia Press.

Edwards, Brent (1998). "The Seemingly Eclipsed Window of Form: James Weldon Johnson's Prefaces." In Robert G. O'Meally (ed.), *The Jazz Cadence of American Culture*. New York: Columbia University Press, pp. 580–601.

Harper, Michael S. (2000). *Songlines in Michaeltree: New and Collected Poems*. Urbana: University of Illinois Press.

— and Walton, Anthony (2000). *The Vintage Book of African American Poetry*. New York: Vintage Books.

Hayden, Robert (1985). *The Collected Poems of Robert Hayden*. New York: Liveright.

Hughes, Langston (1995). *The Collected Poems of Langston Hughes*, ed. Arnold Rampersad. New York: Vintage.

Johnson, James Weldon (ed.) (1931). *The Book of American Negro Poetry*. New York: Harcourt Brace and Company.

Kaufman, Bob (1965). *Solitudes Crowded with Loneliness*. New York: W. W. Norton & Company.

Komunyakaa, Yusef (2001). *Pleasure Dome: New and Collected Poems*. Middletown, CT: Wesleyan University Press.

Locke, Alain (ed.) (1980). *The New Negro*. New York: Atheneum.

Lorde, Audre (2000). *The Collected Poems of Audre Lorde*. New York: W. W. Norton & Company.

Mackey, Nathaniel (1986). *Eroding Witness*. Urbana: University of Illinois Press.

— (2001). *Atet A.D.* San Francisco: City Lights Books.

Moss, Thylias (1998). *Last Chance for the Tarzan Holler*. New York: Persea.

Nelson, Marilyn (1997). *The Fields of Praise: New and Selected Poems*. Baton Rouge: Louisiana State University Press.

Nielsen, Aldon Lynn (1997). *Black Chant: Languages of African-American Postmodernism*. New York: Cambridge University Press.

Phillips, Carl (1992). *In the Blood: The 1992 Morse Poetry Prize*, edited and selected by Rachel Hadas. Boston: Northeastern University Press.

Rampersad, Arnold (1988). *The Life of Langston Hughes, vol. 1, 1902–1941: I, Too, Sing America*. New York: Oxford University Press.

Wright, Jay (2000). *Transfigurations: Collected Poems*. Baton Rouge: Louisiana State University Press.

Chapter 8

Home and Away: US Poetries of Immigration and Migrancy

A. Robert Lee

Our Independence
Day Parade . . .
Five Nations: Dutch, French, Englishmen,
Indians, and we . . .

("Fouth of July in Maine," Lowell 1967: 27)

Rising, rising, rising
we migrants,
mosquitoes,
malcontents,
do hereby defy the Ching emperor . . .

Indentured to dreams
we imagine America,
the soft green breast of an island
almost a mirage beyond our eyes.

(Leong 1993: 24)

México
When I'm that far south, the old words
Molt off my skin, the feathers
Of all my nervousness.
My own words somersault naturally as my name,
joyous among all those meadows: Michoacán,
Vera Cruz, Tenochtitlán, Oaxaca . . .

I don't want to pretend I know more
And can speak all the names, I can't.
My sense of this land can only ripple through my veins
Like the chant of an epic corrido.
I come from a long line of eloquent illiterates
Whose history reveals more than words can say . . .

Washington
I don't belong this far north . . .
I come north
To gather my feathers
for quills
("Visions of Mexico While at a Writing Symposium in Port Townsend, Washington," Cervantes 1981: 45–7)

I

Standard writ has long held that, from the Anglo-Puritan landfall through to postmodern California, the United States has been nothing if not an immigrant nation, an ongoing process of arrival. Not only New England, but *Nueva España* and *Nouvelle France,* bequeath their shaping European passage and geographies. *Gum Sahn,* Gold Mountain in English, reflects the West Coast as America's parallel beckoning, the index of Chinese and other Asian inward population flow. Can it be doubted that immigration, be it across the Atlantic from Britain and Europe, or across the Pacific from Asia and the islands, or as the lure of *el norte* for the Americas to the south, or from the Caribbean to the mainland, together with every manner of internal migration, lies other than at the heart of America's making, as multicultural as it has been ongoing?

Little wonder that this evolution of the "American Grain," in William Carlos Williams's memorable phrase, finds refractions throughout American writing, whether fiction, drama, every manner of autobiographical and discursive work or, wholly in kind, poetry. Robert Lowell, Russell Leong, and Lorna Dee Cervantes, to be sure, supply but a selective literary roster from amid the variously sedimented, and sometimes warring, American legacies of origin, ethnicity, class, gender, and languages far from English. Yet as the opening extracts from their work confirm, and from across the span of the two coasts, they also can be said to exhibit an unmistakable shared interest: that of America's enduring memory of migrant timelines and routes.

Lowell, upper-tier Massachusetts WASP poet, for all his maverick confessionalism and politics, invokes the founding European immigration of "Dutch, French, Englishmen" and their encounter with the "Indians," likely Algonquin, together with the arising "we" of America. The poem's remembrance of a Maine Independence Day parade, full of wry flourish, reflexive, looks to how America, and certainly Anglo-America, has indeed "paraded" its seventeenth century and an ensuing, not to say preemptive, white-cultural or Anglo "mainstream." Leong, a Chinese-American poet raised in San Francisco and longtime editor of *Amerasia*, looks to an exodus from the era of the last Chinese emperor and from the legendary Chinese mainland rebellious regions of Canton and Guandong province. The paradox for these journeyers could not lie more in being "indentured" to their own kind of Asian-Gatsbyesque dream of America, the hardship of Pacific crossing and survival within the "green breast" of hope. Cervantes, her poetry rooted in the *chicanismo* of a blue-collar mestiza-California upbringing, uses the one America of the Pacific northwest to situate the other of Mexico. Her "own words" she thinks of as having been migrantly compounded of silence and quill, Nahuatl and Spanish, and an English, ironically, nowhere to find apter expression than at a writing symposium.

Other poetries of American migration, not only European, Asian, or Mexican but still further beyond, inevitably give their own stylings, the redemption, and sometimes unredemption, of older regimes in the promise of the new. These bespeak the exhilarations of setting forth yet the pains of uprooting, crossings of sea and land, a chosen path or flight, enforced asylum or exile, each, one way or another, the need, the resolve, to make home of away. America as Brave New World has just cause to celebrate triumphs, be it the forging of a "nation of immigrants," a first generation's journeying, the labor and the benefits for later generations, community upward well-being, or new individual freedom. That, however, is not in the least to overlook the caveats.

If America has created a sense of nation what to say of migrant labor, populations often race or color marked and at the bottom of the work-ladder? What sense of migration, and its causes, most appropriately holds for the Afro-America first of Middle Passage slavery, and as postbellum Dixie reimposed Jim Crow in its wake, the northwards Great Migration? More than a million black southerners would head for Harlem, Chicago, or Canada, a "wave of black people running from want and violence" as Toni Morrison calls it in her novel *Jazz* (1992: 33). Has not *chicanismo*, whatever its own historic claims to the southwest and west, and in common with the Caribbean of Puerto Rico, Cuba, and other Latin American populations seeking the dream of *la abundancia*, often enough been thought a "border" culture welcome only as manual labor? Luis Omar Salinas's "Ode to Mexican Experience," with its allusions to the poet's own "Aztec mind" and to "roving gladiators" and "those lost in the wreckage" (Salinas 1980: 23–4) gives a pointer to the fuller human nuance.

What version of immigrant America would best hold for "bachelor" Chinese initially denied their families by the 1882 Exclusion Act, or, against the backdrop of the Spanish-American War of 1898, the Filipino diaspora as colonial-Asian workforce, or each Japanese and Korean passage through Hawaii into the continental USA? In "Minority Poem" the Chinese-Hawaiian poet Wing Tek Lum gives his own cryptic gloss to this history:

> Why
> We're just as American
> As apple pie –
> That is, if you count
> the leftover peelings (Lum 1987: 69)

The issue turns especially acute in connection with America's first peoples, Native Americans, even allowing that many of the tribes, Pequot or Sioux, Anishinaabe or Navaho, and across today's US–Canada and US–Mexico borders, engaged in seasonal moves for food-gathering. A right wording, spoken or written, poetry or otherwise, would be the challenge of any Native writer seeking to capture the "migrant" history consequent upon the homesteader and cavalry wars, imported disease, the massacres, and the deportations into, and out of, "Indian Country" of which the well-named Indian Removal Act of 1830, the Cherokee "Trail of Tears" in 1835, and the surrender and dispatch of Geronimo and his Chiricahua Aspaches to Florida in 1886, were typical. The successive Allotment Acts of 1887 and 1906, and the rise of the reservations, add their shared history. Native poets, no less than novelists and fellow writers of tribal descent, have rightly refused Vanishing American victimry. But from New Mexico's Scott Momaday (Kiowa) to Alaska's Mary TallMountain (Athabaskan), or Simon Ortiz (Acoma Pueblo) to Gail Tremblay (Onandaga-Micmac-French), that is not to understate their recognition of migrancies as anything but self-chosen.

Lowell, Leong, and Cervantes, to reemphasize, give no more than sight lines. Their extracts, however, help to underline how in all its several and overlapping forms, American migrancy can be said to have been taken up in modern poetry quite as much as elsewhere in American culture. Migrations from Europe or Africa across the Atlantic, or from Asia across the Pacific, indicate the one scheme of reference. Migrations within America, Anglo or Irish, northern or southern European, the border southwest or west, tribal or black, or under religious auspices like the Mormons in their trek from New York to Utah, indicate another. None, in all the human flux of leave-taking and arrival, the mix and match of Americanization, has failed to attract the languages of poetry. Beginning from a contextual map of immigrant and migrant America, the account to hand looks to a spectrum of poetic voice: WASP, Euro-American, Jewish, Asian American, Latino/a, African-American and, as a reminder of bearings, Native American.

II

Pilgrim Massachusetts, with the Bay Company or Plymouth Rock as key memorial insignia, and its poets Edward Taylor and Anne Bradstreet – whose lineage leads to Robert Lowell – would quickly be obliged to share their migration. The Irish, Scots, and Scots-Irish became key players, more than five million in all, for whom steerage, indenture, the Great Famine of 1845–7, and even lace-curtain respectability in Boston, Chicago, or San Francisco, provided their own migrant *aides-memoire* among which, from another literary domain, can be included the bittersweet "poetry" of Irish-American retrospect in Eugene O'Neill's 1955 play *Long Day's Journey Into Night.*

The nineteenth century, and the early years of the twentieth, also witnessed the arrival of an estimated seven million Germans; the Scandinavians headed for the upper Midwest; the Italians, Greeks, and other Mediterraneans to the cities; and each Slavic population with its poets like the Belgrade-born Charles Simic with lines like "Touching me, you touch/ The country that has exiled you" from "The Wind" (Simic 1974: 4). Migrancy equally stalks the poetry of the more than two million Poles who sought America, with Adam Miskievicz as their nineteenth-century national poet whose voice continues through to a current Polish-American name like Mark Pawlak in the memorial poems of his first collection, *The Buffalo Sequence*

(Pawlak 1978). Russia has its formidable modern émigré presences, few more consequential than Joseph Brodsky. Jewish America's migrations look to 1820–80s emigration from Germany, the Russo-Polish pogroms, the 1930s flights from the Nazis and, despite marring antisemitism, the rise out of the Lower East Side or other lowly arrival into successful Americanness.

The Arab and Muslim world, a citizenry likewise currently numbered at six million, adds its own human plies and skeins to the trans-Atlantic pathway, migrancies which time and again underwrite landmark collections like *Grapeleaves: A Century of Arab-American Poetry* (Hamod 1988) and *Post-Gibran: Anthology of New Arab American Writing* (Khaled and Samuel 1999). Naomi Shihab Nye's "Steps" succinctly, and delicately, conjures the inscription of a migrant Middle East, with its Arabic into English, upon America's storefronts:

> A man letters the sign for his grocery
> in Arabic and English.
> Paint dries more quickly in English.
> The thick swoops and curls of Arabic letters
> stay moist and glistening till tomorrow when the children
> show up jingling their dimes . . . (Nye 1998: 79)

The Pacific seaboard, and California as prime territory, tells the corresponding story. Inerasably the Native and Latino/a dispensations require full recognition, a massive indigenous and US migrant history. Way stations, direct and indirect, include the western tribes, Cortés and La Malinche, *mestizaje*, the missions, Mexican Independence in 1821, the Mexican Revolution (1910–17), the 1940s *bracero* fieldwork program, Delano and the 1960s *huelgas* (or labor strikes) as led by César Chávez against agribusiness, and barrios and communities from the southwest of New Mexico and Texas to East Los Angeles and the Central and Imperial Valleys. The onetime province of Spain, and then Mexico, it quickly also became a territory competed for by the different currents of Anglo and Euro-American settlement. The relevant poetries, and the migrancies to which they give witness, deservedly continue to invite recognition as borne out in collections like Duane Niatum's *Harper's Anthology of 20th Century Native American Poetry* (1988) and Nicolás Kanellos's *Herencia: The Anthology of Hispanic Literature in the United States* (2002).

Asia's journeyers represent another example of the West's plenty, to embrace Chinese track builders for the Central or Pacific railway,

Chinatowns from Los Angeles to Vancouver, and each Japantown, Manilatown, Little Korea, Little Saigon, or Indo-Pakistani community. This, however, is not to overlook Yellow Peril anti-Asianism, notably the 1882 Exclusion Act or Angel Island – from 1910 onwards a mainly immigrant-Cantonese detention center with its trove of 125 etched-in wall stories and poems of immediate past transit and "all kinds of abuse from these barbarians" (Lai, Lim, and Yung 1980). In *AIIIEEEEE! An Anthology of Asian-American Writers* (1974) and *The Big Aiiieeeee!* (1991), Frank Chin and his coeditors called time on anti-Asianism, the cartoon images, the model minority patronage. Both anthologies, though calls to rally, and greatly controversial for their attacks on Maxine Hong Kingston and Amy Tan, carried the built-in literary tracing of Asian-American settlement. Companion volumes have been plentiful, whether woman-centered like Shirley Geok-Lin Lim et al's *The Forbidden Stitch* (1989) or given to Indo-Pakistani and connected regional migrant memory like Sunaina Maira and Rajini Srikanth's *Contours of The Heart: South Asians Map North America* (1996).

Internal migration has been equally resonant. New Englanders embarked upon their celebrated errand into the wilderness, Boston, Salem, or Amherst as cities upon a hill and to be carried into the mid-west and beyond. New York took up succession as America's premier metropolis, its ever-burgeoning immigrant multiplicity to be found, typically, in Jewish Brooklyn, Italian Hell's Kitchen, 125th Street and Spanish Harlem or, latterly, Russian Brighton Beach. Be it Manhattan's YMHA, or Sixth Street's Nuyorican Poets Café, or any of the Irish, Italian, or other ethnic clubs and meeting places, literary remembrance has been a prerequisite.

Victor Hernández Cruz, leading Nuyorican poet, in his "Loisaida" – Spanglish for Lower East Sider – encompassingly, and symptomatically, invokes a cityscape of those he explicitly names as "immigrants." The spectrum includes Blacks, Poles, Italians, "Broome Street Hasidics," one-time "Mississippi sharecroppers" and, inevitably given his own roots, "Ricans" as derived from the migrant crossovers of Caribbean Tainos, Africa's Moors, and Spain's Andalucians, and from inter-American migration from island Puerto Rico to Manhattan's East Harlem of 116th to 145th Street. Yet at the same time they are to be identified by their wholly contemporary city-American "Pra-Pra" headwear (Cruz 1961: 160–4).

The America of the farms and prairies of Illinois, Iowa, Wyoming, Minnesota, or Idaho, with Chicago pivotal as trade-route and South

Side stockyard, is to be heard as a migrant ethos, if slightly at a remove, in Carl Sandburg's "Chicago," the city as "Hog Butcher," "Stacker of Wheat," and "Freight Handler to the Nation" (Sandburg 1970: 3). The South, whatever the magnolia Jeffersonianism of Virginia, looks also to poor-white migrancy, that of sharecropper and hill and backcountry indenture, and brought through the Cumberland Gap into Appalachia and the Dixie of the eventual Confederacy. Its poets, notably, and among other interests, have included Robert Penn Warren in his Kentucky-centered "Audubon: A Vision" and the James Dickey both of the novel *Deliverance* (1970) and a verse collection seamed in southern reference like *Buckdancer's Choice* (1965). Nor, again, is this to downplay slaveholding's sales and transfers (Dickey's own poem "Slave Quarters" well applies), or Seminole, Cherokee, Chickasaw, and all other Native adjustments to white intrusion and land seizure.

The Mississippi as America's inspirational arterial river, from the Minnesota headwaters to the New Orleans Delta, supplies yet another symbol of migrant change and adaptation. Its human freight, as Herman Melville's *The Confidence-Man* (1857) and Mark Twain's *Huckleberry Finn* (1884) bear witness, runs from homesteaders to steamboat merchants, trapper-hunters to runaway slaves. A poem like Langston Hughes's lyric "The Negro Speaks of Rivers" (Hughes 2001: 36) presents an African-American memory, the Mississippi made over into a blues linking to the Euphrates, Congo, and Nile as coeval rivers of migrant blackness. In the southwest the Rio Grande acts as territorial marker, yet also, from the vexed 1848 Treaty of Guadalupe-Hidalgo to the present-day, the means of every kind of legal and illegal human transit. Much to the point, Jimmy Santiago Baca, born in New Mexico of Chicano and Apache background, orphan, jailee, wanderer, and eventual teacher and poet, entitled his first verse collection *Immigrants in Our Own Land* (1979).

The Rockies, the coastline west and Pacific northwest, all give out their call, whether in consequence of the Lewis and Clarke expedition of 1804–6, The Oregon Trail, or the building of the railroads as the iron horse. So inexorable a westering has become the very stuff of legend, the national mythology of frontier, America as endlessly being peopled and repeopled. It embraces the pioneers and prairie schooners, the Plains Comanche or Dakota's Sioux and all other tribes, the cavalry, the family ranch or smallholding, cowboy and cattle drives, or panhandlers seeking instant fortune in the 1840–50s Gold Rush of the Sierras. Lawrence Ferlinghetti's "Starting From San Francisco"

(1961) invokes this America in a nice reverse-itinerary perspective, a poem as he calls it of "all night Eastward" and "Back and forth, across the Continent" (Ferlinghetti 1961: 5).

California, the Golden State, inevitably acts as mecca, at once Pacific Garden and ocean vista, the nation's ever more populous state. But shadow, once again, there has been, whether Native dispossession under the Spanish and then successor American regimes, or Roosevelt's Executive Order 9066 which, in 1942, and in the aftermath of Pearl Harbor, "relocated" 120,000 Japanese Americans. As to the Pacific, Hawaii has also long taken on its own migrant transformations of identity: kanaka homeland yet haole America, idyll yet sugarcane and other plantation labor for Chinese, Japanese, Filipinos, and Koreans. The poetry reprinted in *The Best of Bamboo Ridge: The Hawaii Writers Quarterly* (1986), from the journal and press established in 1978 by Eric Chock and Darrell H. Y. Lum and whose luminaries include Wing Tek Lum, Cathy Song, and Gary Pak, issues a reminder of how Hawaii has historically been the Pacific's migrant crossroad of Polynesia, Europe, and America.

Even amid the settledness of American family, township, and the eventual cities and suburbs, a defining migrancy persists. For whether millennial voyaging in the name of the would-be New Jerusalem or Atlantis, or each ensuing European and Asian wave, or Native and slave transportation, the effect has been shared, a vast, eclectic, multilingual, and often enough abrasive, surge of Americans-in-the-making. There can be little surprise that tropes of pilgrimage recur in American poetry as elsewhere. The use of pilgrim itself, certainly, with its echo of Bunyan, runs from frontier to western movies. Few icons of America's immigration, in this transfer of peoples, have become better remembered than New York's Ellis Island, a first historic port of entry for so much of Europe, and beyond, during its working life of 1892–1943.

A whole literary iconography arises out of this immigrant-migrant America. It can include nineteenth-century steerage, ethnic city enclaves, the western trek and settlement; Nantucket's whale boats and Commodore Matthew Perry's 1853 landing in Japan; the automobile from the Ford Model T onwards; Steinbeck's Joad family and other dustbowl-era flights; the Pullman, the freight train, or latterly, the Greyhound and Trailways buses; south-to-north hispanic and Filipino field workers; Cuban *balseros* or boatpeople (a tenth of all Cubans have left since Castro's 1959 revolution); fleeing Vietnamese or Haitians; and, in all its Beat counterculture and youth-centeredness, the

1950s–60s of "on the road." Even space travel, under John Kennedy's presidency, became a form of internal American migration, a latest frontier.

The composite effect of migrancy, sought and unsought, and despite the prejudice and exclusions, gives grounds to being thought the very wellspring, as Randolph Bourne (1964) was early to term it, of transnational America. Whether European, Native, African, Asian, Hispanic, Pacific Island, or Middle Eastern in origin, or given to the one or another ethnic, regional, or class formation, or to the interplay of identity, it has made for an America indeed both home and away. Even canonical figures give confirmation. William Carlos Williams could look to English, Puerto Rican, and Jewish stock, and Charles Olson to Swedish and Irish-American parentage.

In the 15th chant from "Song of Myself," the landmark poem first published in 1855, Walt Whitman duly lays down an apt visual cameo with "The groups of newly-come immigrants cover the wharf or levee" (Whitman 1980: 17). In "Howl," exactly a century later, Allen Ginsberg closes his visionary Beat poem with an allusion to "a sea-journey on the highway across America" (Ginsberg 1956: 26). Both verse lines, however different in time or intent, speak linkingly to the America of first arrival, the America of onward journey.

Two celebrated poems give a yet further frame. Robert Frost's "The land was ours before we were the land's," written in 1935, read at the Kennedy inaugural in 1961, and later titled "The Gift Outright," suggests a seeming preordained migrant juncture of people and country. Latterday doubts as to its implication of manifest destiny have not been overlooked ("She was our land more than a hundred years/ Before we were her people" [Frost 1964: 467]). Hart Crane's "The Bridge," even as it sacramentalizes Brooklyn Bridge, warns of the dangers of miscivilizing Whitman's open road – "Macadam, gun-grey as the tunny's belt,/ Leaps from Far Rockaway to the Golden Gate" (Crane 1986: 56).

Whitman, and Ginsberg in his wake, offer voices of testimony and prophecy. Both Frost and Crane imply the necessary attraction of America's expanses of time and space. A myriad of poets, be they so-called mainstream or margin, give every further continuance to America as immigrant or migrant past-into-present. No one would claim, even so, that American poetry, premodern or modern, affords a simply ready-made sheaf of immigration or migrancy poems. Rather it has been a matter of image and echo, at times explicit, at other times oblique, and worked into the poetry's overall directions of interest. But whatever the fashioning, the memories persist of America as ever an ongoing migrant cultural process and creation.

III

Robert Lowell may well supply a link back into New England's founding: the legacies of Atlantic crossing begun with the *Mayflower*; the Puritanism of election theology, congregation, and magistracy; and assuredly his own poetic dynasty of James Russell Lowell and Amy Lowell. But whatever the Brahmin mantle, or longtime assumption of establishment status, New England has in fact been not only the one England for another but, eclectically, an interaction of Native (hence the naming of Massachusetts), Irish, Italian, Jewish, African-American, and other migrant legacies.

Different migrant footfalls even play into New England's vaunted Anglo-Saxonism, and not least its circuit of confessional poetry. In this a key resonant name has to be that of Sylvia Plath. For if her voice, too, was effortlessly thought to be WASP, it draws powerfully on the German roots of her entomologist professor father, Otto Plath, though he was actually born in Poland. In "Daddy" she speaks of him as "a man in black with a Meinkampf look" (Plath 1965: 56). In "Lady Lazarus" he becomes the Aryan patriarch "Herr Doktor" (pp. 16–19). Plath uses German migrancy as extremity, Nazi shadow. This history, in shared graphic reach, is again to be heard in William Heyen's *The Swastika Poems* (1977). But others, and from beyond New England, focus on less negative aspects of Germany.

Theodore Roethke, raised in a German-American family in Michigan, calls up an older imported heritage of country-German good order, *ordnung*, in typical nursery-greenhouse poems like "Cuttings" or "Root Cellar." In his "Frau Bauman, Frau Schmidt, and Frau Schwartz," three "ancient ladies," employees of the family business, serve as the near virtual migrant continuation of a largely nineteenth-century farm Germany ferried into both the mid-west and, hauntingly, into Roethke's own childhood (Roethke 1966: 44). Charles Bukowski, German-born, in his "Near Hollywood," using Los Angeles's "Grand Central Market" as metaphor, explores a migrant perspective well beyond his own. Within a busy overall and multicultural picture to include "the Spaniards all the way from Spain" he invokes the interplay of "old Mexican women . . . arguing with young Japanese clerks," a California shared, however contendingly, by its contributing migrant peoples. Inescapably most of the poetries of Euro-America derive from similar workings of immigrant/migrant memory. Three – Ireland, Italy, and Jewish Europe – do service here.

The poetry of Irish-America draws upon a greatly distinctive body of migrant allusion, whether Susan Howe's "Speeches at the Barriers" in her *The Europe of Trusts* (1990: 97) with its reference-back to "earth of ancient ballad," or John Norton's prose-poem "Com-Plaint" in his *The Light at the End of the Bog* with its "A Difficult people the Irish. Difficult stuck in the past . . ." (Phillips, Reed, Strads, and Wong 1992: 272). This collective memory calls up emigration, blue-collar, poor-white, and "respectable" assimilation (or not), churchgoing and politics, song, or festival like St Patrick's Day. It has been a migrancy whose poets have been suitably diverse.

The "mainstream" voices of Galway Kinnell and Robert Kelly, however mutedly, give one source. Tom McGrath, descended from Catholic-Irish stock and a Gaelic-speaking mother, and the founder of *Crazy Horse* magazine, supplies a vast populist-radical oeuvre. Migrant Irishness surfaces throughout the generation of Terence Winch, as in "The Irish Riviera" from his *Irish Musicians American Friends* (1985) with its memory of fiddler, accordionist, and song during a Rockaway summer; or Susan Firer in her vivid, often irreverent retellings of an Irish American Catholic childhood in *The Lives of the Saints and Everything* (1993) – not least "God Sightings" ("I have never seen all of God/ only the red-glow tip of Her cigarette"); or Eamonn Wall in a poem like "Immigrants" with its pluses and minuses of trans-Atlantic journey ("At night we go home to break our bread./ Our doors are bolted to America./ Our dreams are fastened to no promised land" [Wall 1997]); or the many collections of Edward Byrne, editor of *Valparaiso Poetry Review*. Seamus Heaney, Irishman-in-America, Nobel prizewinner, shows himself wholly alert to Ireland's not only American but global migration. There has also been interwoven ethnic legacy as articulated, and not without tease, in the poetry of the Irish- as well as black-ancestried Ishmael Reed.

In John Ciardi, born in Boston's Little Italy, America looks not only to a distinguished critic and translator of Dante, but a poet of long-standing, whose very titles give an apposite geographic touch, whether his *Homeward to America* (1940) or *The Birds of Pompeii* (1985). His poem "Firsts" calls up the two-way nature of Italian migration, the arriving generation in America, the generation which seeks the Italy behind that arrival:

> At forty, home from traveled intention,
> I could no longer speak my mother's dialect
> I had been in Italy rinsing my vowels.
> She had been in Medford, Massachusetts
> Thickening her tongue on English crusts . . . (Ciardi 1971: 61)

In "The Old Italians Dying" Lawrence Ferlinghetti thinks back on an early generation "telling the unfinished *Paradiso* story" (Ferlinghetti 1979: 4), whereas in "Backyard" Diane di Prima (1990: 114) calls up that generation's nostalgia: "O Brooklyn! Brooklyn! where . . . / the phonograph . . . creaked Caruso come down from the skies;/ Tito Gobbi in gondola; Gigli ridiculous in soldier uniform;/ Lanza frenetic . . ." Whether "Paradiso" or "Brooklyn" both make for America's immigrant Italy, the coexistence of America as Dantean dream and the Little Italy of New York backyard reality. Other poetic versions of the legacy run from Gregory Corso's Beat-centered serious whimsy to Sandra Mortola's vision of feminism from out of the context of patriarchal *Italianitá*, and into a current generation of Gerry LaFemina, Paula Corso, and Daniela Gioseffi. A rueful backward glance, its references both to Dante and TV, is to be heard in Felix Stefanile's well-titled poem "The Americanization of the Immigrant":

> Like Dante
> I have pondered and pondered
> The speech I was born to,
> lost now, mother gone,
> the whole neighborhood bull-dozed,
> and no one to say it on TV,
> that words are dreams. (Stefanile 2000: 59)

Denise Levertov, in "Illustrious Ancestors," summons the Jewish Europe of the "Rav/ of Northern White Russia" (Levertov 1979: 77), her own actual historic ancestor. English-raised of Welsh Christian-mystic and Hasidic background, a US resident from 1947, she would act as one of poetry's best-known voices of the Jewish Atlantic. Looking back to her beginnings in "A Map of the Western Part of the County of Essex in England" she speaks of herself as the onetime "child who traced voyages/ all indelibly over the atlas, who now in a far country remembers" (Levertov 1983: 21).

Diaspora, and America as the Goldeneh Medina, have long won their poetic measure, whether from the perspective of European high culture, in this case ironic, of Philip Levine's "I Was Born in Lucerne"

(Levine 1981: 12–13) or the brute ground-zero of the Nazi camps as in Gerald Stern's "Soap" (1982: 49–51). In Samuel Menashe's "The Promised Land," from his *The Niche Narrows: New and Selected Poems* (2000), he speaks of exile, and by implication the migrancy behind it, as "always/ green with hope" (p. 53). The American poetry which remembers this diasporic history, Europe to America or Israel, and out of a continuum to include Russia, the Warsaw or other ghetto, Freud's Vienna, or Auschwitz or Belsen, along with its treasury of Yiddish writing, belongs to a startlingly extensive gallery. It would be difficult, not to say negligent, to omit a listing of Delmore Schwartz, Louis Zukofsky, Muriel Rukeyser, Stanley Kunitz, Karl Shapiro, Howard Nemerov, or David Ignatow.

Hilton Obenzinger takes on quite another kind of vantage-point. A poem like "This Passover or the Next I Will Never Be in Jerusalem" plays upon the notion of "lost tribe," questioning Zionism as a one-dispensation politics, and with the poet himself nicely, and ambiguously, positioned in California as "a schoolteacher with the Indians" (Phillips et al. 1992: 294). "The X of 1492" might be a roll-call of migrancy as descended from Columbus into Americas both north and south. 1492 is invoked as the historical weave of Catholic Spain's restoration of monarchy and yet Jewish and Arab expulsion. "The Great Expedition" becomes the lure of Asia's gold, the East "discovered" from the West. Columbus himself transforms into the migrant-serial identity of Colón, Italian and Jew, and both Las Casas's St Christopher and "whore" and the "Admiral of Hell" responsible for "the devastation of the Indies" (Phillips et al. 1992: 291, 292, 294). European migrancy with Columbus as its pathfinder, for Obenzinger, becomes a species of contraflow, Jewish dispossession at one with Native American and Palestinian dispossession, an America won and yet always reflective of both indigenous and wider human loss.

IV

"Chinamen in the New World" and "wherever Chinamen mine/ minerals or track trains" – Russell Leong's further phrasings from "In the Country of Dreams and Dust" deliver a telling overlap of time and place, the nineteenth and early twentieth century of immigrant Chinese in America's "mother load" west (Leong 1993). They also lead into the poetry of Asia's overall migrancy, China as one prime source but an Asia also, and equally, of originating geographies from Seoul to Manila, Saigon to Calcutta. Marilyn Chin keenly addresses her own second-generation identity within the China embedded in America in "How I Got That Name" with its "The further west we go, we'll hit east;/ the deeper down we dig, we'll find China" (Chin 1994: 17). Wing Tek Lum (1987) movingly celebrates a past generation's Chinese-Hawaiian migrant hardship in "At a Chinaman's Grave" (Phillips et al. 1992: 209–10). The poetry of Li-Young Lee inscribes his Chinese family's itinerary from Indonesia to Hong Kong, Japan to Pittsburgh, rarely to better effect than in "The Cleaving" from *The City in Which I Love You* (1990). Lee's speaker situates his immigrant face among those of the neighborhood butcher and the larger migrant Asian America about him:

> . . . this Jew, this Asian, this one
> with the Asian face, this one
> with the Cambodian face, Vietnamese face, this Chinese
> I daily face,
> this immigrant,
> this man with my own face. (Lee 1990: 87)

Kimiko Hahn's "Resistance: A Poem on Ikat Cloth" uses the image of traditional fabric to locate her inherited migrant Japanese legacy of womanhood within a multi-America and as a gift of voice to her daughter (Hahn 1989). Lawson Fusao Inada's "Legends From Camp" deftly elaborates the lives, the culture, of the Japanese America carried into the "relocation" of "10 camps, 7 states/ 120,113 residents" (Inada 1992: 7–15). Cathy Song, born of Chinese and Korean parents in Honolulu, takes up that joint migrancy in her "Easter: Wahiawa, 1959" with its remembrance of a grandfather's sugar cane labor (Song 1983: 7–9). Asia-in-America as migrancy finds wholly ongoing poetic articulation, whether Myung Mi Kim's "Into Such Assembly" with its keen Korean immigrant remembrance (Kim 1997: 29–31), or Jessica Hagedorn's (2002: 26–9) "Souvenirs" as a Filipino American poem of transmigration and the ironic interplay of Catholic Manila and California Disneyland, or Thuong Vuong-Riddick's "Seeds" as a roll-call of Vietnam as *patria*, colony, and war-zone and, always, the haunting of America (Tran, Truong, and Khoi 1998), or S. Shankar's "Passage to North America" with its boldly imagined contour of migration from equatorial south India to a Chicago whose "wintry rest/ promises a future beyond history" (Maira and Srikanth 1996: 107–14).

V

If Lorna Dee Cervantes's "Visions of Mexico . . ." calls up the migrancy implicit in her own Chicana make-up, then Rodolpho "Corky" González's anthem-poem, "I Am Joaquín/Yo Soy Joaquín," written in parallel English and Spanish, supplies the unfolding larger canvas. Its opening paragraph serves to summarize the transformation from the historicomythic Aztlán of Mexico into a USA of contested proprietorship:

> La Raza!
> Mejicano!
> Español!
> Hispano!
> Chicano!
> Or whatever I call myself . . . (González 1972: 98)

The poem fills out these keywords in busiest allusion and image, a memorial verse roll-call of transition and the *mestizaje* it has entailed, across pueblo and barrio and a borderlands America of family, politics, labor, belief, and, always, the dialectic of no one but a genuine plurality of language.

Further Chicano/a verse gives abundant confirmation. Carlos Cumpián's "Cuento" wittily offers a reminder of why Aztlán, especially amid the 1960s era of Brown Power, becomes both a call to rally and the reminder of how a people's whole history itself can migrate ("You'll hear more about it soon!" [Cumpían 1990: 62–3]). Pat Mora's "Immigrants" speaks cryptically to first-arrival anxiety, whether the need to "wrap their babies in the American flag," "thick English," or the acceptability of the American son or daughter they have newly parented (Mora 1986: 15). Few Chicano poems take on a more Whitmanesque itinerary sweep than Jimmy Santiago Baca's *Martín and Meditations on the South Valley* (1987), a retracing of his surrogate persona's migrant progress through the south and southwest with its affecting remembrance of the "broken chain of events" and the "embering stick/ I call the past."

Puertorican, Nuyorican – few poets of Caribbean island to New York origins have had greater impact than Tato Laviera, most of all his collection *AmeRícan* (1985) as the portrait of immigrant Manhattan ("we gave birth to a new generation/ AmeRícan"). The eclecticism of "all folklores,/european, indian, black, spanish" finds an enclosing metaphor in the notion of a bridged America:

AmeRícan, across forth and across back
Back across and forth back
Forth across and back and forth
our trips are walking bridges! (Laviera 1985: 94)

Cuban America, overwhelmingly Florida-centered, can look to a poem like Pablo Medina's "Madame America" (Kanellos 2002) with its sense of immigrant challenge – "'Ven' he said, accented/ but impervious, 'dame lo que das'" (English version "'Come'. . . Give me what you give'"). In "English Con Salsa" Gina Valdés teasingly offers a species of summary, "ESL" as "English Surely Latinized," America's English as "English refrito" and "thick as Zapotec tongues" (Valdés 1996). Her poem, in effect, speaks to the vast Hispanic intermigrancy of peoples and languages, a multihemispheric America and its ongoing and widely shared poetic enwordment.

VI

Migrancy may well be an inadequate term for the remembrance of Afro-America's passage out of Africa: the rot, and yet the resilience, of slavery as seizure and transport. Few poems more richly take up these implications than Robert Hayden's three-part "Middle Passage," with its opening irony in citing slaveships named *Jesús, Estrella, Esperanza,* and *Mercy,* and beginning and closing designation of the middle passage as a "voyage through death to/ life upon these shores." Each part acts upon similar paradox: Christian America imprisoning "black gold, black ivory, black seed" on vessels both of slave and sexual cargo; a mariner haunted by past manacled slave-columns from "Gambia, Rio Pongo, Calabar"; and the crossing to "New World littorals" as "unlove," "charnel stench, effluvium of living death," and yet the *Amistad* rebellion led by Cinquez who bequeaths a "deathless" image. Hayden's command could not be more availing, slavery's enshipments from Africa to America as "shuttles in the rocking loom of history" (Hayden 1985: 54, 48, 50, 51, 54).

The silhouette of this coercive migrancy lies everywhere in African-American poetry, not, evidently, its only concern, but a begetting point of reference. Countee Cullen's "Heritage" famously asks *"What is Africa to me?"*. He thinks it "copper sun," "scarlet sea," "jungle track," "heathen gods," yet also *"three centuries removed."* This is migration as left-behind time, life lived in an Afro-America of now as against an

Africa of then, and in which the poem's speaker acknowledges his own costly "double part" (Cullen 1991: 104–8). Gwendolyn Brooks's "To the Diaspora," with Africa this time as also Afrika, speaks of a migrancy from, and to, the Africa not so much there as here – "You did not know you were Afrika./ You did not know the Black continent/ that had to be reached was you" (Brooks 1987: 99). Rita Dove's *Thomas and Beulah* (1986), her wholly accomplished verse history, chronicles an intimate black family migration from Tennessee to Akron and from pre-Depression to postwar America. In its play of memory it tells of yet another kind of black migrancy, lives of domesticity, parenthood, and labor southern-style and northern-style.

For Jayne Cortez the migrancy of Africa is as much to be heard in its dynamic of sound worked consciously, and simultaneously, into sense. In "For the Poets (Christopher Okigbo & Henry Dumas)" (Phillips et al. 1992: 60–2), a dirge and a celebration of two poets racistly killed before their time, she collates, as though in a chant, the Africa of Damballah and "one hundred surging Zanzibars" with the America of Bessie Smith and Harlem. Appropriately she end-lines her verses with "ah"s, "huh"s and "uhuh"s, the Africa-originated call and response of griot and, as in her own case, of an American jazz bard longtime the verse-and-musical collaborator with her husband Ornette Coleman.

Ted Joans, performance poet, trumpeter, and surrealist (typically playful-serious in "I'M FLYING OVER ALABAMA . . . WITH BLACK POWER IN MY LAP" from his "No mo' Kneegrow" [Joans 1969a: 26]), creates a notable run of poems which bear upon a kind of reverse African migrancy. In an Afro-Beat panorama like "Afrique Accidentale," which he describes as "a long rhyming poem of mine of me coming to Timbuktu," the rap asides and improvisations lead into the celebratory "I finally made you/ Timbuctoo/ Yeah!" (Joans 1969b: 4–8). The multiple glosses and spellings of Timbuktu convey an obvious affection for this most fabled of cities. Joans's Afro-America, engagingly, and wholly unmumbo-jumboed with Western condescension, so rejoins the Africa of its beginnings.

VII

Native verse, that of America's first peoples, affords a wholly appropriate place to conclude. Which cultures have better known migrations stretching back into the unknown time of Bering Strait to Tierra Del Fuego and the Caribbean to the Pacific; or undertaken tribal journeyings of coast, woodland, prairie, or pueblo; or more keenly, and at cost, been witness to conquering Euro-migrancy? In "Columbus Day," Jimmy Durham (Wolf Clan Cherokee) calls for a "holiday for ourselves," a "parade" somewhat the opposite of Lowell's in "Fourth of July in Maine." This works to counter the supremacist "bloodline" from Cortez to Eisenhower and to celebrate the "grass" and "every creek" in which Native migrancy has its history (Niatum 1988: 129). For Gail Tremblay in "Indian Singing in 20th Century America" the America spaced by "patterns of wires invented by strangers" and "highways" is to be set against "remembering what supports our life" (Niatum 1988: 193–4). Simon Ortiz's "Wind and Glacier Voices" speaks of "continuing voice," the birth of a daughter within a migrant timeline both present-day and yet, anciently, that of a "glacier scraping . . . thirty thousand years ago" (Ortiz 1992: 114).

It falls to Joseph Bruchac, of mixed Slovak and Abenaki ancestry, to give in his "Ellis Island" an appropriate version of these differing yet joined American migrancies:

> Beyond the red brick of Ellis Island
> where the two Slovak children
> who became my grandparents
> waited . . .
>
> Yet only a part of my blood loves that memory.
> Another voice
> speaks of native lands
> within this nation.
> Lands invaded
> when the earth became owned.
> Lands of those who followed
> the changing Moon,
> knowledge of the seasons in their veins. (Bruchac 1978: 34)

Bruchac speaks from the plies of his own history: Europe, Ellis Island, Native America. But he has certainly not wanted company in seeking a poet's voice for the migrations, literal and figural, of the America-at-large that is always, and more than most, to be thought of as both home and away.

References and Further Reading

Baca, Jimmy Santiago (1987). *Martín and Meditations on the South Valley*. New York: New Directions.

Brooks, Gwendolyn (1987). *Blacks*. Chicago: David Company.

Bourne, Randolph S. (1964). "Trans-national America." In *War and The Intellectuals: Collected Essays, 1915–1919*. New York: Harper and Row.

Bruchac, Joseph (1978). *Entering Onondaga*. Austin, TX: Cold Mountain Press.

Cervantes, Lorna Dee (1981). *Emplumada*. Pittsburgh, PA: University of Pittsburgh Press.

Chin, Frank, Chan, Jeffery Paul, Inada, Lawson Fusao, and Wong, Shawn (eds.) (1974). *AIIIEEEEE! An Anthology of Asian-American Writers*. Washington, DC: Howard University Press.

— (1991). *The Big Aiiieeeee! An Anthology of Chinese American and Japanese American Literature*. New York: Meridian/Penguin.

Chin, Marilyn (1994). *The Phoenix Gone, The Terrace Empty*. Minneapolis: Milkweed Editions.

Chock, Eric and Lum, Darrell H. Y. (eds.) (1986). *The Best of Bamboo Ridge: The Hawaii Writers' Quarterly*. Honolulu: Bamboo Ridge Press.

Ciardi, John (1979). *For Instance*. New York: W. W. Norton.

Crane, Hart (1986). *The Complete Poems of Hart Crane*, New York: Liveright.

Cruz, Victor Hernández (1981). *Rhythm, Content, and Flavor*. Houston, TX: Arte Público Press.

Cullen, Countee (1991). *My Soul's High Song: The Collected Writings of Countee Cullen, Voice of the Harlem Renaissance*, ed. Gerald Early. New York: Doubleday.

Cumpián, Carlos (1990). *Coyote Sun*. Chicago: MARCH/Abrazo Press.

Dove, Rita (1986). *Thomas and Beulah*. Pittsburgh: Carnegie-Mellon University Press.

Ferlinghetti, Lawrence (1961). *Starting From San Francisco*. New York: New Directions.

— (1979). *Landscapes of Living and Dying*. New York: New Directions.

Firer, Susan (1993). *The Lives of the Saints and Everything*. Cleveland, OH: Cleveland State University Poetry Center.

Frost, Robert (1964). *The Collected Poems of Robert Frost*. New York: Holt, Rinehart and Winston.

Gates, Henry Louis and McKay, Nellie Y. (eds.) (1997). *The Norton Anthology of African American Literature*. New York: W. W. Norton.

Ginsberg, Allen (1956). *Howl and Other Poems*. San Francisco: City Lights.

González, Rodolpho (1972). *I Am Joaquín/Yo Soy Joaquín*. New York: Bantam Books.

Hagedorn, Jessica (2002). *Danger and Beauty*. San Francisco: City Lights.

Hahn, Kimiko (1989). *Air Pocket*. New York: Hanging Loose Press.

Hamod, Sam (ed.) (1988). *Grapeleaves: A Century of Arab-American Poetry*. Salt Lake City: University of Utah Press.

Hayden, Robert (1985). *Robert Hayden: Collected Poems*, ed. Frederick Glaysher. New York: Liveright.

Heyen, William (1977). *The Swastika Poems*. New York: Vanguard Press.

Hughes, Langston (2001). *The Collected Works of Langston Hughes, Vol. 1: The Poems 1921–1940*, ed. Arnold Rampersad. Columbia and London: University of Missouri Press.

Howe, Susan (1990). *The Europe of Trusts*. Los Angeles: Sun and Moon.

Inada, Lawson Fusao (1992). *Legends From Camp*. Minneapolis: Coffee House Press.

Joans, Ted (1969a). *Black Pow-Wow: Jazz Poems*. New York: Hill.

— (1969b). *Afrodisia: Old & New Poems*. New York: Hill.

Kanellos, Nicolás (ed.) (1995). *Hispanic American Literature: A Brief Introduction and Anthology*. New York: HarperCollins.

— (ed.) (2002). *Herencia: The Anthology of Hispanic Literature of the United States*. New York: Oxford University Press.

Kim, Myung Mi (1997). *Under Flag*. Berkeley, CA: Kelsey St. Press.

Lai, Him Mark, Lim, Genny, and Yung, Judy (eds.) (1980). *Island: Poetry and History of Chinese Immigration on Angel Island 1910–1940*. Seattle: University of Washington Press.

Laviera, Tato (1985). *AmeRícan*. Houston, TX: Arte Público Press.

Lee, Li-Young (1990). *The City In Which I Love You*. Brockport, NY: BOA Editions.

Leong, Russell (1993). *The Country of Dreams and Dust*. Albuquerque, NM: West End Press.

Levertov, Denise (1979). *Collected Earlier Poems, 1940–1960*. New York: New Directions.

— (1983). *Poems 1960–1967*. New York: New Directions.

Lim, Shirley Geok-lin, Tsutukawa, Mayumi, and Donnelly, Margarita (eds.) (1989). *The Forbidden Stitch: An Asian American Women's Anthology*. Corvallis, OR: Calyx Books.

Lowell, Robert (1967). *Near the Ocean*. New York: Farrar, Straus & Giroux.

Lum, Wing-Tek (1987). *Expounding the Doubtful Points*. Honolulu: Bamboo Ridge Press.

Maira, Sunaina and Srikanth, Rajini (eds.) (1996). *Contours of The Heart: South Asians Map North America*. New York: Asian American Writers' Workshop.

Mattawa, Khaled and Hazo, Samuel (eds.) (1999). *Post-Gibran: Anthology of New Arab American Writing*. Syracuse, NY: Josor/Syracuse University Press.

Menashe, Samuel (2000). *The Niche Narrows: New and Selected Poems*. Jersey City, NJ: Talisman House.

Mora, Pat (1986). *Borders*. Houston: Arte Público Press.

Morrison, Toni (1992). *Jazz*. New York: Alfred A. Knopf.

Niatum, Duane (ed.) (1988). *Harper's Anthology of 20th Century Native American Poetry*. San Francisco: Harper.

Nye, Naomi Shihab (1998). *Fuel: Poems by Naomi Shihab Nye*. New York: BOA Editions

Ortiz, Simon (1992). *Woven Stone*. Tucson, AZ: University of Arizona Press.

Pawlak, Mark (1978). *The Buffalo Sequence*. Port Townsend, WA: Copper Canyon Press.

Phillips, J. J., Reed, Ishmael, Strads, Gundars, and Wong, Shawn (eds.) (1992). *The Before Columbus Foundation Poetry Anthology*. New York: W. W. Norton.

Plath, Sylvia (1965). *Ariel*. London: Faber and Faber.

Prima, Diana di (1990). *Pieces of a Song*. San Francisco: City Lights Books.

Roethke, Theodore (1966). *The Collected Poems of Theodore Roethke*. New York: Doubleday.

Salinas, Luis Omar (1980). *Afternoon of the Unreal*. Fresno, CA: Abramás Publications.

Sandburg, Carl (1970). *The Complete Poems of Carl Sandburg*, revised and expanded edn. San Diego and New York: Harcourt Brace Jovanovich.

Simic, Charles (1974). *The Silence*. New York: Braziller.

Song, Cathy (1983). *Picture Bride*. New Haven, CT: Yale University Press.

Stefanile, Felix (2000). *The Country of Absence*. West Lafayette, IN: Bordighera.

Stern, Gerald (1982). *Paradise Poems*. New York: Random House.

Tran, Barbara, Truong, Monique T. D., and Khoi, Luu Truong (eds.) (1998). *Watermark: Vietnamese American Poetry and Prose*. New York: Asian American Women's Workshop.

Valdés, Gina (1996). *Bridges and Borders*. Tempe, AZ: Bilingual Press.

Wall, Eamonn (1977). *Iron Mountain Road*. Cliffs of Moher, Ireland: Salmon Publishing.

Whitman, Walt (1980). *Leaves of Grass*, Variorum Edition of The Printed Poems, vol. 1, eds. Sculley Bradley, Harold W. Blodgett, Arthur Golden, and William White. New York: New York University Press.

Williams, William Carlos (2000). *In The American Grain*. New York: New Directions.

Winch, Terence (1986). *Irish Musicians/American Friends*. Minneapolis, MN: Coffee House Press.

Wing, Tek Lum (1987). *Expounding The Doubtful Points*. Honolulu: Bamboo Ridge Press.

Chapter 9

Modern Poetry and Anticommunism

Alan Filreis

In one way or another, poets have always been involved in political life. Even the most resolutely inward-turning or formalist of writers have written what might be called a poetry of social encounter; even apolitical poets are wont to commend the poem as a social text. Major events or catastrophes tend to bring the social text to the fore, of course, and the American twentieth century is a period full of such moments. We would be right to suspect that most readers and critics of modern American poetry do not quite agree with Theodor Adorno's famous dictum, "To write poetry after Auschwitz is an act of barbarism" (Adorno 1983: 34), because they sense, as for example the poet Lyn Hejinian does, that poetry after genocide has a more, rather than less, compelling role to play in intellectual life – as an alternative to official language. "Poetry after Auschwitz must indeed be barbarian," Hejinian has said, because "it must be foreign to the cultures that produce atrocities. As a result, the poet must assume a barbarian position, taking a creative, analytic, and often oppositional stance, occupying (and being occupied by) foreignness – by the barbarism of strangeness." The generation of American poets with whom Hejinian has been associated – members of the so-called "Language writing" school and others – were "shocked into awareness of atrocity" by the American military involvement in Vietnam (1954–75) and turned to poetry in the mid- and late 1970s as a means of challenging the dominant idea that language is natural – "that we speak this way because there is no other way to speak." In redressing the "social fraud" of official American language these poets sought writing as a difficult sincerity, a new realism. Even when writing about her family life, Hejinian is always at least implicitly a political poet because the honesty of her language refuses to reproduce that fraud, and "fraud produces atrocity" (Hejinian 2000: 325–7).

In the long run of American poetry across the twentieth century, before Auschwitz and after, there were eras in which poets' politics tended to be overt, when radicalized poets castigated others for whom the social text remained implicit, hidden, or unconscious. Conversely there were eras in which it was the political poet who suffered rejection by those who felt that poems should not take political positions or that beautiful poems inherently did not – that there was something ugly about political statements made in verse. The American 1930s (which can be bounded as 1929–41 or 1927–44, depending on how scrupulously one follows decades) was the first sort of era; the initial period of Cold War (1949–60 or 1945–63) was of the latter sort. It is difficult to separate study of the poetry of the 1930s from the skeptical way in which it was viewed in the 1950s by critics and the poets themselves. As political crises heated up in the earlier period – the onset of economic depression, the rise of antifascism in response to the National Socialist state in Germany and Fascist states in Italy and then Spain, a new wave of challenges to civil rights in the US South – poets were confronted with the seemingly reasonable option of joining or closely affiliating with the Communist Party of the United States (CPUSA). (The strategy of the international communist parties beginning in 1935 – the "Popular Front" policy of including liberals – made affiliation even more convenient.)

But by the late 1940s and 1950s American communists and former communists were routinely attacked for their beliefs, and the sort of poems communists had written in the 1930s went out of style. Communists were said to have written hamhanded, overexplicit, unlyrical verse. Ideological confidence, dubbed dogmatism, was said to be anathema to lyricism. No person who had signed on to a definitive political program could write a good lyric poem and in that poem be consistent with his or her politics. Actually the relationship between modern poetry and communism in the United States in the twentieth century was dynamic and complex – no less complex than the relation between art and ideology generally. Yet anticommunism, in the world of poetry, especially in the peak Cold War years, served as a simplifying and reductive force. To the extent that anticommunists conceded that their approach to the writing of the communist movement was reductive, they were at least willing to justify it on the grounds that the art produced during the heyday of communism was itself so simple that a counterreductiveness was not just warranted but had an ethical basis. Of all literary genres, poetry in particular was at stake, because, of course, poetry is deemed inherently resistant to simplification.

Our concern here is to begin comprehending American political poetry in the context of modernism, a project that requires denying the dictum that communists could not be communists and engage the modernist style. To achieve this understanding, we must first know how political poetry could be understood by anticommunists as – to adapt a phrase that critic Alfred Kazin once used (1951: 398) against the communist novel – *against the poem itself.* The realignment of modernism and communism had to entail some kind of forgetting or smoothing over of the political crises of the 1930s that had so compelled writers as scattered across the modernism–communism spectrum as William Carlos Williams, Walter Lowenfels, George Oppen, Norman Rosten, Alfred Kreymborg, Dorothy Van Ghent, Genevieve Taggard, the imagist-communist Whittaker Chambers, Naomi Replansky, the lumberman Joe Kalar, Eda Lou Walton, Claude McKay, Kenneth Patchen, Louis Zukofsky, Norman MacLeod, Lola Ridge, Isidor Schneider, Frank Marshall Davis, the surrealist Bob Brown, Stanley Burnshaw, Martha Millet, Maxwell Bodenheim, Carl Rakosi, the great sonneteer Edna St Vincent Millay, Muriel Rukeyser, and so on.

Consider, for example, the judgment the anticommunist poet Louise Bogan made against the poems of Muriel Rukeyser: in a radical's poems one senses a distaste for the individualized feeling; radicals write poems with a "seriousness . . . unrelieved by . . . moments of lightness" (Bogan 1951: 92). Poetry *had* to be about human passion, the emotional sourcework of a deep coherent self. Any refusal to explore or disclose that subjective depth was a subversive sign, and such a heretical view was another quality shared by the remnant of the 1930s left and by advocates of the "New American Poetry" as it emerged out of modernism in the late 1950s (and was gathered in Donald Allen's influential book *The New American Poetry* in 1960). Most suspicious to anticommunists was the "progressive depreciation of the value of personality" in the writing of radicals, as conservative political theorist Frank Meyer put it in *The Moulding of Communists.* The communist was incapable of forming an "attachment to another person – filial devotion, love, or friendship – *deep enough* to create values independent" of abstract political belief (Meyer 1961: 130, 46).

Instances of this critique abound. The poet-editor Henry Rago, later the editor of the influential *Poetry* magazine, reviewed Genevieve Taggard's book *Slow Music* (1947) and saw only "her humorless faith" in the writing, but no humanity. He "wear[ied of] following Miss Taggard around" as she wrote poems mindlessly historical and mechanically incurious about form. Taggard's poetry actually did not count, for Rago, as poetry. Poetry was not "poetic comment on the news." And "poetry is not about crisis, it is the resistance to and escape from crisis, but of course only those people sensitive enough to know what crisis is will take the trouble to resist it!" The logic of Rago's critique is circular: he does not even credit as poetry Taggard's line, "Let it [poetry] have heart-beat," because he is not convinced the poet herself has a heartbeat (Rago 1947: 289–91). Taggard, who had served as treasurer of the League of American Writers, a communist writers' "front" organization, was not, to Rago, among those poets "sensitive enough" to present human depth. Her linguistic surfaces were like those of the newspaper headline, of the clipped subjectless language used by reporters and political commentators.

But what if that kind of language was itself the poem's concern? In agonizing over the declined role of the poet, it might have plenty of heart. Taggard's poem called "Poet" – published in the communist literary weekly, *New Masses* – begins straightforwardly enough, with a speaker, a poet indeed, who has worked in the fancy high-minded mode:

> Tragic meaning was my altitude.
> Took it for mine, felt it lift
> Very high, learned to live holding it behind diamond eyes . . .

But that is the last we see of the subject in a poem of five six-line stanzas. Increasingly the poem is about the poet's linguistic choices – about lines that are end-stopped or not, about poetic units of measure that can be slowed or sped up. Yes, the poem's "line" is the "party line" of the time: poets have a responsibility to widen the scope and role of poetry to include "the crisis hurrying." But because the metrical heart of this poem-about-poetry beats with that urgency, the party line must be in the poetic line. Prosody and grammar have ethical aspects. The commentator's stinting language (lacking subject, missing articles, etc.) of which Rago complains is the basis of the communist poet's claim to aesthetic relevance. Here are the final lines of Taggard's "Poet":

> Toiled in unit of slow going; in the line as it stops;
> With stop after stop, the signal awaited. One
> In the lock with all, chained but never slave.
> Here sweat out struggle nothing-sweeter than history.
> Web of feet, working over dark bloody ground.
> Heart plunging neatly, spasm on spasm. (Taggard 1944)

The poet of rhetorical and stylistic "altitude" comes finally to be associated with a disturbance of the lyric line. The poet willing to write "Here sweat out struggle nothing-sweeter than history" brings the disengaged conventional tragic mode, with its obvious subjects and objects (poets and historical matters), down to the level of the line. The poem has heart, all right; its humanity, though, is in the meter of "spasm." Here party line and disruption of lyric convention converge.

By the late 1940s and 1950s it was simply assumed, as Rago assumed of Taggard, that poets who were or had been affiliated with the communist movement wrote verse that was plain, descriptive, didactic, tonally grim, and had learned little or nothing from the language of the modern poetic revolution, with its emphasis on the "word as such." It made no difference that communist poets like Taggard did wrestle with their poetry *as aesthetic problems*. For conservative poet E. Merrill Root, it simply made no difference that in the late 1930s the magazine called *The Harvard Communist* had "*combine[d] avant garde experiments* with Communist ideology": notwithstanding such experiments, which imply an awareness of poetry's formal problems among the students who edited and wrote for the magazine, the "style of the magazine," Root claimed, "is *pure* party jargon" (Root 1955: 28–30). The poems Root quoted when he made this judgment – and the rest of the verse published in the *Communist* – can hardly be said to have succeeded in their linguistic experiments, and while thematically many follow the CPUSA line, as language they cannot rightly be called jargon. For conservatives like Root, communist writers' stiff certainty mooted *a priori* any connection to the poetic *avant garde*. Yet by complaining about young collegiate poets, Root was going after small game.

Had he aimed for bigger game, he might have sought after William Carlos Williams – already by the mid-1930s an eminent modernist who then entered a brief period in which his populism and enthusiasm for American working people converged with the ideas of the Popular Front. There can be no doubt that Williams's 1935 poem "The Yachts" evinces the very sort of certainty that drove the excommunist

E. Merrill Root further and further rightward. Williams wanted to write a poem describing his recollection of the impressive America's Cup yacht races he had seen off Newport, Rhode Island. Notwithstanding the grandness and beauty of the scene, he was angry that the magnificent skills of a small privileged class were supported by the work of a nation of impoverished people. His personal response seems almost too obvious to us now and could easily have made for a poem of the sort that anticommunists later deemed the inevitable result of communist infiltration into modern writing. But if anything was inevitable about Williams' desire to craft his economic views into verse, it was that he would seek for radicalism a correlative poetics. He decided to begin with, and then abandon, Dante's *terza rima*, the rhyme scheme of interlocking rhymes written in iambic tercets (three-line stanzas): *aba bcb cdc ded* (and so forth). Why would a poet, presumably striving for a reputation of competence, eschew a stanza form just a few lines after taking it up? Would that not draw too much attention to the poem's failure, or at least indecision? This choice helped convey the poem's theme of social desperation amidst luxury and apparent surety, which Williams borrowed from literary history and then radicalized: the scene from Dante's *Inferno* where Dante and Virgil must cut through the arms and hands of the damned who float beneath them and attempt to sink their craft. Williams's poem begins thus:

The Yachts

contend in a sea which the land partly encloses
shielding them from the too-heavy blows
of an ungoverned ocean which when it chooses

tortures the biggest hulls, the best man knows
to pit against its beatings, and sinks them pitilessly.
Mothlike in mists, scintillant in the minute

brilliance of cloudless days, with broad bellying sails
they glide to the wind tossing green water
from their sharp prows while over them the crew crawls . . .
(Williams 1986: 388)

Later, in its final three stanzas, the poem shifts from its depiction of the boats contending with a restless ocean (the "moody" sea "lapping their glossy sides, as if feeling/ for some slightest flaw but fails completely") to the nightmarish scene of a sea of human bodies, Depression-era people in agony, the "ungoverned" watery world the society that permits them to live impoverished lives, the waves their hands pulling at the yachts. The shift seems abrupt although it is thematically prepared at the beginning:

> Arms with hands grasping seek to clutch at the prows.
> Bodies thrown recklessly in the way are cut aside.
> It is a sea of faces about them in agony, in despair
>
> until the horror of the race dawns staggering the mind,
> the whole sea become an entanglement of watery bodies
> lost to the world bearing what they cannot hold. Broken,
>
> beaten, desolate, reaching from the dead to be taken up
> they cry out, failing, failing! their cries rising
> in waves still as the skilled yachts pass over. (Williams 1986: 389)

One interpreter of this poem, Thomas Whitaker, deems it to be "limited . . . by the lack of preparation (and hence justification) for that sudden shift." He argues that we accept the abrupt move from precise natural depiction to surrealistic radicalism because of what we know about history and economics beyond Williams's words. We "assent to it as a paradigm of something known outside the poem rather than find it inherently revelatory" (Whitaker 1968: 121). Whitaker's complaint can be understood as political code. One doesn't need to be a deep reader to conclude that his point is antipolitical: he's complaining that the leftist position animating Williams in this poem is an extraneous or extrapoetic matter, that the poem must be taken on its own terms, that "knowing" of the Depression and economic crisis as the poem's historical background is one thing and interpreting the poem as revolutionary quite another. Yet if the point of "The Yachts" is to depict the discovery – I take it to be the speaker's discovery of the radical nature of his economic views – of the "relentless tyranny exercised by its own beautiful instruments" (Whitaker 1968: 120), we must also consider that a poem is always at every point in danger of becoming just such a beautiful instrument. "The Yachts" is written to enable Williams to think in this critical way about the form his writing takes. So it is a matter for Williams of an ethical poetics that he abandon the *terza rima* that assured or certified his engagement with art *and* that he abruptly cast off "objective description" (Schneider 1945: 5) for didactic political symbolism.

The radicalism of "The Yachts" depends on that abruptness or discontinuity, and these qualities are inherent in the poem's form even as the typical virtue of a great poem is its flow or continuity. Yet the party line against the Party line was roughly this: what is inherent in poetry is good; what is "outside" it threatens its integrity as art. Note, for example, the way in which the Soviet Union's criticism of the superficiality of American poetry of the day (it was 1947) was refuted by T. O'Conor Sloane, director of the Catholic Poetry Society of America: "If a few . . . poets are moved to lyricize for political purposes," Sloane announced, it "has [no] bearing on the quality or value inherent in their work" (*New York Times* 1947). The false connection of aesthetic value and "political purposes" was itself seen as a form of communist charlatanism. Ray B. West, editor of *Western Review*, argued that revolutionary writers of the 1930s were "less interested in literature than they were in other matters . . . primarily social." He claimed that on the whole "such communities dislike, if they do not hate, genuine literary achievement." West added that the by-then defunct communist writers' clubs of the 1930s, such as the John Reed Clubs – though they were crucial as oases of support for unemployed writers developing their craft in a barren time – were, to his mind, "well-remembered, but little lamented" (West 1958: 4).

For critic William Van O'Connor the "upheavals of the thirties" did draw experimental poets out of their usual isolated state, but "the pendulum swung too far the other way," verse got too involved with politics and "became the poetry of a party," thus "forcing out aesthetic" concerns (O'Connor 1947: 36). Leo Gurko's history of poetry in a book called *The Angry Decade* was similarly quick and dirty: "Why there should have been an outpouring of notable verse during the second decade of the century and not during the fourth, may be due at bottom to . . ." – whereupon Gurko's readers are treated to his musings on the "accident" of history (Gurko 1947: 258–9). But he meant that it was *no* accident that the Red Decade was a barren time for poetry. He agreed with John Chamberlain, who wrote: "By taking "*control* of *writing* in the thirties, the Communists managed to *poison* the intellectual life of a *whole* nation – and the poison has lingered on" (Chamberlain 1952). Now the "big job" was "to *extract* the poison."

No "notable verse"? The communist-modernist problem inspired two great books of poems by Williams, *An Early Martyr* (1935) and *Adam & Eve & the City* (1936) as well as his series of short "proletarian portraits"; fueled the emergence of the "objectivist" poets, three of whom took the communist movement seriously (two, George Oppen and Carl Rakosi, joined the Party); and, in the person of poet and *New Masses* editor Stanley Burnshaw, who criticized Wallace Stevens for his disengagement, enabled the left–right dialectic in Stevens's "The Man with the Blue Guitar" (1936–7). "Blue Guitar" is the poem in which Stevens confronts the literary left most perceptively; it is also the poem in which he makes his most explicit allusions to modernism. In the opening cantos of this long work, people referred to only as "they" are modernism's alleged communist detractors (Filreis 1994: 248–90). Here is the first canto:

> The man bent over his guitar,
> A shearsman of sorts. The day was green.
>
> They said, "You have a blue guitar,
> You do not play things as they are."
>
> The man replied, "Things as they are
> Are changed upon the blue guitar."
>
> And they said then, "But play, you must,
> A tune beyond us, yet ourselves,
>
> A tune upon the blue guitar
> Of things exactly as they are." (Stevens 1997: 135)

The speaker introduces the guitarist, a figure of the artist or of the poet. But before the guitarist himself can speak from his position (he is literally making his art by bending his body over his instrument and he has an aesthetic point of view as well), his unnamed detractors criticize him. "They" are the detractors. The poem begins by creating the impression that readers should already know who would insist that the guitarist play "things exactly as they are." The speaker of later cantos eventually emerges from a dialectic of opposing (and then overlapping) aesthetic positions. The reality that is *changed* on the blue guitar is not only the sort of change the blue guitarist already knows how to make, as a cubist or surrealist. Finally, he also changes the way he makes his changes. The detractors, whose complaints are absorbed by the speaker, enable this higher order of change.

No "notable verse" that engages the communist-modernist problem? If it weren't for Kenneth Fearing's association with communism as one of the original "Dynamo" poets, who would know (or rightly care) that his poem "Literary" didn't simply give expression to modernists' antibourgeois impulse, their repudiation of the means of mainstream literary publishing? Fearing's demotic, chatty, comic, digressive style made Allen Ginsberg's to some degree possible and arguably supported the venturing of New York School poets (such as Frank O'Hara) into their antic, free, antiliterary style. Here is the first stanza of Fearing's "Literary":

> I sing of simple people and the hardier virtues,
> by Associated Stuff Shirts & Company, Incorporated,
> 358 West 42d Street, New York, brochure enclosed;
> Of Christ on the Cross, by a visitor to Calvary, first class;
> Art deals with eternal, not current verities, revised from last week's
> Sunday supplement;
> Guess what we mean, in *The Literary System*; and a thousand noble
> answers to a thousand empty questions, by a patriot who
> needs the dough. (Fearing 1940: 79)

In "What If Mr. Jesse James Should Some Day Die?" Fearing heaps scorn upon capitalism's big shots:

> Where will we ever again find food to eat, clothes to wear, a roof
> and a bed, now that the Wall Street plunger has gone to his
> hushed, exclusive, paid-up tomb?
> How can we get downtown today, with the traction king
> stretched flat on his back in the sun at Miami Beach?
> (Fearing 1940: 47)

The critic M. L. Rosenthal called this "the true poem of the early thirties," the kind of poem "that aroused the . . . ire of pure esthetes [and] Southern Agrarians." Its immediacy, clarity, and oratorical style "was declared to be not poetry but propaganda" (Rosenthal 1944: 215). And yet in poems like "Resurrection" Fearing's writing is "remarkable in its lyrical telescoping of personal emotion with sensuous imagery and critical thought" (p. 217), and like many poets involved with communism between the wars Fearing "could hardly avoid the thousand experimental and symbolistic influences of the times" (p. 208).

Rosenthal was the first to treat seriously the poetics of Fearing, and indeed was one of the earliest fans of 1930s poetry generally among

American critics. As he came of critical age in the late 1940s, Rosenthal knew many poets, Fearing and Rukeyser among them, who refused to succumb to the new fashionable separation of modernism and radicalism. In fact, as Rosenthal wrote, poets "*played with*" the "esthetic war between conservatives and radicals" (emphasis added). He meant that communists and modernists (including some modernists who were communists) wrote poems, poem by poem, that were *sometimes* generalizable as "modernist" but that no pattern imposed on "thirties poets" by mid-century critics revealed the actual cut and style of the poetic line, let alone the content, political or otherwise (Rosenthal 1957). For instance, the communist editors of *The Left*, a magazine produced in Iowa in the early 1930s, deemed *apolitical* those who made the *distinction* between modernist and left-wing poetry; their magazine was subtitled "A Quarterly Review of Radical and Experimental Art." "I suspect that 'esthetic' and 'Marxist,'" wrote the critic Kenneth Burke (1932) in a letter to Isidor Schneider, "should not seem so different in emphasis as do 'esthetic' and 'sociological.'" Richard Wright, whose ideas about poetry we have been taught to think of as premodern and unnuanced, published an article in the communist *New Challenge* in 1937 declaring that T. S. Eliot and Gertrude Stein represented a "gain in human thought" and needed to be *materia poetica* for the radical writer (p. 55). The "proletarian" writer Edward Dahlberg told a friend in 1933 that his current writing project was a marriage of Karl Marx and Marcel Proust. Dahlberg introduced a new book of Kenneth Fearing's poems in 1935 – the book that included "Literary" – with the judgment that Fearing's "fantastic patterns of slang and speech," his rhetorical derangements, made him something of a *symboliste* "with Marxian insights" (Dahlberg 1935: 11).

Burke, even in those politically charged days more modernist than communist (it was already 1936), was in any case a close advisor and theoretical mentor to a number of communist poets; among them was the communist poet Isidor Schneider, who always agreed with his friend Burke that the idea of radical writing composed "as though nothing but a shoddy sentence were really 'virtuous,'" was not just crude but politically ineffective. Communists in the 1930s had often written "of strikes," of course, but the fact is that they also had written love poems (Filreis 1994: 198, 346 n.94) and lacy imagist ditties (Schneider 1929), had conducted "elfin experiments" in verse (Untermeyer 1945: 336); had sometimes quoted "passages from revolutionary poems which are plainly precious" (Burnshaw 1936: 20–1); had loved and imitated "the orotund, rolling prose of Sir Thomas

Browne" (Conroy 1968: 49); and had praised "the little lyricists . . . who are finding a place in the memories of people who can and do, upon occasion, quote the great poets of the past" (Schneider 1932).

Nor later, during the Cold War, was it possible to predict what communist poets who associated themselves with the 1930s milieu felt should be the *poetic* response to the anticommunist purge of poetry in the 1950s. Experimentalism was part of the heretical mix, as was honor due modernist experimenters. In a striking lyric published in *Mainstream*, Richard Davidson, the best of the communist confessional poets of the late 1950s, presented a portrait of the poet as a "young rebel": this poet mourns the radical martyr Joe Hill, adores the pro-Soviet singer-actor Paul Robeson, supports progressive presidential candidate Henry Wallace, and . . . *reads Proust* (Davidson 1960). Isidor Schneider deeply admired the evasive, circumlocutious novelist Henry James and was willing to say so in the communist papers (Schneider 1945). Radical Joe Freeman revered the work of the modernist painter Piet Mondrian. Muriel Rukeyser, along with her communist "sense of righteous indignation," worked hard to make her poems "an amalgam of modern styles" (Bogan 1951: 92). Given the actual details of individuals' poetic practice, there was (and is) simply no prediction or accurate generalization accounting for what version of the modernist aesthetic one would find in the work – in the actual writing – of any given left-wing poet at mid-century.

Again and again, the very presence of communism among American poets threw off some of the most nuanced poetry critics of the second half of the century. Even the subtlest among them fell into the anti-ideological pattern. This is surely the case with Richard P. Blackmur's rebuke in 1945 of Muriel Rukeyser. Blackmur read Rukeyser's book of poems, *Beast in View* (1944), and decided that her "amorphous" meters failed. Actually Blackmur's judgment was harsher than that: her meter was not even "representative of the tradition of craft in English poetry"! This prosody, claimed Blackmur, had "nothing to do with the speed and little to do with the shape of the poetry." Without overtly conceding that his bias against Rukeyser's use of "direct perception, reportage, and *the forces to which she gives in*" – a transparent euphemism for communism (for communist culture was generally associated with documentary) – was a repudiation of political poetry and its modes, Blackmur was able to speak of the poet's poor metrical control as a drag on otherwise *strong* generic and even topical aspects of the blank verse (Blackmur 1945: 346–7). What book was Blackmur reading? *Meter* was hardly the thing that could truly have irked him when coming to these metrically regular lines:

> The *girl* whose *fa*ther *raped* her *first*
> *Should* have *used* a *lit*tle *knife*

That passage of Rukeyser's beautiful "Gift-Poem," emphatically (and appropriately) iambic, was almost but not quite in a ballad stanza – a ballad wrenched just slightly, aided by the thematic violence:

> The girl whose father raped her first
> Should have used a little knife
> Failing that, her touch is cursed
> By the omissive sin for life, . . . (Rukeyser 1944: 34)

perhaps disappointing as a piece of rhyming, but *not* because of its *meter*. In the end Blackmur's many readers learned summarily that Muriel Rukeyser was "confused about sex" (this noted in an essay otherwise oblivious of thematic considerations) and were instructed to imagine "what she ought to have done and could do" in her poetry "at some future stage of itself": instead of the "rough blank verse," "rough rhyme," "half rhyme," reportage, the immediacy of direct perception which "usually takes over the verse," there would be more formal lyrics like these (of John Fletcher):

> Lay a garland on my hearse
>   Of the dismal yew;
> Maidens, willow branches bear;
>   Say, I died true.

Blackmur meant that Rukeyser should follow "the *form*" (Blackmur's emphasis) although not the sentiment of such traditional lines. It is difficult to imagine that the connection between Rukeyser's "rough" language and her "confus[ion] about sex" was not connected *thematically* to this judgment. Rukeyser, who was already being red-baited, was beginning to be aware that the criticisms of poetic form by otherwise sensitive critics sometimes now covered homophobic and antiradical reactions. She overheard publishers talk about the gay poet Robert Duncan's writing – that it "lacked . . .'moral fibre'" – the same "strength of [Fletcher's] sort of form" Blackmur called for. In 1944, Duncan had come out as a homosexual in the magazine *Politics*, and, Rukeyser observed, "the echoes have not faded." She heard a poet say of Duncan: "Intellectual torment. Sexual confusion." "Now the two touchstones of American sentimental reactions," she wrote, "are . . . the names of communism and homosexuality[,] signals to the unsure for fear-trigger response that will be identical" (Rukeyser 1948: 49).

R. P. Blackmur (1945: 346–7) had gone looking in *Beast in View* for lines of verse that might come "to the strength of th[e] sort of *form*" he had found in the English lyric tradition – and then, turning back to Rukeyser, discovered these lines:

> The world is full of loss; bring, wind, my love,
> My home is where we make our meeting-place,
> And love whatever I shall touch and read
> Within that face. (Rukeyser 1944: 16)

Yet this poem – Rukeyser's sweet-sad poem "Song" – beautiful as it is, is not at all typical of the political and sexual radicalism of *Beast in View*, which Blackmur eviscerated without feeling the need to refer to politics at all – only to the failures of form, and to a (vague, unnamed) "force" to which Rukeyser the poet submitted herself (Blackmur 1945: 346–7).

This sort of averting to form was much more effective than if Blackmur or many another anticommunist critic had felt any obligation to spell out the emerging antipolitical counteraesthetic that would mostly bury the work of Rukeyser and would obliterate other left-wing poets from the poetic landscape. The praise of Rukeyser's "Song," a completely integrated lyric effort, implicitly cast doubts on the disruptions of poems like Rukeyser's marvelous "Who in One Lifetime," where the difficulty of the first line becomes the medium for the convergence of domestic/sexual and wartime/international radicalisms. The poem begins by identifying itself, by date, as a wartime poem:

> *June 1941*
> Who in one lifetime sees all causes lost,
> Herself dismayed and helpless, cities down,
> Love made monotonous fear and the sad-faced
> Inexorable armies and the falling plane,
> Has sickness, sickness. Introspective and whole,
> She knows how several madnesses are born,
> Seeing the integrated never fighting well,
> The flesh too vulnerable, the eyes near-torn.

> She finds a pre-surrender on all sides:
> Treaty before the war, ritual impatience turn
> The camps of ambush to chambers of imagery.
> She holds belief in the world, she stays and hides
> Life in her own defeat, stands, though her whole world burn,
> A childless goddess of fertility. (Rukeyser 1944: 37)

One begins this poem trying to decipher the grammar of the first line. Is it an interrogatory without a question mark, asking who sees lost causes? Rather, "who in one lifetime" is the grammatical subject of a fragment – *it is she who* has witnessed the war-torn world and "has," or feels, or, more properly, comprehends, sickness. So much has happened by June 1941. Vocabularies collide somewhat ungrammatically. "Love" could also be the subject and "made" thus a transitive verb, making a noun have a quality (love has been made monotonous). But the noun follows the modifier (monotonous fear), so that it might refer to the *kind* of fear love makes. Or monotony may be made into fear by love. Domestic and geopolitical qualities are confused, as then, after love, there are armies: an "and" ("and the sad-faced . . .") seems colloquial, a parataxis (creating a connection between unconnectable parts). This is not the way history is usually told (*and* then this happened, *and* then this, and so on). Or perhaps the connection makes sense and love is meant to be making other objects into other qualities, "sickness, sickness" being the quality love bestows on the armies no one can stop as on the ground falling out from under their feet. The cause that is lost is that level, sure ground: connection between sentences and phrases; the normal, logical way in which history, in language, proceeds. And yet, of course, the poem is grounded and assured by the blessings of literary history: it's a Petrarchan sonnet, with an octet and sestet, a lyric diction, and a rhyme scheme sufficient to remind us of its formal pedigree.

"Who in One Lifetime," dated "June 1941" in the text – the great turning point in World War II, when the Soviet Union joined the Alliance and a second front opened – is about a woman, not herself a warrior, who upon finding "pre-surrender on all sides" discovers the abandonment of prewar treaties, the language of peace betrayed – "turn/ The camps of ambush to chambers of imagery." She presents a poem as a form of infuriated feminized helplessness, which, she implies, serves us as a model not for just *one* lost cause, but for *all.* Is "Who in One Lifetime" a "communist" poem? Does it follow the platform of a radical political party? These are not simple questions.

Nonetheless, the skeptical or antipolitical critic, assuming the answers to these questions are *ipso facto* yes, might well attack the poem on *aesthetic* grounds. The poem itself allows for this. What enables the poet to "turn/ The camps of ambush to chambers of imagery"? Is it the sonnet itself, a classic "chamber of imagery," a result of "ritual impatience"? The speaker maintains "belief in the world" by epitomizing the ultimate paradoxical form for a political woman poet, "A childless goddess of fertility." The c-rhyme in the sestet, which is supposed to rhyme *abcabc* (one of several conventional options for a Petrarchan sonnet), should be *imagery/fertility*. But after *sides/hides* and *turn/burn*, that final rhyme is odd and disappointing, and metrically the line falls a beat short. Poets have long derived a sense of clarity and unity from the sonnet. This is a sonnet made in and about June 1941 – a time of extraordinary unity among allies, when antifascism finally seemed ubiquitous and the war seemed possible to win – that undermines its expression of "belief in the world" by enacting, through its form, the very "ritual impatience" that normally renders the agony into the solaces of poetry, especially in time of war. The antifascist poet, rather than feeling clarification at the re-entry into the war of the world's one communist government, is confused by what it means. The work of reconstructing the political context – a context of which the poem is evidence and to which it contributed – is difficult. But attentive readers of American political poetry of the twentieth century need to engage in such effort.

Then there is the work, also difficult, of reading the poem *as poetry* while maintaining an awareness of a history of ideological readings that have already distorted the poem's career among the readerly public. In historical terms, such distortion is the "social fraud" perpetrated by official American language about radicalism – the language against which political poets at the end of the century, such as Lyn Hejinian, sought redress in organizing or constructing the process (in other words, *the writing*) of their own writing. Hejinian's *My Life*, written in the 1980s, is a political portrait of the young artist as a languaged self passing through periods – especially the late 1940s and 1950s – in which language seemed to her a social fraud. "[D]eceptive metaphors," such as the trope that nations were dominos falling in predicted order to Soviet communism, "establish[ed] the pretense that language is 'natural' – that we speak this way because there is no other way to speak" (Hejinian 2000: 324). And so the American political poet, after the demise of communism and the fading even of anticommunism, still seeks in poetry an alternative to that naturalness.

References and Further Reading

Adorno, Theodor (1983). "Cultural Criticism and Society." In *Prisms*. Cambridge, MA: MIT Press, pp. 19–34.

Allen, Donald (1960). *The New American Poetry*. New York: Grove Press.

Bogan, Louise (1951). *Achievement in American Poetry, 1900–1950*. Chicago: Henry Regnery.

Blackmur, R. P. (1945). "Notes on Eleven Poets," *Kenyon Review*, 7(2): 339–52.

Burke, Kenneth (1932). Letter to Isidor Schneider. October 3, correspondence box "A-L," Isidor Schneider Papers, Butler Library, Columbia University.

— (1936). Letter to Isidor Schneider. January 12, correspondence box "A-L," Isidor Schneider Papers, Butler Library, Columbia University.

Burnshaw, Stanley (1935). "Turmoil in the Middle Ground," *New Masses*, 17: 41–2.

— (1936). "Notes on Revolutionary Poetry," *New Masses*, 10: 20–1.

Chamberlain, John (1952). "A Reviewer's Notebook," *The Freeman*, August 11: 777.

Conroy, Jack (1968). "Home to Moberly," *Missouri Library Association Quarterly*, 29: 49–61.

Dahlberg, Edward (1933). Letter to Joseph Warren Beach, January 3, Beach Papers, University Archives, University of Minnesota.

— (1935). "Introduction." In *Poems by Kenneth Fearing*. New York: Dynamo Press.

Davidson, Richard (1960). "A Garden of Chicago," *Mainstream*, 13: 34–38.

Duncan, Robert (1944). "The Homosexual in Society," *Politics*, 1: 209–11.

Fearing, Kenneth (1940). *Collected Poems of Kenneth Fearing*. New York: Random House.

Filreis, Alan (1994). *Modernism from Right to Left*. New York: Cambridge University Press.

Freeman, Joseph (1953). Letter to Floyd Dell. April 14. "De reserve box," Floyd Dell Papers, Newberry Library.

Gurko, Leo (1947). *The Angry Decade*. New York: Dodd, Mead and Company.

Hejinian, Lyn (1980). *My Life*. Los Angeles: Sun & Moon Press.

— (2000). *The Language of Inquiry*. Berkeley: University of California Press.

Kazin, Alfred (1951). "Ideology vs. the Novel," *Commentary*, 11: 398–400.

Meyer, Frank (1961). *The Moulding of Communists*. New York: Harcourt, Brace & World.

New York Times (1947). "Poets Here Scorn Soviet Attack on Work," January 7: 25.

O'Connor, William Van (1947). "The Isolation of the Poet," *Poetry*, 70: 28–36.

Rago, Henry (1947). "The Immediate is the Irrelevant," *Poetry*, 69(5): 289–91.

Root, E. Merrill (1955). *Collectivism on the Campus*. New York: The Devin-Adair Co.

Rosenthal, M. L. (1944). "The Meaning of Kenneth Fearing's Poetry," *Poetry*, 44: 208–23.
— (1957). "A Note on Tradition in Poetry," *Nation*, May 11: 419.
Rukeyser, Muriel (1944). *Beast in View*. Garden City, NY: Doubleday, Doran and Co.
— (1948). "Myth and Torment," *Poetry*, 72: 48–51.
— (1949). *The Life of Poetry*. New York: Current Books.
Schneider, Elisabeth (1967). "The Yachts," *Explicator* 25(5): 5, 7.
Schneider, Isidor (1929). "Dawn." Typescript of poem box 21, folder 29, *Poetry* magazine papers, 1912–35, Regenstein Library, Chicago.
— (1932). "Hard Luck of Poets," *New York Times*, April 9, 1932, sec. 1, 16.
— (1945). "Probing Writers' Problems," *New Masses*, October 23: 23.
Stevens, Wallace (1997). *Collected Poetry & Prose*. New York: Library of America.
Taggard, Genevieve (1944). "Poet," *New Masses*, 50(3): 12.
— (1947). *Slow Music*. New York: Harper & Row.
Williams, William Carlos (1986). *The Collected Poems of William Carlos Williams*, ed. A. Walton Litz and Christopher MacGowan, vol. I. New York: New Directions.
Wheelwright, John (1972). *Collected Poems of John Wheelwright*, ed. Alvin H. Rosenfeld. New York: New Directions.
Whitaker, Thomas B. (1968). *William Carlos Williams*. Boston: Twayne.
Untermeyer, Louis (1945). "War Poets and Others," *Yale Review*, 35(2): 335–8.
West, Ray B. (1958). "On Beginnings, Middles, and Ends," *Western Review*, 23: 4.
Wright, Richard (1937). "Blueprint for Negro Writing," *New Challenge*, 2: 53–65.

Chapter 10

Mysticism: Neo-paganism, Buddhism, and Christianity

Stephen Fredman

Introduction

"Mysticism" is an inexact term that covers a broad range of religious and quasi-religious phenomena. Loosely conceived, mysticism refers to the knowledge or experience gained by an individual that purports to effect a direct relationship to absolute reality or the divine. In practice, mystical knowledge or experience is said to erase the boundaries that maintain a limited conception of the self, and, by so doing, to give rise to a pervading sense of unity, ecstasy, or love. Mysticism as so defined can be found within monotheistic and polytheistic religions and in nontheistic Buddhism; it also appears in less well-defined religious movements, such as the tantric sects of Hinduism and Buddhism, the gnostic sects of early Judaism and Christianity, and the occult sects in European culture beginning in the Renaissance. To highlight the importance of mysticism for twentieth-century American poetry, this chapter will explore the relations of the poetry to three forms of mystical practice: neo-paganism, Buddhism, and Christian mysticism. In terms of its impact upon the poetry, the most prevalent of the three forms is neo-paganism, which comprises a number of non-Christian occult movements, such as Hermeticism, alchemy, Theosophy, and primitivism. Buddhism gained a surprisingly strong foothold in American poetry of the second half of the century – particularly the schools of Zen and Tibetan Buddhism. The most prominent strains of Christian mysticism have been the incarnational, which can open into nature mysticism, and the *via negativa*, which approaches the ineffable by stripping away all limited conceptions of the divine and the self. It is also important to note that because these three mystical traditions contain overlapping ideas and practices, many poets have been attracted to more than one of them.

Before looking at the ways specific poets and poems interact with these forms of mysticism, it will be helpful to think about why mysticism appeals to American poets and about what sorts of effects it has on their poetry and poetics. Since mystical movements are often esoteric and thus at odds with dominant ideologies, the first thing to notice about mystical literature is its countercultural status: although mystical beliefs and experiences have contributed to literary masterworks such as the Chinese and Japanese poetry arising from Zen, the Sufi poetry in Persian of Rumi and Hafiz, the Christian mystical poetry of Dante's *Paradiso* and of St John of the Cross, and the American transcendentalist works of Emerson, Thoreau, and Whitman, each of these literary monuments was seen as countercultural when it was created. For American poets in the twentieth century, recourse to mysticism also acts as a countercultural gesture. Rather than speaking for the liberal mercantile values of the society, poets have often taken a critical stance, addressing through mystical means what they see as moral and political shortcomings of capitalism and consumerism. Emphasizing individual experience over social conformity, mysticism has provided poets an alternative way of knowing from which to mount attacks and offer opposing values. By claiming the kinds of knowledge that mysticism underwrites, the poets have taken on dominant American institutions and attitudes and shown them to be at variance with both the individualist and the communalist ideals at the heart of American democracy. For instance, many poets have criticized the spiritual blindness they discern in the acquisitiveness and self-promotion arising from American capitalism and imperialism. Although it is true that an Emersonian individualism can lead to two kinds of self-realization – the mystical and the entrepreneurial – which may go hand-in-hand, poets have tended to view these two sorts of individualism as diametrically opposed. In the works of the mystically inclined poets, self-exploration is usually a route not to ego-inflation but to a kind of self-effacement that opens onto the social virtues of love, compassion, and solidarity.

Paradoxically, the poetry that promotes solidarity and compassion can sometimes do so through exclusionary means, and this too reflects an aspect of the influence of mysticism. For instance, one of the most pronounced qualities of the avant-garde wing of twentieth-century American poetry is its initiatory stance: like heads of mystical brotherhoods, poetic gurus propound esoteric doctrines demanding that one be initiated in order to understand them. Doctrines like Ezra Pound's Vorticism, Louis Zukofsky's Objectivism, Charles Olson's Projectivism, Robert Bly's Deep Image, and Charles Bernstein's Language Poetry are purposefully obscure, asking fellow poets or readers to make a kind of mystical leap by accepting a set of intuitive or nonrational propositions. The esoteric quality of American avant-garde poetics acts as a gateway, inviting "believers" into the fold while keeping out those imagined to be too obtuse or wrongheaded to understand. Adherence to one of these movements becomes more than an aesthetic decision, for the adherent receives an esoteric key that ties the poetry and poetics to celestial, political, or erotic realms. In this sense, we could say that there is a "mystical" style surrounding many of the movements in twentieth-century American poetry, and this accounts, in part, for what some consider the inflated claims made by these movements to a philosophical or quasi-religious stature.

Neo-paganism

The twentieth-century American poet who most knowingly and effectively set himself up as master of a poetic cult was Ezra Pound. Through his close association in London (where he lived from 1908–21) with the Irish poet W. B. Yeats and a number of the other occultists – G. R. S. Mead, A. R. Orage, and Allen Upward – Pound became convinced of the need to fold into the worldwide poetic lineage he was assembling a historical series of occult movements. This intertwining of poets with pagan and neo-pagan figures made it possible for him to claim that each of the poems he admired was in some way an embodiment of a mystical doctrine or illumination. Likewise, from the London occultists Pound seems to have acquired, at least in part, the oracular, even pontifical, style that dominates his poetry and his prose. Pound's pronouncements on aesthetic, social, and economic issues in his epic poem, the *Cantos*, and in his prose are delivered as though from the mouth of a "master," whose direct access to knowledge (gnosis) guarantees their authority. As a result of this immersion in mysticism Pound acquired a threefold influence upon later poets. First, he became the exemplar of the poet-as-guru, offering a mystical doctrine that ties poetry to other realms, including politics, economics, religion, nature, and the erotic. Second, he assembled a tradition of "illuminated" writers who partake of the "Spirit of Romance," such as Ovid, Apuleius, the Troubadours, Guido Cavalcanti, and Dante (Pound 1968), who also become touchstones for later poets. Not only did the specific poets that Pound lauded become objects of study for later poets, but he also bequeathed to them the habit of assembling such a tradition. Third, he demonstrated how to write a modern poetry in which the mystical and the factual intersect – a tendency in American writing that began with Emerson, Thoreau, and Whitman and has flourished during the twentieth century.

Mystical tendencies were in full flower as the modern arts developed at the beginning of the twentieth century, contributing, for example, to such seminal twentieth-century breakthroughs as abstraction in painting, sculpture, and cinema (Tuchman 1986: 17–61). The occult movements that sprung up at this time (and then returned periodically throughout the century) advocated two interlocking sorts of investigations aimed at uncovering hidden truths: the rediscovery of "ancient wisdom" and the conduct of modern experiments in expanding the senses – through meditation, contemplation, trance, divination, magic, drugs, and so forth. The ancient wisdom was exhumed from classical pagan and "primitive" sources, while the experiments carried on by psychic pioneers in the modern era laid "claim to knowledge of a scientific nature which is inaccessible to the accepted methods of positive, objective scientific research" (G. R. S. Mead, quoted in Tryphonopoulos 1992: 25). The ultimate object and source of these two mutually reinforcing forms of knowledge was the divine, but at a more instrumental level the two derived their authority from opposing entities: tradition and science. The occult tradition consists of texts and artifacts strung out in a long and loosely connected history that begins in Classical Greece and the Hellenistic Era, although many of its texts posit an even earlier pseudo-source in Ancient Egypt (Tryphonopoulos 1992: 24–5). Practitioners of the experiential component often adapt scientific terminology, inventing fields such as "psychic research" in an attempt to overcome the restrictions of a positivist epistemology by using its vocabulary to describe magical knowledge. As a "way of knowing" that places itself in between science and normative religion – often borrowing the vocabulary of one to counter the arguments of the other – the modern occult can be characterized as "a neo-pagan piety that is polytheistic, fleshly, erotic and ecstatic rather than a Christian or Jewish piety that is monotheistic, otherworldly, ascetic and revealed" (Surette and Tryphonopoulos 1996: xvii).

For Pound, the Eleusinian Mysteries of Athens, the most renowned religious mysteries of the classical world, represent one of the two basic poles of culture – which he sees as residing "Between KUNG and ELEUSIS" (*Canto* 52; Pound 1970: 258), that is, between the ethical order, exemplified for him by Confucius, and the spiritual order, exemplified by the Athenian Mystery cults. The myth behind the rites of Eleusis is that of Demeter, the Earth Mother or Grain Mother (Ceres in Latin), and her daughter Persephone, or Kore (Proserpine), who is carried off to the underworld by Hades (Dis or Pluto). In her disconsolate wandering in search of her daughter, Demeter finds her way to Eleusis, outside Athens, where she has a temple built and then retreats inside it – with devastating consequences for the fertility of the natural world, including human beings. Demeter petitions Zeus and ultimately wins the release of Persephone, but because the girl has eaten some pomegranate seeds she must return to Hades for part of every year. With Persephone set free, Demeter restores fertility and reveals the rites of the Mysteries. Scholars have remained uncertain to this day about the actual content of the rites, but we know that there were two major rituals at Eleusis, one of initiation and purification, the other of revelation and mystical union (Ferguson 1982: 52–4).

In "Persephone's Ezra," Guy Davenport (1981) argues that Pound's career from beginning to end takes guidance from Persephone, the goddess of springtime clarity, beauty, and purity, who appears in his writing in many different forms but always signifying a direct knowledge of the nature and beauty of living things. The speaker of "The Tree," the poem that Pound places at the inception of his poetic career (it opens *Personae,* his collected shorter poems), says that he "stood still and was a tree amid the wood" and that he learned "the truth of things unseen before" (Pound 1926: 3) – in other words, knowledge granted in the Eleusinian mysteries. During the mysteries, the gods were thought to have provided initiates with an expanded state of consciousness that gave them a sense of identification with nature and especially with natural fertility. As a result of this kind of identification, the speaker of the poem says, ". . . I have been a tree amid the wood/ And many a new thing understood /That was rank folly to my head before" (ibid.). The figure of Persephone as the embodiment of a neo-pagan connection to the gods and nature recurs many times throughout the *Cantos*. In *Canto I*, for instance, Pound recounts the moment in the *Odyssey* when Odysseus, seeking counsel on how to get home, slaughtered sheep as a sacrifice and "Poured ointment, cried to the gods,/ To Pluto the strong, and praised Proserpine" (Pound 1970: 4); in *Canto XLVII*, Pound's Odysseus is advised, "First must thou go the road/ to hell/ And to the bower of Ceres' daughter Proserpine" (p. 236). In the quest for a way through the chaos of the modern world, Pound takes Persephone as a signpost of the release from hell and of the promise of regeneration through natural/divine forces.

Alongside the Eleusinian cult in Classical Greece, there were also Orphic and Pythagorean cults, which likewise had mythical underpinnings and involved rites of initiation and salvation. The Orphic and Pythagorean cults attracted Pound's followers Robert Duncan and Charles Olson, who saw their Black Mountain poetry movement as a modern-day version of such a cult, transposed to the realm of poetry. Olson, for instance, cites the Pythagorean cult as a model for a new initiatory cult of poetry in his poem "The Praises" (Olson 1987: 96–101). Both poets also take up the Greek myths as primary poetic material. Duncan employs the myth of Cupid and Psyche – a myth with quest features similar to that of the Demeter and Persephone myth – as the backbone of his "Poem Beginning with a Line by Pindar" (Duncan 1993: 54–62). All three poets were also involved to varying degrees with the occult tradition that succeeded the Greek mystery cults – a pagan tradition that continued to develop in the West in the philosophies of gnosticism and Neoplatonism, which in turn gave birth to a long succession of occult movements that spanned the period from the middle ages to the nineteenth century: Catharism, alchemy, Kabbalah, Hermeticism, Rosicrucianism, Freemasonry, Swedenborgianism, and spiritualism (Tryphonopoulos 1992: 31–48). Near the end of the nineteenth century, these occult strains were brought together and cross-fertilized with Hinduism and Buddhism by Helena Petrovna Blavatsky. The movement she founded, Theosophy, had a pervasive influence upon the arts of the early twentieth century and was the principal form of the occult that reached Yeats and Pound.

Pound resembles Blavatsky in the sense that he believes there is one principle of knowledge, available at all times and places, which the initiated can receive through synthesizing the clues hidden in prior occult thinkers and through direct experience. Responding to a challenge by his friend T. S. Eliot to give a succinct statement of his beliefs, Pound answers by throwing his allegiance behind the neo-pagan tradition: "Given the material means I would replace the statue of Venus on the cliffs of Terracina. I would erect a temple to Artemis in Park Lane. I believe that a light from Eleusis persisted throughout the middle ages and set beauty in the song of Provence and of Italy" (Pound 1973: 53). Eliot's own relation to mysticism is very different, but equally complex and extensive. Over the course of his career, Christian mysticism takes pride of place in his work, although both early and late he set Christian mysticism in dialogue with Hinduism and Buddhism (Kearns 1987). In *The Waste Land,* however, neo-paganism becomes the dominant form of mysticism, although Eliot uses its symbols in strikingly ambivalent ways. Its dominance stems particularly from Eliot's reliance upon Jessie Weston's *From Ritual to Romance,* which he says provided him with "not only the title, but the plan and a good deal of the incidental symbolism of the poem" (Eliot 1971: 50). Unlike *The Waste Land*'s other primary source, Sir James Frazer's anthropological treatise, *The Golden Bough,* Weston's book is a work of Theosophy – which helps account for the myriad occult images populating the poem (Surette and Tryphonopoulos 1996: 73–96).

Notwithstanding Eliot's distrust in *The Waste Land* of the poem's occult symbols, many other poets have found an occult synthesis attractive because it creates a symbolic language that invests the images of poetry with a mystical potency. Not only do the symbols of the occult have a multilayered and multivalent quality, but they can be seen as magically efficacious in their own right: "the occult image is not merely a symbol, but in a transformation that is the poet's dream the symbol creates what it signifies" (Materer 1995: xiv). H. D. (Hilda Doolittle), a poet who was extremely close to Pound when they were young, takes this belief in the mystical potency of the poetic symbol farther than perhaps anyone but Yeats. In her *Trilogy,* for instance, written during World War II, H. D. presents the artist as a spiritual healer capable of restoring a dying civilization to health. Out of her experience of the destruction wrought by the Blitz in London, she depicts a symbolic psychic transformation that she hopes will effect an actual regeneration of the gravely wounded world. *Trilogy* is shot through with occult investigations and syntheses of religious symbols from many times and places. In one section, for example, the work of the poet is presented as analogous to that of the alchemist:

> Now polish the crucible
> and in the bowl distill
>
> a word most bitter, *marah,*
> a word bitterer still, *mar,*
>
> sea, brine, breaker, seducer,
> giver of life, giver of tears;
>
> now polish the crucible
> and set the jet of flame
>
> under, till *marah-mar*
> are melted, fuse and join
>
> and change and alter,
> mer, mere, mère, mater, Maia, Mary,
>
> Star of the Sea,
> Mother. (H. D. 1983: 552)

In alchemy, chemical compounds in a crucible are distilled over a flame, provoking a sequence of transformations meant to lead to an ultimate or quintessential element, the *prima materia* or philosopher's stone. In *Trilogy* the alchemy is not a literal chemical transmutation but a linguistic one, so that the mixing of *marah* (Hebrew: bitter) with *mar* (Spanish: sea) results in a series of multilingual puns that tie the sea to the maternal through bitterness (linking possibly the bitter memories of H. D.'s near-death when her daughter was born to the alchemical breakdown of compounds into salty and bitter elements). Applying an imaginative heat to the crucible containing divine figures from different religions (Maia, Mary) and words from different languages (French, English, Spanish, Greek, Latin, Hebrew), H. D.'s alchemical punning confers on the words a mystical potency beyond their everyday usage and effects a linguistic synthesis that mimics and calls forth a synthesis of figures from various myths and religions. In content, this mystical conjunction of the sea with bitterness and maternity is not too dissimilar from Walt Whitman's conjunction of the sea with death and maternity in "Out of the Cradle Endlessly Rocking." They contrast, though, in that Whitman personifies the sea as an "old crone rocking the cradle," who whispers "the low and delicious word death" (Whitman 1973: 252–3), while H. D. engages the words of her poem as if they were themselves occult symbols, made capable, through her patient and sensitive ministrations, of causing psychological and spiritual change.

The foremost inheritor of H. D.'s poetic and occult sensibility was Robert Duncan. In his vast unfinished study of twentieth-century poetry, *The H. D. Book,* Duncan casts American poetry in a decidedly occult key, with H. D., rather than Pound, Eliot, Frost, or Stevens, as its central figure. *The H. D. Book* explores the occult world behind modern American poetry, mainly in H. D.'s generation but also in Duncan's. Duncan's ability to unravel the role of the occult in poetry and poetics is as skillful as it is because Duncan himself grew up in a family that believed in and practiced Theosophy. As he writes in *The H. D. Book,* the mystical and magical investigations of his parents, grandmother, and aunt became the lore that haunted his childhood:

> [I]n the inner chamber, the adults, talking on, wove for me in my childish overhearing, Egypt, a land of spells and secret knowledge, a background drift of things close to dreaming – spirit communications, reincarnation memories, clairvoyant journeys into a realm of astral phantasy where all times and places were seen in a new light, . . . of most real Osiris and Isis, of lost Atlantis and Lemuria . . . Egypt was the hidden meaning of things, not only Greek things but Hebrew things. The wand of Hermes was the rod of Moses, and my grandmother studied hieroglyphics as she studied Hebrew letters and searched in dictionaries for the meaning of Greek roots, to come into the primal knowledge of the universe. (Duncan 1968: 5)

As an adult, Duncan remained an active investigator into the occult, but he did so not as a believer, in the manner of H. D. or Yeats, but as a kind of anthropologist of exotic psychic states, exploring the most far-flung realms of human meaning-making for the poetic, psychological, and even social powers they could release. "Although he did not literally believe in occult doctrines, they were so natural to him that he has employed them with complete assurance. In this confidence he resembles many intellectual Christians and Jews in mainstream culture who are imbued with the spirit rather than the letter of their religions" (Materer 1995: 108). Duncan is so much at home with the occult that in "The Architecture: Passages 9," a poem in which he describes the house he inhabits with his partner, the painter Jess (Collins), he sets the scene by invoking not only the architecture, the furnishings, and the music playing, but also the books:

> from the bookcases the glimmering titles arrayed keys
> Hesiod . Heraklitus . *The Secret Books of the Egyptian Gnostics . . .*
>
> *La Révélation d'Hermès Trismégistes*
> *Plutarch's Morals: Theosophical Essays*
> *Avicenna*
> *The Zohar*
> *The Aurora* (Duncan 1993: 81)

These "keys" to a hidden mystical tradition comprise Greek mythology and philosophy, gnosticism, Hermeticism, Hellenistic Theosophy, Islamic Sufism, Jewish Kabbalah, and the Christian mysticism of Jacob Boehme. For Duncan, as opposed to a believing occultist, these keys open up not the literal truths of reality but rather the truths of reading. Duncan probes the occult much as Freud works with dreams – in order to tease out correspondences among different levels of reality, so that psychic structures can be laid bare.

As a "born" Theosophist, Duncan had a certain level of comfort with *outré* doctrines that other poets beginning to write in the 1940s and 1950s did not share. One of the threads woven into his theosophical upbringing, for instance, was the Kabbalah, which Duncan refers to in the two quotations above when he mentions the study of hidden meanings in Hebrew letters and when he points to *The Zohar* (the most renowned of all Kabbalistic texts) among his books. Although the Jewish mystical tradition of the Kabbalah had been incorporated into Christian occult circles during the Renaissance, it didn't begin to have an influence outside those circles until Gershom Scholem published his first scholarly treatment of the subject, *Major Trends in Jewish Mysticism*, which was made available in English in 1954. Many concepts from the Kabbalah figure importantly in Duncan's work and an entire volume of his poetry, the 1958 *Letters*, is undergirded by Kabbalistic conceits. It is not surprising that Kabbalah would appeal to a poet because it is a kind of alchemy that engages with the materials of writing: the word, the letter, and the book. Kabbalah contains all of the levels of occult "work" – magical practice, meditation and contemplation techniques, visionary excursions, and spiritual and psychological self-transformation – all of them carried forth through investigations of language and writing. Out of his occult background and explorations, Duncan in turn became the instigator of lifelong research by Jewish poets such as Jerome Rothenberg, David Meltzer, and Jack Hirschman into the Jewish form of mysticism. Meltzer, for instance, who edited a journal devoted to Kabbalah, *Tree*, and an anthology of Kabbalistic texts, *The Secret Garden*, calls Duncan "my exemplar" in Kabbalah studies (Meltzer 1998: x) and credits Duncan with introducing him to the works of Scholem.

Curiously, Charles Olson, whose poetry, like Duncan's, draws from many strands of neo-paganism, was not enticed but was threatened by Duncan's occult proclivities. In "Against Wisdom as Such," Olson accuses his fellow Black Mountain poet of being deceived by the false "wisdom" (the secret doctrines and symbols) of the occult and therefore of not taking responsibility for his own acts of meaning-making: "the poet cannot afford to traffick in any other 'sign' than his one, his self, the man or woman he is. Otherwise God does rush in. And art is washed away, turned into that second force, religion" (Olson 1997: 262–3). As soon as "wisdom" is separated from individual experience and formulated in a general statement, it becomes false, for "wisdom, like style, is the man," rather than the doctrine or the symbol (p. 261). Olson insists that value can be found only in individual people and their attempts to gain knowledge of the world and of themselves:

> There are no hierarchies, no infinite, no such many as mass,
> there are only
> eyes in all heads,
> to be looked out of (Olson 1983: 33)

By finding out the truth for oneself, through experiential knowledge, one remains an "artist" rather than being fooled by a "religion." In discussing the occult in this chapter, we have been stressing that it encompasses two ways of knowing: exploring recondite texts and engaging in mind-expansion through experiential knowledge. Olson combines the two in his very active sense of what "history" is. Citing the first Greek historian, Herodotus, Olson claims that " *'istorin* in him appears to mean 'finding out for oneself' instead of depending upon hearsay" (Olson 1970: 20). Olson spends his writing life as such an "historian," probing deeply into recondite texts in order to locate primary instances of human experience:

> PRIMARY DOCUMENTS. And to hook on here is a lifetime of assiduity. Best thing to do is *to dig one thing or place or man* until you yourself know more abt that than is possible to any other man. It doesn't matter whether it's Barbed Wire or Pemmican or Paterson or Iowa. But *exhaust* it. Saturate it. Beat it. And then U KNOW everything else very fast: one

> saturation job (it might take 14 years). And you're in, forever. (Olson 1997: 306–7)

For Olson, the sifting of historical documents becomes a kind of occult practice, whose purpose is to chart the bases of human experience in order to have a complete measure of human capacity. To do this, Olson chose the early history of Gloucester, Massachusetts, as his "*one place*" and spent 20 years researching every aspect of it and writing *The Maximus Poems* to report his research, his breakthroughs, and resultant new recognitions.

Buddhism

Olson makes a good figure for a transition to the subject of Buddhism because his two most famous essays, "Projective Verse" (Olson 1997: 239–49) and "Human Universe" (pp. 155–66), express a philosophy that has many affinities to Buddhism, especially to Zen as it was being received in the 1940s and the 1950s through the writings of D. T. Suzuki. In "Projective Verse," there are several aesthetic points that align with Zen values: the focus, as in meditation, upon breath as a central component of poetic composition; the admonition that the poet move from one perception to the next without stopping to cogitate ("in any given poem always, always one perception must must must MOVE, INSTANTER, ON ANOTHER!" [p. 240]); and the proposal of a new aesthetic of "objectism," which is "the getting rid of the lyrical interference of the individual as ego, of the 'subject' and his soul, that peculiar presumption by which western man has interposed himself between what he is as a creature of nature . . . and those other creations of nature which we may, with no derogation, call objects" (p. 247). In "Human Universe," Olson likewise decries self-centeredness, idealism, and any thought process that creates or depends upon an isolated self or ego, urging a recognition that "the skin itself, the meeting edge of man and external reality, is where all that matters does happen, that man and external reality are so involved with one another that, for man's purposes, they had better be taken as one" (p. 161); he also participates in the Buddhist emphasis on radiant awareness in the here and now by asserting that active alertness is the highest form of human endeavor: "If there is any absolute, it is never more than this one, you, this instant, in action" (p. 157).

Making these statements about the proper disposition needed for writing poetry and the proper relationship of the individual toward the world, Olson joins the Buddhists in taking a resolutely countercultural stance on core American values. If American culture bases so many of its ideals upon the furtherance of individual self-interest – lauding the person who can "take charge" and promoting the "pursuit of happiness" and the American Dream of getting ahead – Buddhism stresses letting-be, nonattachment, the cessation of desire, and the illusory nature of the "self." The one value that American culture and Buddhism share in common is freedom, although Buddhism gives a much more radical interpretation of it than lack of governmental control and the ability to do as one pleases: Buddhism seeks freedom from suffering and desire and the mental freedom that comes with enlightenment. American poets have been drawn to Buddhism, it seems, by its opposition to so many of the values with which they were raised, and in surprising numbers they have pursued its complex and demanding philosophy. An anthology of contemporary American poetry influenced by Buddhism, *Beneath a Single Moon* (1991), edited by Kent Johnson and Craig Paulenich, prints work by 45 poets, including Olga Broumas, John Cage, Diane di Prima, Allen Ginsberg, Susan Griffin, Sam Hamill, Michael Heller, Robert Kelly, Jackson Mac Low, George Quasha, Leslie Scalapino, Andrew Schelling, Armand Schwerner, Gary Snyder, Lucien Stryk, Nathaniel Tarn, Anne Waldman, and Philip Whalen. Although this is an extremely diverse group of poets, Snyder, in his Introduction to the anthology, maintains that their poetry shares a set of qualities: "They are unsentimental, not overly abstract, on the way toward selflessness, not particularly self-indulgent, wholehearted, nonutopian, fluid (that is, able to shift shapes), on the dry side, kindhearted, unembarrassed, free of spiritual rhetoric and pretense of magic, and deeply concerned with the questions of knowing" (Johnson and Paulenich 1991: 8).

Of the poets listed above, the three most prominently associated with Buddhism are Cage, Ginsberg, and Snyder. For all three, Buddhism has been a shaping element, both aesthetic and philosophical, for much or all of their mature work. Snyder gives a succinct list of the central tenets of Buddhism: "The marks of the Buddhist teachings are impermanence, no-self, the inevitability of suffering, interconnectedness, emptiness, the vastness of mind, and the provision of a Way to realization" (Johnson and Paulenich 1991: 7). If most mystical philosophies and practices seek to unite the self with the divine, Buddhism turns mysticism inside out by asserting that there is no self and no divine. For Buddhists, the absolute is a void and all forms that exist, including the "self," are inherently empty and without permanence. In a world characterized by impermanence and shackled with suffering due to desire (for unreal objects and states), the proper way to act is to let things happen, rather than to try to direct them, and to cultivate an attentive but desireless stillness and silence.

For John Cage, who divides his life into the periods before and after meeting the Zen scholar D. T. Suzuki, the cultivation of silence and nonintervention constitute not only a spiritual but also an ethical, an aesthetic, and even a political principle. Cage's first and most influential book of writings, *Silence* (1961), discusses the implications of attending to silence for a new understanding of music. Interspersed with Zen and Zen-like stories, a number of which are gathered into his famous 1959 musical composition *Indeterminacy*, *Silence* includes poem-lectures with Zen-inspired topics, such as "Lecture on Nothing," "Lecture on Something," and "Where Are We Going? and What Are We Doing?" These poem-lectures, like much of Cage's music, are composed using chance operations (often involving the *I Ching*, the ancient Chinese book of divination), in order to circumvent the controlling function of the ego. Not only does Cage rely upon chance, but he often writes indeterminate works in order to make each performance unique and to sharpen the attention of both the performers and the audience. This attitude of welcoming the unforeseen and sharpening attention reaches its culmination in Cage's most renowned piece, *4′33″*, during which a pianist plays no notes and signals the succession of three movements by opening and shutting the keyboard. What the audience hears is the ambient sound both inside and outside the concert hall, which Cage refuses to separate from the concept of "music." Subsequent poets have taken Cage's example in two directions. Jackson Mac Low has composed a vast output of poetry using chance operations and indeterminate means for the past half-century, with Buddhist texts and poetic forms prominent among the materials from which he works. David Antin has turned the poem-lecture composed by chance into the spontaneous talk-poem delivered without notes to a unique audience; like Cage, he draws attention to the crucial importance of the present moment and he debunks the American faith that "experts" can solve the problems of individual and social life.

Beat writers of the 1950s and 1960s, such as Allen Ginsberg, Jack Kerouac, Diane di Prima, and Philip Whalen, took Buddhism as a central preoccupation and saw Gary Snyder as its American ideal. In his 1959 novel *Dharma Bums*, Kerouac enshrines Japhy Ryder (Snyder) as an ascetic, studious, free loving, anarchist, ecstatic mountain climber. Snyder's pursuit of Zen took him on extended stays to Japan, where he learned Japanese and studied Buddhism under several roshis in traditional monasteries. No matter how traditional Snyder's Zen training, his poetry always presents Buddhism as a natural human birthright, at home as much in the American West as in Asia. In an early poem, "Hunting," he rhapsodizes about the birth of a baby, "Baby, baby, noble baby/ Noble-hearted baby," and then switches gears abruptly:

> One hand up, one hand down
> "I alone am the honored one"
> Birth of the Buddha.
> And the whole world-system trembled. (Snyder 1966: 73)

The most natural occurrence, the birth of a child, can also evoke the most miraculous occurrence, the birth of the Buddha. The "Noble-hearted baby," by suddenly assuming the iconographic posture of a Buddha, represents the absolute freshness, benevolence, fearlessness, and contentment of the "natural mind," the enlightened state.

Allen Ginsberg also cultivates the "natural mind" in his poetry, contending that writing poetry and sitting for meditation share many features in common, such as regarding the activity as a "process" rather than looking for a "product"; learning to let go of predictable thought patterns; cultivating a direct, "purified" perception of the objects of the world; and recognizing that the mind is larger than the thoughts within it (Johnson and Paulenich 1991: 94–100). Ginsberg's slogan for this spontaneous, attentive method of composition is "First Thought, Best Thought," and it corresponds closely to Kerouac's "spontaneous bop prosody." Ginsberg first discovered Buddhism in 1953, led to it, like many other artists and thinkers, by the writings of D. T. Suzuki (Fields 1986: 210). In 1962 he traveled to India in search of a guru, stopping in Israel on the way to see if Martin Buber might fit the bill. In India, Ginsberg met many gurus and visited many holy sites, but he didn't find the teacher he was looking for until he met the Tibetan guru, Chogyam Trungpa, Rinpoche, in 1970 (pp. 310–11). Ginsberg became deeply involved with Trungpa's Naropa Institute, in Boulder, Colorado, and founded there with Anne Waldman the Jack Kerouac School of Disembodied Poetics, which has hosted courses on poetry and spirituality for the past 30 years.

Ginsberg's Buddhist spirituality made the greatest public impact during the 1960s and 1970s, when he crisscrossed the United States and much of the world, reading his poetry, chanting mantras, and singing the songs of William Blake to vast audiences in stadiums and at protest marches. In his 1966 poem "Wichita Vortex Sutra," Ginsberg lambastes the duplicitous language used to justify the Vietnam War ("McNamara made a 'bad guess'/ 'Bad Guess?' chorused the Reporters./ Yes, no more than a Bad Guess, in 1962" [Ginsberg 1984: 398]) and contrasts it to the language of sacred magic. Invoking an eclectic garland of saints and deities as "Powers of imagination," Ginsberg proceeds on their authority to work his own magic by creating a new mantra:

> I lift my voice aloud,
> make Mantra of American language now,
> I here declare the end of the War! . . .
> Let the States tremble,
> let the nation weep,
> let Congress legislate its own delight
> let the President execute his own desire
> (Ginsberg 1984: 407)

In Tantric Buddhism and Hinduism, a mantra is a syllable or group of syllables imbued with the power to bring into being the deity or state of mind it invokes. In this case, Ginsberg aimed his mantra at causing the Vietnam War to cease and then turned the language of political power ("Congress legislate," "President execute") into a language of ecstasy ("delight," "desire"). Summoning the vast mystical traditions of India to participate in his political goal of stopping the war, Ginsberg made Buddhism a public force to be reckoned with during the tumultuous war years.

Christian Mysticism

The third form of mysticism may be the least exotic and therefore the least countercultural of the three types we are exploring, but in the work of American poets Christian mysticism often combines with other forms, making for a poetry much less orthodox than might at first appear. T. S. Eliot, for instance, who strove in much of his poetry and prose to present an orthodox Christian face, engaged the occult tradition in *The Waste Land*, as was mentioned above, and maintained a lifelong dialogue with the Indic traditions of Buddhism and Hinduism, which he first studied in detail as a graduate student in philosophy at Harvard. His most mystical poem, *Four Quartets*, ends with the following lines:

> And all shall be well and
> All manner of thing shall be well
> When the tongues of flame are in-folded
> Into the crowned knot of fire
> And the fire and the rose are one. (Eliot 1971: 145)

These lines combine words of pious acceptance by the English mystic Julian of Norwich (in the first two lines) and the central symbol of Dante's *Paradiso*, the rose, with the Indic image of fire at the crown of the head, which symbolizes enlightenment, and the tongues of flame that descended on Jesus's disciples at Pentecost. During the course of the poem the fire and the rose draw many other meanings toward them, but in each of the poem's central images there is a conversation taking place between Western and Eastern mystical traditions (Kearns 1987).

The most characteristic form of Christian mysticism in Eliot's work is the *via negativa*, which itself has affinities to the Hindu philosophy of Vedanta. In both spiritual undertakings, all the attributes that have been assigned to the divine are discarded one by one (Vedanta: *neti neti*, "not this, not this"), so that what remains is the unbounded Absolute. As opposed to occultism, which sees language as having a magical potency, the *via negativa* finds all words to be inadequate and all images to be delusory. The *via negativa* is not an easy path, for it involves the virtual unmaking of the personality. At a certain stage, the mystics speak about a "dark night of the soul" in which everything is thrown into question and the soul seems completely lost. The most famous exponent of the *via negativa* is the poet-saint John of the Cross, for whom Eliot had a lifelong affection. In "East Coker," the second of the *Four Quartets*, Eliot writes, "I said to my soul, be still, and let the dark come upon you/ Which shall be the darkness of God" (Eliot 1971: 126), and then shortly afterward he paraphrases from St John of the Cross's *Ascent of Mount Carmel* (Hay 1982: 174–5):

To arrive where you are, to get from where you are not,
    You must go by a way wherein there is no ecstasy.
In order to arrive at what you do not know
    You must go by a way which is the way of ignorance.
In order to possess what you do not possess
    You must go by the way of dispossession.
In order to arrive at what you are not
    You must go through the way in which you are not.
(Eliot 1971: 127)

This is a classical exposition of the *via negativa*, for which paradox is the most natural figure of speech. In order to transcend the individual self, this philosophy counsels a stripping away of everything that undergirds the limited ego. The process is a frequently painful self-annihilating one, whose purpose is to break down the barriers between the ego and the divine so that a merging can finally take place. A more recent poet, Fanny Howe, sees this breakdown as occurring most effectively in relation to other people. In this way, she joins post-modern and liberation theologies in locating the mystical *via negativa* in the realm of ethics. Howe and other contemporary Catholic theologians draw inspiration particularly from women thinkers on the cusp between Judaism and Christianity, such as Simone Weil and Edith Stein, and owe their greatest theoretical debt to the Jewish philosopher Emmanuel Levinas, who contends that our ethical obligation to the Other is prior to Being itself. For Levinas, this insistence upon the inescapability of the Other (both other people and the otherness of the divine) grows out of his reaction to the Holocaust. In Howe's poetry, fiction, and prose meditations, her self-abnegating devotion to otherness derives also from the liberation theology of Gustavo Gutierrez and from her own experiences of racism in an interracial marriage. A committed Roman Catholic, Howe explores not only her own sense of the mystery of the Other but also Christianity's open relations to its "others," such as Judaism and Hinduism.

Denise Levertov carries within her personal heritage this interface of the Jewish and Christian: one of her paternal ancestors was Schneur Zalman, who founded a still-flourishing sect of Hasidism called Habad, and one of her maternal ancestors was a Welsh preacher named Angel Jones of Mold. Her father crossed over from Hasidic Judaism to Christianity and became an Anglican priest, but he passed on the Hasidic heritage to his daughter and continued to pursue Jewish–Christian dialogue. The Hasidic delight in uncovering the sparks of the divine in the ordinary world dovetails for Levertov with the sense of immanence or sacramentality that informs her incarnational form of mysticism: "Hasidism has given me since childhood a sense of marvels, of wonder . . . The Hasidim were a lot like the Franciscans[:] in both movements there was a recognition and joy in the physical world. And a sense of wonder at creation, and I think I've always felt something like that" (Gelpi 1993: 262). In her 1961 poem "Matins" she addresses this "Marvelous Truth," asking it to "confront us/ at every turn," to

> dwell
> in our crowded hearts
> our steaming bathrooms, kitchens full of
> things to be done, the
> ordinary streets.
>
> Thrust close your smile
> that we know you, terrible joy. (Levertov 1983: 62)

Although Christian faith lies mostly implicit at this early stage of her career in the title of the poem, "Matins," and the phrase "terrible joy" that seems to refer to Jesus's incarnation as the source of the "Marvelous Truth," a deeply committed religious orientation becomes more and more pronounced over the course of Levertov's career.

Like Levertov, the other American poets who draw on Christian mysticism join the poets who explore Buddhism and neo-paganism in one particularly salient stance: because they all find the dominant values of American culture, whether Protestant or secular, to be too restrictive, they cross cultural boundaries in search of spiritual and ethical nourishment. For many poets eager to test the full range of human experience, tribal or prehistoric cultures also exert a powerful magnetism. This can be felt, for instance, in the ethnopoetics movement that includes writers such as Jerome Rothenberg, David Antin, Gary Snyder, Dennis Tedlock, and Nathaniel Tarn, or in the archeologically inspired poetry of Charles Olson, Robert Kelly, Armand Schwerner, Clayton Eshleman, Gustaf Sobin, Nathaniel Mackey, or Anne Carson. The paradox of mysticism is that by turning inside to explore hidden depths the poets have been led outside and across socially constructed boundaries of religion, nation, race, and time. American poetry informed by mysticism offers moments of attentive cross-cultural dialogue, something for which the contemporary world evinces a glaring need.

References and Further Reading

Cage, J. (1961). *Silence*. Middletown, CT: Wesleyan University Press.

Davenport, G. (1981). "Persephone's Ezra." In *The Geography of the Imagination: Forty Essays*. San Francisco: North Point, pp. 141–64.

Duncan, R. (1968). "From the *H.D. Book*, I.5: Occult Matters," *Stony Brook*, 1/2: 4–19.

— (1993). *Selected Poems*, ed. R. Bertholf. New York: New Directions.

Eliot. T. S. (1971). *The Complete Poems and Plays 1909–1950*. New York: Harcourt.

Ferguson, J. (1982). *Encyclopedia of Mysticism and Mystery Religions*. New York: Crossroad.

Fields, R. (1986). *How the Wild Swans Came to the Lake: A Narrative History of Buddhism in America*, revised edn. Boston: Shambhala.

Friedman, S. S. (1981). *Psyche Reborn: The Emergence of H.D.* Bloomington: Indiana University Press.

Gelpi, A. (1987). *A Coherent Splendor: The American Poetic Renaissance, 1910–1950*. Cambridge, UK: Cambridge University Press.

— (ed.) (1993). *Denise Levertov: Selected Criticism*. Ann Arbor: University of Michigan Press.

Ginsberg, A. (1984). *Collected Poems 1947–1980*. New York: Harper.

Hay, E. K. (1982). *T. S. Eliot's Negative Way*. Cambridge, MA: Harvard University Press.

Howe, F. (2003). *The Wedding Dress: Meditations on Word and Life*. Berkeley: University of California Press.

H. D. (Hilda Doolittle) (1983). *Collected Poems 1912–1944*, ed. L. Martz. New York: New Directions.

Johnson, K. and C. Paulenich (eds.) (1991). *Beneath a Single Moon: Buddhism in Contemporary American Poetry*. Boston: Shambhala.

Johnston, D. (2002). *Precipitations: Contemporary American Poetry as Occult Practice*. Middletown, CT: Wesleyan University Press.

Jonas, H. (2001). *The Gnostic Religion*, 3rd edn. Boston: Beacon Press.

Kearns, C. M. (1987). *T.S. Eliot and Indic Traditions: A Study in Poetry and Belief*. Cambridge, UK: Cambridge University Press.

Levertov, D. (1983). *Poems 1960–1967*. New York: New Directions.

Materer, T. (1995). *Modernist Alchemy: Poetry and the Occult*. Ithaca, NY: Cornell University Press.

Meltzer, D. (ed.) (1998). *The Secret Garden: An Anthology in the Kabbalah*. Barrytown, NY: Station Hill Press.

O'Leary, P. (2002). *Gnostic Contagion: Robert Duncan and the Poetry of Illness*. Middletown, CT: Wesleyan University Press.

Olson, C. (1970). *The Special View of History*, ed. A. Charters. Berkeley, CA: Oyez.

— (1983). *The Maximus Poems*, ed. G. Butterick. Berkeley: University of California Press.

— (1987). *Collected Poems,* ed. G. Butterick. Berkeley: University of California Press.
— (1997). *Collected Prose,* ed. D. Allen and B. Friedlander. Berkeley: University of California Press.
Pound, E. (1926). *Personae: The Collected Shorter Poems of Ezra Pound.* New York: New Directions.
— (1968). *The Spirit of Romance.* New York: New Directions.
— (1970). *The Cantos of Ezra Pound.* New York: New Directions.
— (1973). *Selected Prose 1909–1965.* New York: New Directions.
Snyder, G. (1966). *A Range of Poems.* London: Fulcrum Press.
Surette, L. and D. Tryphonopoulos (eds.) (1996). *Literary Modernism and the Occult Tradition.* Orono, ME: National Poetry Foundation.
Tuchman, M. (ed.) (1986). *The Spiritual in Art: Abstract Painting 1890–1985.* New York: Abbeville Press.
Tryphonopoulos, D. (1992). *The Celestial Tradition: A Study of Ezra Pound's* The Cantos. Waterloo, ON: Wilfred Laurier University Press.
Whitman. W. (1973). *Leaves of Grass,* ed. S. Bradley and H. Blodgett. New York: Norton.

Chapter 11

Poets and Scientists

Peter Middleton

Twentieth-century American poets have been acutely aware that poetry is not the central art of their time, let alone a discourse that shapes the entire culture. Ezra Pound wrote a critique of the modern poet's dilemma early in the century, in "Hugh Selwyn Mauberley," his portrait of a poet who feels out of place in the modern world. "The age demanded an image/ Of its accelerated grimace," an art like "a prose kinema, not, not assuredly, alabaster/ Or the 'sculpture' of rhyme" (Pound 1977: 98). Modern society wants speed, movies, change. The fictional poet Mauberley responds by trying to withdraw into poetic reveries shaped by traditional poetic language. Pound himself thought this was self-destructive and took the opposite tack. Like many modernists, he believed, in the words of an art historian, "that artists can be scientists, and new descriptions of the world be forged under laboratory conditions, putting aside the question of wider intelligibility for the time being" (Clark 1999: 10). Between 1910 and 1920 he developed a poetics that relied heavily on contemporary sciences, notably electromagnetism and biology, because he was convinced that: "The arts and sciences hang together. Any conception which does not see them together in their interrelation belittles them both" (Bell 1981: 83). One of his best-known ideas, that it was time to replace the image in poetry with the more dynamic idea of a "vortex" of creative energies, derived from its use in late nineteenth-century physics by Hermann von Helmholtz. Pound felt that scientists needed poets:

> For the modern scientist energy has no borders, it is a shapeless "mass" of force; even his capacity to differentiate it to a degree never dreamed by the ancients has not led him to think of its shape or even its loci. The rose that his magnet makes in the iron filings, does not lead him to think of the force in botanic terms. (Pound 1954: 154)

Modern culture is failing to find ways of visualizing and therefore thinking fully about the electromagnetic field that creates the beautiful shapes in the steel dust. Poets could help find new ways of imagining and verbalizing the supersensory worlds that science is revealing.

Pound was one of the earliest poets to recognize that the rapid transformations of twentieth-century science and technology made demands on the poet for which the poetic responses of Romanticism to an earlier stage of scientific development were no longer adequate. These new demands could neither be ignored nor answered without a new poetics. Ignore science and technology and your poetry would be irrelevant, but try to meet the demands they made directly and you appeared to risk losing the poetry (becoming no more than a poor imitation of the movies). But why did science and technology seem so important to Pound and later American poets? Is it true, as the critic Douglas Bush wrote in 1950, that "all poetry has been conditioned by science, even those areas that seem farthest removed from it" (Bush 1950: 151)? Have poets really reacted against what he calls the "positivistic and mechanistic habit of mind" of science? The poet William Carlos Williams said that a poem was simply a "machine made of words" (Williams 1988: 54), adding that he meant that every part of the poem must contribute to its effects. The metaphor, however, effectively says that poems are conditioned by science and this is fine, there is nothing wrong in thinking of poetry as one of science's products, a verbal machine.

The career of William Carlos Williams shows just how complex the relation between poetry and science has been. In 1902 this 19-year-old scientist who would become one of the most significant American poets of the twentieth century began his medical studies at the University of Pennsylvania Medical School. There he met Ezra Pound and was encouraged to follow a parallel career as a modernist poet. By thinking about the changes wrought by science and technology during Williams's career, and their effect on his poetry, we can begin to grasp the scale of the transformations that took place in the last hundred years, and how and why they have influenced American poetry in diverse ways.

The world of 1902 is not far away in time and yet in terms of the everyday environment in America today it is remote, for this was a world with no radio, television, or computers, and even without the electricity supplies to power such equipment. Companies were only just beginning to build the series of generating stations and dams like Niagara that would provide the electrical power for the new industries. There were no airplanes, and few automobiles and telephones (it was not possible to phone across the continent), making distance a much more tangible lived experience than it is today. The medicine that Williams was studying had no cures for disease (and few means of preventing it other than the smallpox vaccine), no antibiotics, no drugs for tuberculosis, no antiviral treatments, no anesthesia except dangerous chloroform, and surgery was still very difficult. The secret of blood groups had been discovered only two years earlier; before that blood transfusions were so risky as to be largely impossible. Far from the young scientist and poet feeling that he was living in a benighted world, however, he probably felt very excited about the future because scientists were making many new discoveries, and the new technologies of the photograph, the telephone, the bicycle, and the automobile were exciting great interest. Only a few years earlier, in 1895, x-rays had been discovered by William Röntgen and their medical uses immediately recognized. During the next three decades of the twentieth century the rapid development of these and other new technologies must at times have seemed dazzling, and even if the pace of development slowed somewhat, by the time of Williams's death in 1963 he was living in a new world: astronauts had been in orbit, television could show the launch live to every house in the country, everyone traveled by car or airplane, and telephones were ubiquitous. There were new dangers too: people lived in fear that the entire world could be destroyed by atomic bombs. Technology has continued to alter society since his death, and in the last two decades the pace of change has accelerated again as the computer, the Internet, the cell phone, and digital photography began to alter social interaction in ways that we have yet to fully understand.

How did Williams's poetry respond to the demands of this scientific age? His interest in Albert Einstein suggests one answer: the discoveries of science compel poetry to replace old images and themes. In 1905, while Williams was still at university, the young Einstein published the first of his papers on the physics of relativity that would quickly make him the most famous scientist in the world. By 1921 when he visited the United States he was a celebrity, and Williams wrote a poem likening "Einstein and April," in which the scientist's new knowledge brings the same joy as the arrival of daffodils in spring. Now, says Williams, "oldfashioned knowledge is/ dead under the blossoming peachtrees" and "it is Einstein/ out of complicated mathematics/ among the daffodils – / spring winds blowing/ four ways, hot and cold,/ shaking the flowers" (Williams 1986: 133), who provides new poetic material. Where poets once wrote about the joy of renewal in terms of the natural landscape of plants and flowers, now they can employ scientific progress as a better metaphor for hope and transformation. But there is a paradox here. The logic of the poem makes the flowers represent poetry or "oldfashioned knowledge" and therefore the poem itself is a kind of flower that manages to perform its own "complicated mathematics" in order to be able to acknowledge the arrival of this new spirit. Many other poets would try to perform this feat and make flowers perform mathematics. Sometimes this would involve no more than using metaphors and images derived from modern science – electrons, x-rays, black holes, and genes – for their poems. Alice Fulton speaks for many when she says: "I often lift scientific language for my own wayward purposes. That isn't to say I play fast and loose with denoted meanings. I'm as true to the intentions of science as my knowledge allows. But my appropriations from science are entwined with other discourses, other ideas" (Fulton 1999: 179).

One way to reconcile the new science and the older poetics did suggest itself to Williams. The poet could observe the world with "scientific" attentiveness. Williams's poetry persistently offers precise direct observation of people and landscapes, rather than treating the world as a dictionary of potential symbols for poetic expression, and many later American poets have also thought that poetry could respond to science's precision of observation by striving for a similar accuracy of report in their own medium. Denise Levertov was one such, and wrote a whole poem, "O Taste and See," that although addressed to readers of poetry, treats them as a teacher might address apprentice scientists, telling them to be better observers: "the world is/ not with us enough," so we should sharpen every sense, even our sense of taste, to "bite/ savor, chew, swallow, transform// into our flesh" the "grief, mercy, language/ tangerine, weather" and other phenomena around us (Levertov 1983: 125). In the process she does what many poets have done, and implicitly challenges the strict materialism of science, in this case its confining of reliable observation to the senses of sight and sound.

Such beliefs in the potential of poetry to sharpen our powers of observation are widespread among poets. When Audre Lorde says that "poetry is the way we help give name to the nameless so it can be thought" and "lays the foundations for a future of change" (Lorde 1984: 37), she might be describing the passage of modern science, which has had to find ways of imagining and naming the supersensible world of atoms, for instance, even though she is ostensibly referring to elusive personal and political experiences. One of the most thoroughgoing observers of the natural world, Gary Snyder, writes poems that are deeply committed to the principles of ecological fieldwork advocated by scientists such as Eugene P. Odum. Snyder came to believe that (adopting the terms of the Navaho ceremony) "science walks in beauty" (Snyder 1974: 84). Some of his poems actually emulate the type of fieldwork advocated by Odum's *Fundamentals of Ecology* (e.g., "Control Burn" in *Turtle Island*). Over the years Snyder's interest in biology has grown to the point where he can repeatedly affirm that "language is, to a great extent, biological" (Snyder 1999: 329). Given that he also thinks of poetry as a playful art of language, it is easy to extrapolate to the idea that poetry itself is a manifestation of biology (Snyder 1990: 17).

Williams thought that such poetic fieldwork was not enough for poetry to stay abreast of science. Poetry also ought to acknowledge the existential impact of new concepts like Einstein's theory of Relativity. In a lecture given in 1948 Williams made a plea for a new conception of poetry:

> How can we accept Einstein's theory of relativity, affecting our very conception of the heavens about us of which poets write so much, without incorporating its essential fact – the relativity of measurements – into our category of activity: the poem? Do we think we stand outside the universe? Or that the Church of England does? Relativity applies to everything, like love, if it applies to anything in the world. (Williams 1954: 283)

A new "variable foot" is needed in place of the old fixed metrics so that the poem's measure can perform in accord with what is now known of our relation to the material world. Whether or not this new metric really does embody the principles of the new cosmology is questionable; what it does do is offer an exemplary strategy to poets who wish to be scientific. It tells modern American poets to find new poetic methods homologous to the most salient features of the new scientific theory. Charles Olson's "field" of the poem, the breaking down and recombining of linguistic units from the word to the sentence in unfamiliar orders by Language Poets, or Jorie Graham's extended poetic narratives of the time of changing perception – these are just a sample of the many attempts to create a poetic form capable of representing the world revealed by new scientific discoveries. Gertrude Stein's account of her development of a writing of the "continuous present" typifies the desire of many American poets to make their poetry a form of inquiry as up to date as new scientific ideas. Like Williams she believed that the poet should recognize the new scientifically conceived universe: "So far then the progress of my conceptions was the natural progress entirely in accordance with my epoch" (Stein 1967: 190–91). A poet could provide what the "age demanded" without sacrificing poetry.

Williams was aware of yet another transformation brought about by the development of science that poetry should acknowledge: the way technology was altering the form and texture of everyday life, even our very sense of self. One of his most effective ways of writing about this was to place himself as a poet inside the automobile that was changing America's relation to its vast continental space. Between the time Williams was a medical student and the writing of *Spring and All* in 1923, millions of automobiles were produced, a great proportion of them the result of Henry Ford's mass production of the Model T. The automobile appears in a number of Williams's poems from that period. He takes his children to the countryside, drives to an isolation hospital or to deliver a baby, and reflects on modern life in America where alarmingly the "pure products of America go crazy," and sometimes there is: "No one/ to witness/ and adjust, no one to drive the car" (Williams 1986: 217–19). To be modern is to feel that you are in a runaway car of technological and cultural change. His most searching reflections on the new sense of being in the world that resulted from having four wheels instead of two legs is set out in the poem "In Passing With My Mind" from *Spring and All*, where the ambient world becomes a "nameless spectacle" as a result of this speed and enforced anonymity that enclosure in a metal vehicle brings. He evokes this "disembedding" effected by modern transport and communications (Giddens 1990: 21) in the enigmatic opening lines: "In passing with my mind/ on nothing in the world// but the right of way /I enjoy on the road by //virtue of the law – / I saw." The ambiguity is never quite resolved because the gerund has no object (passing what – a house, judgment?) and so the lines seem to say that his mind was somehow out of the world, detached from what he saw. Technology has altered perception and the work of the senses, fundamentally altering the ground of ordinary experience.

No single poet could cover all aspects of the changes brought about by science and technology, but Williams certainly tried. Many poets have gone no further than to allude through images and metaphors to the inventions, entities, and theories offered by science. Some poets have followed the line of close observation, as if the poet were a linguistic researcher out in the field. Others have tried to find poetic equivalents for the new experience of living in the material universe offered by the new physical and biological sciences. A few have been ambitious enough to try to merge theory and experiment into an intellectual inquiry capable of standing alongside the achievements of science. There have been three other kinds of response that have also been important as we shall see in a moment: to treat science as if it were a failed poetry responding to a secular condition; to denounce science and scientists for their complicity with warfare and such horrors as the atomic bomb; and to expose false sciences – especially race science – as the ideological interests of one social group.

When Williams described the poem as a "machine," he was writing an introduction to a small volume of poems published during World War II, that begins: "The war is the first and only thing in the world today" (Williams 1988: 53). This war is also the primary feature of the history of science and technology in the twentieth century, and divides our history into two distinct phases. Before the war no one science dominated public perception of its activities, and technology was the most visible sign of science's achievement (it is important to emphasize that although technology is dependent on scientific development, other economic, political, and social factors are necessary too; America's leading role in technology has been possible because of its immense economic power as well as the quality of its science). As a result of World War II the entire way science was organized altered. Now science was big. Small laboratories and individual researchers were increasingly replaced by large teams of scientists working with massive equipment such as linear accelerators and later, DNA sequencers. Defense funding after the war made physics far and away the most important of the sciences until the early 1970s, when genetics research emerged as a medical and commercial success and attracted massive investment.

Prewar responses to science were not all as temperate as those of Williams, as we can see if we look at the poetry of Hart Crane and

Wallace Stevens, who respectively embraced science and cold-shouldered it. Of all the modernist poets, Crane was the most awed by science and its new technologies, and asked most sharply what the new science and technology was doing to the human world. Would the products of science "carve us/ Wounds that we wrap with theorems sharp as hail" (Crane 1984: 86)? The poem sequence "The Bridge" puts into practice his avowed conviction that "poetry is an architectural art . . . inclusive of all readjustments incidental to science and other shifting factors related to that consciousness" (Waggoner 1950: 162). The last line of "To Brooklyn Bridge" – "And of the curveship lend a myth to God" (Crane 64) – refers to the curve of the bridge and also alludes to Einstein's theory that the space of the universe is curved, making this triumph of engineering a visual sculpture of the General Theory of Relativity. Crane feels the same tension between scientific materialism and the desiring imagination as other poets, but unlike the doubters he is convinced that it is possible to integrate the two. "Cape Hatteras" depicts a world in which airplanes, radio, power stations, explosive shells, and the vast architectures of the city and manufacturing industry have transformed the landscape that his presiding poetic deity, Walt Whitman, celebrated little more than half a century earlier. The poem asks a question that remains potent today. "Walt," he asks, "tell me, Walt Whitman, if infinity/ Be still the same as when you walked the beach" (p. 86). In a confused, almost surreal, image he sees the entire universe become an engine "murmurless and shined/ In oilrinsed circles of blind ecstasy!" (p. 87). Now instead of a soul we are "an atom in a shroud" (p. 86) and in place of God's spirit speaking out of a cloud we hear the engine of an airplane. The clash of linguistic registers is sharp, even manic, as if the new age of science and technology demands a feverish rhetoric, "launched in abysmal cupolas of space,/ Toward endless terminals, Easters of speeding light" (p. 90).

Can poetry be effective any longer, Crane asks, when "dream cancels dream in this new realm of fact"? Some of his contemporaries thought that this new realm was just another form of imagination, and that poetry was more necessary than ever to prevent us giving it too much credence. Kenneth Rexroth mocks this new world of fact in a poem with an apparently scientific title, "Inversely as the Square of their Distances Apart." Poetry turns out to have understood such a dynamics of the attraction between bodies already, in its devotion to lovers who are "mysteries in each others arms" and "falling/ Like meteors, dark through black cold/ Toward each other" (Rexroth 1966: 148). Rexroth does not intend this to be a serious critique of science. Wallace Stevens, however, devoted almost his entire output to finding poetic dreams or "fictions," as he called them, whose validity could withstand this new materialist knowledge. He creates a poetic landscape filled with plants, animals, trees, winds, seas, light, and people (albeit somewhat allegorical figures), and apparently empty of cars, airplanes, telephones, atomic bombs, or genetic experiments. This absence is highly significant. The philosopher Mary Tiles points out that "it could be argued that there is already a 'philosophy of technology' (a theoretical view and set of attitudes towards technology) implicit in the long-standing philosophical tradition of ignoring technology" (Tiles 2000: 485), and the same can be said of poetics.

The ignoring of science and technology in an age in which they are dominant is still a poetics of science and technology, and this is what we find in Stevens's poetry. It continually asks implicitly what it means to live in a world that appears to be fundamentally independent of human meanings and desires, the world of the scientists, who in their attempt to "find the real" (Stevens 1955: 404) imagine that the movement of particles and forces, and the evolution of organisms, take place outside any teleology. Stevens has no confidence in the pictures of reality offered by these scientists or "Rationalists, wearing square hats," who can only imagine "right-angled triangles" (p. 75) while living in "an old chaos of the sun" (p. 70). But unlike many of his contemporaries he doesn't think that the scientists are wrong because they are materialists and believe we should be "completely physical in a physical world" (p. 325). He thinks the failure of scientists to imagine the botany in the rose among the iron filings disqualifies them entirely as thinkers who might command belief. There cannot any longer be an "enthroned" imagination, only a constantly changing imaginary, "like a thing of ether that exists/ Almost as predicate" (p. 418). This idealism is a rejoinder to a scientific realism whose reliance on mathematics, hypotheses, theories, and models of supersensible realities makes it in the eyes of many poets no more than a new and not very persuasive mythmaking, replacing the pantheon of gods with a zoo of subatomic particles.

The poets published by Donald Allen in his key anthology *The New American Poetry* (1960) were both impressed and disturbed by the atom bomb and the growth of science that made it possible. Donald Allen and Robert Creeley made a new selection of this poetry in *The New Writing in the USA* (1967) and chose poetry that makes these concerns even more explicit than they were in the earlier volume.

Creeley's introduction begins: "Nothing will fit if we assume a place for it" (Allen and Creeley 1967: 17), and echoes the Baconian scientific method of letting new empirical evidence confirm, refute, or revise theory. Poetry needs to be aware of physics according to Creeley, because that "understanding most useful to writing as an art is, for me, the attempt to *sound* in the nature of the language those particulars of time and place of which one is a given instance, equally present. I find it here" (p. 24). This is the poet as scientist, attentive to the particulars of time and space, whether manifest in a landscape, the stars, or matter, or even within the self. Among the poets we find Lew Welch playing the field researcher and challenging his readers to "step out onto the Planet./ Draw a circle a hundred feet round" and see how many things they can locate that "nobody understands" (p. 78); and Jack Spicer ruefully noting that neither the distances he feels in his lovelorn condition, nor the distances he finds in poetry, behave like the scientists say – "Distance, Einstein said, goes round in circles" – which would mean that both love and poetry would always renew themselves. Even the wave-particle duality of the California beach – "the tidal swell/ Particle and wave/ Wave and particle/ Distances" (p. 269) – holds no hope of relief. Science is everywhere in the poems in this anthology. John Ashbery, that most urbane aesthete among poets, appears to be talking in "The Ecclesiast" (and perhaps also "These Lacustrine Cities") about the scientific revolution: "you see how honey crumbles your universe/ Which seems like an institution" (p. 25).

Creeley was a close friend of Charles Olson, whose theory of "composition by field" (Olson 1966: 17) was one of the strongest influences on the postwar generation of poets. Olson borrows his metaphor for poetic structure from the physics of energy, and his writings repeatedly suggest that he thinks of this relation between poetry and physics as fundamental. At Black Mountain College where he taught and was the final Rector, he devised a plan for a research institute that would emulate the work of Princeton's Institute of Further Studies led by the physicist J. Robert Oppenheimer, director of the Manhattan Project that developed the atomic bomb. Olson probably had a deeper understanding of the transformations of knowledge brought about by science than any other poet of his time. Even archeology was being transformed into a science in the 1950s by leading archeologists such as Lewis Binford, and its findings regularly appeared in the science journals. Olson titled his collected poems *Archeologist of Morning*, thereby saying that he too was a poet-scientist.

Almost wherever one looks in Olson's writings he is trying to enlist the reader into a shared research project, even when the nature and details of this inquiry are deliberately left unresolved, so that quite often what remains is the abstract form of investigation and the concomitant invitation to trust in the validity of what is being reported and proposed. This is very noticeable in his major long poem sequence *The Maximus Poems*. He offers an appeal to data: "There is evidence/ a frame// of Mr Thomson's / did// exist . . ." (Olson 1983, 163); the methodological statement: "in *Maximus* local/ relations are nominalized" (p. 149); the archeological science: "the Continental Shelf// was Europe's/ first West, it wasn't/ Spain's/ south: fish,/ and furs,// and timber,/ were wealth,/ neither plants, / old agricultural/ growing, from// Neolithic . . ." (p. 128); and everywhere the excitement of discovery usually associated with scientific research.

The other science that has had a great cultural influence in the late twentieth century, and the most dominant for the past three decades, is molecular biology and the genetics research it has made possible. This science has had an increasing impact on poetry because DNA is now treated as a language, and poets are usually quick to respond to any new understanding of language. A strand of DNA consists of a long series of triplets of nucleic acids, of which there are just four different kinds – adenine (A), cytosine (C), guanine (G), and thymine (T). Writing the acids as letters readily gives rise to the idea that the genes that enable life to reproduce itself themselves form a code. A specific set of three nucleic acids instructs the cell to make a specific amino acid, the building block of protein out of which all living organisms are formed. When Heinrich Matthaei and Marshall W. Nirenberg took the first step of working out the code in 1961, they relied on the idea that the cell's productive and reproductive capacity was made possible by the use of a language. Molecular biology went on to develop this model much further and was soon talking of sentences, translation, commas, mistakes, and transcription in the molecular process, treating the basic cellular processes that sustain life as texts. Over the decades since these first discoveries it has become possible to wield an apparently godlike scientific power and move genes from one type of organism to another to create new life never seen before. This technology is known as the use of recombinant DNA, and it has suggested a new form of inquiry, the splicing or recombining of these fundamental "words" into new configurations or sentences to find out what sort of life the new sentences would create.

The growing prestige of this new science of the organism as a linguistic artefact suggested to some poets that not only were the unconscious and ideology structured like language, so was all organic life, and this gave linguistic experimentation an irresistible glamour. Some poets even constructed entire works in which the sentences are cut loose from one another, and placed into numerically generated sets. Ron Silliman called this "the new sentence" (Silliman 1987: 91), and put this recombinant poetics into practice in *Tjanting.* This constructivist work takes the form of paragraphs whose sentence count follows the Fibonacci series (in which each number is the sum of the two preceding ones, a progression found widely in nature). The poet and critic Lytle Shaw describes the process in metaphors that merge physics and molecular biology, saying that the text works by "using internal mutation and shifts in contexts to question the self-evidence, the atomistic givenness of a citation" (Shaw 1998: 120). A typical passage of *Tjanting* unfolds like this: "Cat laps up rainwater from saucer. Four out of five cosmic rays from outer space are mu-mesons. A barrel of bottles spills into a dumpster. White-orange rock with veins of green. Many shades of blue in the sky. Gull raises wings & the wind lifts it up" (Silliman 1981: 75). The sentences model the inquiring scientific intelligence, running across many questions from the most domestic (feeding the cat tuna) to the most political (military bases), and in every case there are implicit questions to which these sentences are partial answers. The scope of these sentences is such that they imply the desire to represent the range of a mind's everyday activity, its linguistic production, and the types of thought the "words warp" – the memories, self-awareness, perceptions, and scraps of communicative interaction. Lyn Hejinian, whose quasi-autobiographical prose poem *My Life* is also composed of "the new sentence," insists that for her "the language of poetry is a language of inquiry, not the language of a genre" (Hejinian 2000: 3).

Physics and molecular biology are only the most prominent of many diverse sciences. The success of science encouraged researchers throughout the twentieth century to try to extend its methods into all areas of human life, so that by the end of the century there had been attempts to generate scientific projects on art, society, emotion, sexuality, and race. The two final chapters of one of the most important studies of how science works, *The Structure of Science* by Ernest Nagel (1961), are devoted to sociology and history respectively. He asks whether they can and should be scientific, and concludes that they should:

> However acute our awareness may be of the rich variety of human experience, and however great our concern over the danger of using the fruits of science to obstruct the development of human individuality, it is not likely that our best interests would be served by stopping objective inquiry into the various conditions determining the existence of human traits and actions, and thus shutting the door to the progressive liberation from illusion that comes from the knowledge achieved by such inquiry. (Nagel 1961: 606)

Archeology, anthropology, and many areas of sociology and psychology have clearly benefited from this approach, but its limits have not always been recognized. Scientists study what the world is like independently of what it means to you and me as individuals.

Many thinkers believe that some crucial aspects of our cultural and personal lives cannot be viewed in this way because what an action (or event or object or person) means to you or me makes it what it is. Objectivity of the kind that science works for would be irrelevant in such cases. The great prestige of science has meant that issues such as urbanization or nuclear deterrence have sometimes been treated as if they were purely scientific, and poets have then not surprisingly taken issue with such methods. Poets read scientific accounts of the city or race in a prestigious journal like *Scientific American* and challenge the underlying assumptions, as did George Oppen in his poem *Of Being Numerous*, which is a rejoinder to studies of the city published in *Scientific American* and elsewhere that treated the metropolis as a scientific problem to be solved rather than a political or cultural challenge. As far as Oppen is concerned, when we study a city like New York, "the emotions are engaged," our imaginations are mutually at work, and the result is "a language, therefore, of New York" (Oppen 2002: 164), and because it is a language, poets as the artists of this language can make it into poetry.

Of all the extensions of science into areas where its methods were not appropriate, twentieth-century debates about race were the most egregious, as Elof Axel Carlson's (2001) recent study of the supposed science of eugenics reminds us. Although the association of eugenics with Nazism discredited its ideas about racial purity, until as late as the end of the 1960s various forms of science were still being used to legitimate racist ideas and policies. A. L. Kroeber, one of America's leading anthropologists in the first half of the century, and a scientist who did not believe that one race could be superior to another, wrote in 1934 that "races which differ anatomically also differ in some degree physiologically and psychologically" (Unesco 1956: 72). Such supposedly scientifically based beliefs were regularly used to argue that African Americans were less intelligent than European Americans. *Science*, the leading American science journal read by scientists themselves, published in 1964 an article by Dwight J. Ingle on "Racial Differences and the Future," which laments that "there is no possibility that a comprehensive program to upgrade the genetic and cultural heritage of all the races will be undertaken for several decades" (Ingle 1964: 379). He argues explicitly for a eugenics program that would entail sterilizing women from what he calls "substandard" cultures. Ingle's arguments were losing ground by that time, and such articles stopped appearing after the mid-1960s, but even the most enlightened of the race science articles remained racist.

Consider one which appeared in the August 1968 issue of *Scientific American* entitled "A Study of Ghetto Rioters," with the subtitle "Why do Negroes riot? An analysis of surveys made after the major riots of 1967 in Detroit and Newark indicates that some of the most familiar hypotheses are incorrect" (Caplan and Paige 1968). Though the essay ostensibly tries to articulate a political as well as a scientific discourse on the issues, for black American readers this insistence that they could be the objects of scientific study would readily be felt as a denial of their humanity in the name of science. Where was the companion article on why whites behave in specific ways? Newark as it happens was the home of one of the leading African-American poets, Amiri Baraka, and his poetry of the period of the 1960s and 1970s needs to be read against this backdrop of racial theories claiming to be scientific. This is why his poems of the time say to his black readers, "the black man will survive America./ His survival will mean the death of America," or "you must be a new reality alive now" (Baraka 1979: 147). The stereotypical American was a white scientific American who believed that race science was a picture of reality. Nikki Giovanni writing "bout those beautiful beautiful beautiful outasight/ black men/ with they afros/ walking down the street" (Randall 1971: 320) is countering not only dominant images of beauty, but the eugenicist slur on "substandard culture" that had been given currency by science. This is why Ishmael Reed's poem "Badman of the Guest Professor" includes the founding scientist of genetics research, Charles Darwin, among the poets and novelists (T. S. Eliot, William Faulkner, Ernest Hemingway, and Shakespeare) who are "you know, white-folkese/ business" (Randall 1971: 287).

By the 1990s poets were showing more confidence both in the insights offered by science and in their ability to comprehend them.

This has partly been brought about by a new understanding of the internal history and sociology of science. The American-Korean poet Myung Mi Kim says in an interview recorded in 1996 that she is "reading about/around geopolitical space and the politics of time in some sort of tandem with [her] desire to track the history of scientific knowledge" (Lee 2000: 98) especially anatomy. In her serial poem *Commons,* a meditation on the causes and consequences of the imperialist use of violence, she includes passages from Early Modern accounts of the dissection of dogs and human beings, where the absence of both moral judgment and emotional reaction points to a willingness to subject other territories to similar analysis. One poem begins: "Abnormalities included growth retardation, fasciation, malformation, and variegation, with the latter being most prominent. As to variegation of leaves, the white portion took a linear, spotty, and cloudy form and turned completely white in extreme cases. The shade of white varied" (Kim 2002: 53). This unidentified passage (we probably read it as a citation from a scientific report on the aftereffects of biological or chemical warfare but it could be a poetic invention), demonstrates how even the most rigorous scientific language cannot free itself of cultural value. Placed in the field of high attention to inferential possibility that constitutes the poem it also reads as an account of the struggle between peoples differentiated by skin color.

Mei-mei Berssenbrugge's poem *Endocrinology* (1997) raises similar questions about the clash between genetic accounts of human behavior that treat genes and behavior as independent of the meaning that they have for human beings, and those that believe that subjective response is an integral element of the world too. Jena Osman shares this interest in exploring the dissonance, as the epigraph to her poem "The Periodic Table As Assembled by Dr Zhivago, Oculist" demonstrates. Joan Retallack is cited as saying: "I once heard a scientist who loves poetry say, the language of science and the language of poetry have in common that they are both natural languages under stress" (Osman 1999: 26). Osman's poem is printed in the book *The Character* (1999), but this is a flattened out version of a hypertext poem (Osman 2003) in which the reader selects elements from the periodic table and these lead to further screens where it is possible to enact "chemical reactions" that combine phrases and words according to an underlying computer program.

Science has been the most powerful image of how a democracy should work. For many scientists and their supporters in government and education, science represented an ideal of democratic, egalitarian, international community that stood out like a beacon in the face of nationalism, war, and genocide. As we have seen, many of the poets learned their science from the *Scientific American*, and for much of the century the title of this magazine would have appeared to them to be a tautology: to be American was to be scientific and to be scientific was to be American in spirit. From the 1940s onward, leading intellectuals such as Robert K. Merton suggested that, in the words of the historian David A. Hollinger, "ordinary citizens would live by the code of the scientist" (Hollinger 1996: 158). This would mean, as the president of Harvard James B. Conant proposed, that people should aspire "to behave scientifically in social environments very different from the one in which science actually proceeds" (p. 162). This cosmopolitan ideal of a community of citizens committed to truth and the good of humankind could help discredit science as well. Eugenics and nuclear bomb research both offered ample counterexamples that could be used to call into question the entire scientific project, but it was the expansive optimism among scientists that the "code of the scientist" could be extended to the study of human societies and applied to what were once thought of as moral or aesthetic problems, that elicited the most sustained resistance from poets.

Scientists in the twentieth century never did recognize the importance of poetry as Pound had hoped they would. "The traffic between science and art is . . . almost always one-way," according to the editors of an anthology of poems about science, *A Quark for Mister Mark* (Riordan and Turney 2000: xiii), published at the millennium. Scientists still think of poetry as antiscientific. When Erwin Schrödinger, one of the most important twentieth-century physicists whose ideas on genetics inspired the discoverers of DNA, James Watson and Francis Crick, speculates freely about how cells overcome entropy, in a concluding passage in *What is Life?* (1944), he mocks himself like this: "Well, this is a fantastic description, perhaps less becoming a scientist than a poet" (Schrödinger 1967: 79). Twentieth-century American poets who acknowledge that the world has been transformed by science, both by its ideas of what constitutes life and matter and by the technologies its theories and discoveries have made possible, do not think of their work as a turning away from truth to fantasy. Science has provided the measure of intellectual inquiry to which many poets aspire; it has offered the most advanced forms of socially organized understanding; it has provided paradigms and core metaphors for poetics; and its varied, subtle ways of controlling the degree of surety and assertion in its written forms prefigures much of the treatment of language in poetry. Yet just as scientists mostly ignore poetry, poets don't spend much time explicitly discussing its influence on their work either. Is it possible that just as poetry has been deeply reshaped by the development of science and technology, science itself has been influenced in ways yet to be measured by the achievements of twentieth-century American poetry? Scientific autobiographies suggest this may sometimes be the case (Beckwith 2002: 40), but this is a history yet to be written. For now, we must reluctantly agree that "the traffic between science and art is . . . almost always one-way," even though modern poets have offered many insights into the workings of science in the course of their poetry's "romance with science's rigor, patience, thoroughness, speculative imagination" (Hejinian 1989: 24) that scientists may one day find valuable.

References and Further Reading

Allen, D. (ed.) (1999). *The New American Poetry*. Berkeley and Los Angeles: University of California Press.

— and Creeley, R. (eds.) (1967). *The New Writing in the U.S.A.* Harmondsworth, UK: Penguin.

Armstrong, T. (2001). "Poetry and Science." In Neil Roberts (ed.), *A Companion to Twentieth-Century Poetry*. Oxford: Blackwell, pp. 76–88.

Baraka, A. (1979). *Selected Poetry of Amiri Baraka/Leroi Jones*. New York: William Morrow.

Beckwith, J. (2002). *Making Genes, Making Waves: A Social Activist in Science*. Cambridge, MA: Harvard University Press.

Bell, I. F. A. (1981). *Critic as Scientist: The Modernist Poetics of Ezra Pound*. London: Methuen.

Berssenbrugge, M. (1997). *Endocrinology*. Berkeley, CA: Kelsey St. Press.

Bush, D. (1950). *Science and English Poetry: A Historical Sketch, 1590–1950*. Oxford: Oxford University Press.

Carlson, E. A. (2001). *The Unfit: A History of a Bad Idea*. Woodbury, NY: Cold Spring Harbor Laboratory Press.

Caplan, N. S. and Paige, J. M., "A Study of Ghetto Rioters," *Scientific American*, 219(2): 15–21.

Carter, S. (1999). *Bearing Across: Studies in Literature and Science*. Lanham, MD: International Scholars Publications.

Clark, T. J. (1999). *Farewell to an Idea: Episodes from a History of Modernism*. New Haven, CT: Yale University Press.

Clarke, B. and Henderson, L. D. (2002). *From Energy to Information: Representation in Science and Technology, Art, and Literature*. Stanford, CA: Stanford University Press.

Crane, H. (1984). *Complete Poems,* ed. Brom Weber. Newcastle upon Tyne, UK: Bloodaxe Books.

Fulton, A. (1999). *Feeling as a Foreign Language: The Good Strangeness of Poetry.* Saint Paul, MN: Graywolf Press.

Giddens, A. (1990). *The Consequences of Modernity.* Cambridge, UK: Polity Press.

Hejinian, L. (1989). "The Person: Statement," *Mirage: The Women's Issue,* 3: 24–5.

— (2000). *The Language of Inquiry.* Berkeley and Los Angeles: University of California Press.

— (2002). *My Life.* Los Angeles: Green Integer.

Hollinger, D. A. (1996). *Science, Jews, and Secular Culture: Studies in Mid-Twentieth Century American Intellectual History.* Princeton, NJ: Princeton University Press.

Ingle, D. J. (1964). "Racial Differences and the Future," *Science,* 146(3642): 375–9.

Judson, H. F. (2001). "Talking about the Genome," *Nature,* 409, 15 February: 769.

Kay, L. E. (2000). *Who Wrote the Book of Life? A History of the Genetic Code.* Stanford, CA: Stanford University Press.

Kim, M. M. (2002). *Commons.* Berkeley: University of California Press.

Kragh, H. (1999). *Quantum Generations: A History of Physics in the Twentieth-Century.* Princeton, NJ: Princeton University Press.

Lee, J. K. J. (2000). "Conversation with Myung Mi Kim." In K. K. Cheung (ed.), *Words Matter: Conversations with Asian American Writers.* Honolulu: University of Hawaii Press, pp. 92–104.

Levertov, D. (1983). *Poems, 1960–1967.* New York: New Directions.

Lorde, A. (1984). "Poetry is Not a Luxury." In *Sister Outsider: Essays and Speeches.* Freedom, CA: Crossing Press, pp. 36–9.

Nagel, E. (1961). *The Structure of Science: Problems in the Logic of Scientific Explanation.* New York: Harcourt, Brace & World.

Olson, C. (1966). *Selected Writings,* ed. Robert Creeley. New York: New Directions.

— (1983). *The Maximus Poems.* Berkeley and Los Angeles: University of California Press.

Oppen, G. (2002). *New Collected Poems,* ed. Michael Davidson. New York: New Directions.

Osman, J. (1999). *The Character.* Boston: Beacon Press.

— (2003). "The Periodic Table As Assembled by Dr Zhivago, Oculist." <http://wings.buffalo.edu/epc/authors/osman/periodic/>.

Pound, E. (1954) *Literary Essays of Ezra Pound,* ed. T. S. Eliot. London: Faber and Faber.

— (1977). *Selected Poems.* London: Faber and Faber.

Randall, D. (ed.) (1971). *The Black Poets.* New York: Bantam.

Rexroth, K. (1966). *The Collected Shorter Poems.* New York: New Directions.

Riordan, M. and J. Turney (2000). *A Quark for Mister Mark.* London: Faber and Faber.
Rukeyser, M. (1949). *The Life of Poetry.* New York: William Morrow & Co.
Schrödinger, E. (1967). *What is Life? With Mind and Matter and Autobiographical Sketches.* Cambridge, UK: Cambridge University Press.
Shaw, L. (1998) "The Labor of Repetition: Silliman's 'Quips' and the Politics of Intertextuality." In T. A. Vogler (ed.), *Ron Silliman and the A.L.P.H.A.B.E.T.* Santa Cruz, CA: Quarry West, pp. 118–33.
Silliman, R. (1981). *Tjanting.* New York: Great Barrington, MA: The Figures.
— (1987). *The New Sentence.* New York: Roof Books.
Snyder, G. (1974). *Turtle Island.* New York: New Directions.
— (1990). *The Practice of the Wild.* San Francisco: North Point Press.
— (1999). *The Gary Snyder Reader.* Washington, DC: Counterpoint.
Stein, G. (1967). *Look at Me Now and Here I Am: Writings and Lectures 1911–1945,* ed. Patricia Meyerowitz. London: Peter Owen.
Steinman, L. M. (1987). *Made in America: Science, Technology, and American Modernist Poets.* New Haven, CT: Yale University Press.
Stevens, W. (1955). *The Collected Poems of Wallace Stevens.* London: Faber and Faber.
Tiffany, D. (2000). *Toy Medium: Materialism and Modern Lyric.* Berkeley: University of California Press.
Tiles, Mary (2000). "Technology, Philosophy of." In W. H. Newton-Smith (ed.), *A Companion to the Philosophy of Science.* Oxford: Blackwell, pp. 483–91.
Unesco (1956). *The Race Question in Modern Science.* London: Sidgwick & Jackson.
Waggoner, H. H. (1950). *The Heel of Elohim: Science and Values in Modern American Poetry.* Norman: University of Oklahoma Press.
Williams, W. C. (1954). *Selected Essays of William Carlos Williams.* New York: New Directions.
— (1986). *The Collected Poems of William Carlos Williams, Volume I 1909–1939,* ed. A. Walton Litz and Christopher MacGowan. New York: New Directions.
— (1988). *The Collected Poems of William Carlos Williams, Volume II 1939–1962,* ed. Christopher MacGowan. New York: New Directions.

Chapter 12

Philosophy and Theory in US Modern Poetry

Michael Davidson

Affirming Nothing

Poetry's relationship to philosophy has had a long, if vexed, history. Plato's division of the two spheres in *The Republic* begins a tradition of disputation over the ability of poetry to engage ideas. For Plato, poets traffic in mere imitations of ideal forms; philosophers engage those forms dialectically and thus have a greater role to play in the *polis*. For every poet who claimed, as Shelley did, that poets are the "unacknowledged legislators of the world," there are those who assert, with Sir Philip Sidney that "the poet . . . nothing affirms" or with W. H. Auden that "poetry makes nothing happen." Yet many major poems are philosophical in scope and intent (one thinks of Pope's "Essay on Man" or Wordsworth's *The Prelude*), and a good deal of philosophical writing could be called extended prose poetry (the works of Nietzsche or Wittgenstein being the obvious examples). And philosophers have often relied on poetry to illustrate a point. Even a philosopher as skeptical about poets as Plato relied on Homer for many of his examples, and it would be hard to imagine the work of modern philosophers like Heidegger, Derrida, or Agamben without their use of Holderlin, Mallarmé, or Dante. The separation of spheres seems to depend less on the topics a poem or philosophical treatise engages than on what constitutes their respective means of expression. If our model for philosophy is a systematic treatise such as Kant's *Critique of Judgement* or Heidegger's *Being and Time*, then poetry would have a hard time claiming parity. And likewise, if one's model for poetry is the short condensed lyric, then philosophy might seem overblown and repetitive. Thus the primary issue in philosophy and poetry's claims to truth is the limits of the medium.

With the modernist period, the separation of poetry and philosophy becomes less tenable as classical disciplinary categories blur and mimetic models of poetry fall away. With Mallarmé or Rimbaud in the late nineteenth century, poetry ceases to exist in a secondary relationship to ideas but announces its foundational, constitutive status. Poetry becomes "part of the res itself and not about it," as Wallace Stevens said (Stevens 1968: 473). The modernist belief in a pure "Word," divorced from any originating force or prediscursive meaning, challenges Plato's and Aristotle's mimetic criteria and allows for the possibility that poetry may *be* a form of knowledge, not its amanuensis. As modern theorists have shown, the fact that poetic language refuses to obey strict grammatical or logical rules suggests that it may illustrate an indeterminacy at the heart of language itself and, as a result, may illustrate the fallacy of a grounded Logos or metaphysical absolute. To some extent we might say that if modern poetry didn't exist, modern philosophers would have to invent it.

At the very moment when the division between the two fields was breaking down, it was resurrected in the modern university through the development of the liberal arts curriculum. The emergence of "modern literature" in Humanities programs and of creative writing as a discipline have tended to separate "writers" from "critics," poets from English teachers, and placed philosophers across campus in another building – perhaps in Humanities but increasingly in Cognitive Science or Computer Engineering. Where nineteenth-century figures like Coleridge, Emerson, or Arnold wrote in a number of genres – criticism, reviews, translation, or philosophical speculation – in addition to poetry, their prototypes since the 1940s have become "poet-critics" whose livelihood comes not from journalism or public lectures but from academic appointments. With the dominance of theory and cultural studies within the Humanities and the decline of traditional generic and historical categories, poetry's very existence seems jeopardized. Some schools of poetry have embraced cultural theory into work that blurs the boundary between imaginative and critical practice, while others have repudiated such cross-fertilization, turning, in a rearguard action, to more traditional forms of rhymed and metered verse. We might ask, then, what is the work of poetry in an age of critical theory? What has become of the modernist ideal of fusing, as Mallarmé said, all "earthly existence" into a single "book"? How has US modern poetry redefined the traditional divisions between words and ideas? These will be the operative questions in subsequent pages.

"Till Human Voices Wake Us": Modernism and the Problem of Other Minds

> One must have a mind of winter
> To regard the frost and the boughs
> Of the pine-trees crusted with snow (Stevens 1968: 9)

Wallace Stevens's opening to "The Snow Man" poses a conundrum for the modern poet's relationship to ideas: in order to represent winter adequately the poet must become winter – become a snow man. In doing so, however, he loses the ability to distinguish and assess. He is suspended between the "Nothing that is not there and the nothing that is," between an apprehending mind distinct from nature and the bare reality upon which such apprehension depends. D. H. Lawrence had faulted Walt Whitman for participating in only one half of this paradox, seeking to merge with the world and thereby losing his individuality. The wages of romantic participation, Lawrence felt, is death. Stevens, by refusing to take sides in the question of imagination versus nature, recognizes the fateful complicity between the two – between the mind's "rage to order" (Stevens 1968: 130) and the chaotic world that demands words to describe it. The poem oscillates between the twin poles of its double negative and as a result produces a third thing – the "modern" poem. If, for Stevens, that poem is inherently philosophical, it is not because it embodies ideas beyond the poem but because it engages them as formal and linguistic problems of poetry itself.

Stevens's plight is that of many US poets who faced an epistemological crisis in the first decades of the twentieth century in which knowledge could no longer be validated either by empirical evidence or spiritual fiat. The romantic testimony of a Shelley or Whitman which claimed a participatory identification with the world seemed increasingly naïve in the face of modern secularism and technology. Doctrines of Symbolism and Impressionism offered an aesthetic *cordon sanitaire* against mass culture but fatally separated the poet from the world by positing an artificial nature within the artwork entirely at odds with physical nature. Without traditional religious or metaphysical solutions to social change, on the one hand, and the increasing allure of modernity itself (science, technology, positivism) and mass culture on the other, poets who came of age in the early decades of the twentieth century confronted an increasingly secularized deracinated world. For these poets, subjectivity was both their greatest burden and their major theme, but the issue was not so much the question of whether the self exists separate from God or Nature, but the extent to which "I" exists in relationship to other minds. Hence the first great philosophical crisis to which modernist poets addressed themselves was the question of solipsism.

The inaugural generation of American modernists confronted the crisis of subjectivism and solipsism by various means and through several philosophical traditions. The most characteristic response to this crisis was the creation of memorable personae – such as T. S. Eliot's Prufrock or Ezra Pound's Hugh Selwyn Mauberley or Stevens's comic Crispin in "The Comedian as the Letter C" – that gave a voice to an age without moorings. The dry ironic tone that marks so many poems of the 1910s was inherited from late nineteenth-century French poetry (Laforgue and Corbière) and Browning's monologues, but it was no less a defensive reaction to the growth of cities and the presence of new racial and ethnic others immigrating into those cities. Eliot's influential theory of impersonality – the idea that the new poet must extinguish personality in order to write within a tradition – was only one version of a latter-day Kantianism among many poets of the era. Eliot was also influenced by the work of British philosopher, F. H. Bradley, upon whom he wrote (but never completed) his PhD thesis at Harvard. In his *Appearance and Reality*, Bradley stresses the idea that one's experience forms a closed circle in which "every sphere is opaque to the others which surround it," a phrase that Eliot incorporated into his notes to *The Waste Land* (Eliot 1962: 54). While this suggests an isolated or monadic view of the self, it helps explain the point of view of Eliot's speaker in "The Love Song of J. Alfred Prufrock" whose inability to interact with others stems from seeing himself as bound by a private sphere of experience. Prufrock is paralyzed by self-consciousness, waiting in a spiritless void for "human voices [to] wake us, and we drown" (Eliot 1962: 7). Bradley's "finite centers" provided Eliot with a powerful image of a dissociated consciousness in which emotion and thought are separate, in which, as Eliot said of Victorian poets, although they "think," they "do not feel their thought as immediately as the odor of a rose" (Eliot 1975: 64). The poetic solution to the crisis of solipsism for Eliot is to recuperate an affective relationship to ideas, to embody emotion through an "objective correlative" or rhetorical structure that would universalize, rather than personalize, emotion.

For Eliot's colleague, Ezra Pound, the crisis of solipsism was not a psychological but a cultural and stylistic matter. Pound had little use for formal philosophy, deriving his thinking about Imagism and Vorticism from T. E. Hulme's neo-classical belief in a "hard dry" technique to circumvent the "messiness" of natural orders. Although it was hardly a systematic philosophical movement, Imagism – its adherents including Pound, H. D., and Richard Aldington – was based on a concern for the moment, freed from "time and space limits" and implicitly freed from the contingencies of personal psychology. Pound's famous Imagist criteria – economical language, condensation of expression, musical phrasing – addressed the rhetorical inflation and moral smugness of late Victorian verse and provided a surgical cure. Utilizing Bergson's ideas of duration and simultaneity, Pound hoped to retrieve from the monotonous temporality of the time clock and the factory whistle, "magic moments" of insight and clarity. In his subsequent work, Pound turned increasingly to Neoplatonic mysticism and Confucian theology to buttress these ideas. These philosophical ideas merged a belief in a radiant world beyond the quotidian with a patriarchal, and ultimately authoritarian, social ethos that would be fulfilled in Pound's embrace of Mussolini's Fascism in the 1930s.

Pound and Eliot's worries over the dissolution of individual consciousness to what Pound called an "accelerated grimace" of modern life were motivated by cultural concerns relating to the role of art in modern society. They drew on the work of philosophers like Bradley and Bergson or aestheticians like Hulme for support, but their solutions involved the creation of voices of the age with which they, as poets, would not be confused. In contrast, Gertrude Stein or William Carlos Williams felt that modernity in its bewildering variety and novelty offered a positive opportunity to forge a new consciousness. Instead of creating distancing personae to finesse the problem of alienation, they appropriated Jamesian and Deweyan pragmatism to view identity as a series of multiple perspectives on a shifting reality. Stein was influenced in her early writing by her Radcliffe professor, William James, whose theory of consciousness as a "stream" provided an important model for narrative technique. Stein applied James's ideas of the stream of consciousness to early prose works such as "Melanctha" and *The Making of Americans*, but they could be said equally to have influenced her subsequent poetic portraits and plays. In these highly fragmented, repetitious works, Stein drew on Jamesian ideas of temporality to manifest, as she said "the person as existing and as everything in that person entered in to make that person . . ." (Stein 1957: 176). In experiments conducted while a student of psychology and medicine, Stein argued that consciousness is not something that could be changed or modified but is fixed from birth. Identity is revealed not so much in what people say but how they repeat the same patterns of speech over and over again in what she called a "continuous present." Stein categorized different types of characters based on their differing repetition patterns, referring to each person's character as his or her "bottom nature." This characterology permitted Stein to distinguish between identity ("I am I because my little dog knows me") and what she called "entity," the self uncontaminated by historical causation or family influence. Entity is for existence what the aesthetic is for art.

William Carlos Williams, while never a systematic philosopher, attempted throughout his life to dig down into first things and discover the primordial conditions that underlie language. Unlike his contemporaries, Williams never mourned the loss of the gods or the decline of Western civilization. Rather he relished the fact that a world without metaphysical first principles was new, that it was possible to start over again in an Adamic act of invention. Like the Romantics before him (and with the inspiration of avant-gardists like Marcel Duchamp), Williams wanted to destroy the world in order to make it new. Poetic destruction – or what Stevens called "decreation" – involved a Nietzschian attack on reason, logic, and system and a corresponding investment in the earth and processes of nature. "No ideas but in things," is his famous objectivist claim in *Paterson*, which does not mean that there are no ideas but that ideas must be embodied and materialized. Appropriately enough, his one foray into philosophical thought, a collection of jottings and essays, was to be titled *The Embodiment of Knowledge*. As a program for poetry, such embodiment involves focusing on the thingness of things, on the textures and surfaces of ordinary objects – including words. Williams's early lyrics in *Spring and All* and *Descent of Winter* were designed to strip language of conventional associations, create unexpected linkages between words, and allow the verse line to replicate acts of consciousness. At the same time, by hewing closely to the thing itself – whether red wheelbarrow or shards of green glass in a hospital courtyard – the poem would assert its value as a thing among other things.

Williams's commitment to everyday language and objects influenced a movement of young writers of the 1930s known as the Objectivists, which included George Oppen, Carl Rakosi, Louis Zukofsky, Charles Reznikoff, and Lorine Niedecker. The Objectivists were featured in a 1931 issue of Harriet Monroe's *Poetry Magazine* and in *The Objectivist Anthology* edited by George Oppen and Louis Zukofsky. Despite the name, Objectivism was not a variant of Eliot's impersonality; the focus was less on the poet's objectivity as detachment than on the poem *as* object. The Objectivists sought to restore the materiality of language to the poem while gaining greater access to the *realia* of everyday life. In order to achieve this objectivist position, the poet must eliminate all traces of what Zukofsky called "predatory intent," those elements that reduce the poem to an advertisement or statement. The poem should achieve "rested totality . . . the apprehension satisfied completely as to the appearance of the art form as an object" (Zukofsky 1967: 13). There were several philosophical influences on Objectivist thinking, the first of which was provided by the material conditions of the Depression of the 1930s and the importance of Marxism as a social and economic philosophy. Louis Zukofsky incorporated passages from Marx's *Capital* into his epic poem, *"A,"* and Charles Reznikoff wrote his long documentary poem, *Testimony*, out of law trials concerning workplace injuries. Marxism provided a social ethos for young writers committed to social change, and whether as members of the Communist Party, like Oppen or Rakosi, or as sympathetic fellow travelers, the Objectivists fused their formal experiments with social issues.

Another important influence on the Objectivists was provided by the mathematician and philosopher, Alfred North Whitehead, whose *Science and the Modern World* and *Process and Reality* outlined an "objectivist position" to counter the limits of romantic idealism. Whitehead defined his position as "seeking forms in the facts," a formula that could apply to all of the Objectivist poets. But his was not another form of empiricism. Whitehead states that "things pave the way for the cognition, rather than vice versa. The objectivist holds that the things experienced and the cognizant subject enter into the common world on equal terms" (Whitehead 1967: 89). This is a credo repeated by George Oppen in many of his poems that try to reconcile what he called in "Of Being Numerous" "the shipwreck/ Of the singular" with a world of discrete objects (Oppen 2002: 116). For a writer, the idea that the individual is constructed in relation to things, offers the promise that "... the nouns do refer to something; that it's there, that it's true, the whole implication of these nouns; that appearances represent reality, whether or not they misrepresent it" (Oppen 1969: 163). Although the Objectivists tended to use an ocular metaphor in referring to the focus that the poem should achieve, they never implied a perspectival relativism. Rather, their poems attempted to register the oscillation between the "something" that the nouns represent and the recalcitrant words that mediate direct participation. Clarity does not end in a description of the thing in itself but in what Oppen, quoting Heidegger, called "the arduous path of appearance."

The Objectivist focus on the materiality of the poem, however motivated by Marx's labor theory of value, was equally indebted to Pound's Imagism with its emphasis on clarity and precision. Only by maintaining the integrity of the poem and the clarity of language could use-value be returned to poetry in any meaningful way. But for other activist poets of the 1930s, Marx's political and economic theories were translated into a partisan poetics that rejected avant-garde formal strategies in favor of more unmediated representations of social exploitation and class struggle. In the work of Edwin Rolfe, Muriel Rukeyser, Richard Wright, Langston Hughes, and others, "philosophy" meant political philosophy and class analysis. Unlike Stevens with his lush verbal surfaces, or Pound with his haiku-like Imagism, poets on the Left saw art not as an end in itself but as a means for achieving revolutionary consciousness. Poets became polemicists, essayists, muckraking journalists, and many poems of the period aspired to the condition of documentary film or WPA (Works Progress Administration) photo essay.

The social theory of art had emerged forcefully among black intellectuals within the Harlem Renaissance of the 1920s over the question of cultural traditions. The key question for race leaders of this period was a question of alliances: whether they should aspire to what W. E. B. DuBois called a "talented tenth" elite that would raise the race by deploying white cultural values, or whether they should be organic intellectuals who utilized the vernaculars and idiolects of ordinary black people. Within poetry this took the form of a debate over traditional forms versus vernacular language, typified in the first case by Countee Cullen, Anne Spencer, or Claude McKay, who wrote formal, metered verse, and Langston Hughes or Sterling Brown who wrote in vernacular idioms. The debate was fleshed out in Alain Locke's influential 1925 anthology, *The New Negro* which served as a manifesto for the "Talented Tenth" and in significant journals of the day, such as *The Crisis* and *Opportunity*. Locke had received his PhD in philosophy from Harvard and brought his interests in German metaphysics and French culture to bear on his theories of racial uplift. DuBois also revered German culture, spending two years of postdoctoral study at the University of Berlin. As a graduate student at Harvard, he worked with eminent philosophers of the day such as William James and Josiah Royce. To some extent this Eurocentric emphasis among African-American intellectuals has marked debates over the success of the Harlem Renaissance, causing Langston Hughes to worry over what he saw as the "racial mountain" of white culture that faces the innovative Negro writer who wishes to draw on Afrocentric cultural resources.

During the 1930s and 1940s, partly in response to the ideological claims of political poetry during the Depression and to the ongoing avant-garde in urban centers, a group of Southern poet-critics developed a more systematic criticism based on the poem's supposed autonomy and formal integrity. The New Critics – John Crowe Ransom, Robert Penn Warren, and Allen Tate – developed their theories of poetry within an Agrarian attack on modern urbanism and mass cultural decadence using Eliot's criticism as a basis and Kant's aesthetics as a backbone. Kant's belief, stated in his *Critique of Judgment*, that the work of art exhibits a kind of purposiveness without purpose became a key to New Critical attitudes toward poetic value. Ransom was the most overtly Kantian critic of the group, setting out his ideas of poetic ontology to combat what he called "physical poetry," represented by Imagism which, he felt, fetishized things for their own sakes, and "Platonic poetry," a poetry of ideas embodied by Tennyson's work but which, presumably, would include the partisan poetry of the Depression era. Ransom's alternative was what he called "metaphysical poetry," which attempts to synthesize both "physical" and Platonic schools in a "miraculist fusion" of universals and particulars. Ransom's metaphor is drawn from religion – the spirit made flesh – and in many of their essays, the New Critics suggest that they sought a secular incarnation in poetry to replace a lost spiritual plenitude in the modern world.

These metaphysical and theological concerns among the New Critics were buttressed by a description of the poem as an autotelic or self-enclosed entity. The ideal poem would be one that relies not on authorial intention or biography but on formal mastery and organic coherence. Irony is the dominant trope for such a poem since it displays the author's ability to achieve distance from the poem's subject and give rhetorical structure to what would otherwise be personal confession. Conflict, tension, and ambiguity were highly valued features, not as social imperatives (the poem should not depict personal crisis or class struggle) but ideally as rhetorical solutions, a "pattern of resolved tensions" or "balanced oppositions." Finally, the ideal poem would be organic, all parts, as Cleanth Brooks said, "related to each other, not as blossoms juxtaposed in a bouquet, but as the blossoms are related to the other parts of a growing plant" (Brooks 1971: 1042).

The New Criticism was the first indigenous attempt at a systematic theory of literature that would vie with the sciences for rigor. As both a theoretical and practical criticism it became enormously influential as a pedagogical tool during the 1940s and 1950s when it was implemented within the expanded university system of the postwar era. The New Criticism was disseminated through a series of teaching anthologies such as Cleanth Brooks and Austin Warren's *Understanding Poetry*, which first appeared in 1938, and journals such as *The Sewanee Review* and *the Kenyon Review*. It was also the first major appearance of "theory" as a self-conscious attempt to outline the methods, principles, and means of artistic production. Although the New Criticism is principally remembered as a system of formal elucidation (close-reading) of texts it was also motivated by cultural attitudes about the role that such texts were to play in modern society. And because many of the New Critics were also poets, they were able to illustrate in practice the literary and cultural values they endorsed.

With the expansion of the postwar university system to returning veterans on the GI Bill, and the establishment of creative writing as a disciplinary area, poets increasingly found academic positions as a way of providing job security and income. A shortlist of major mid-century poets who held academic jobs would include Ransom, Tate, and the other New Critics and younger poets such as Robert Lowell, John Berryman, Anthony Hecht, Richard Eberhardt, Adrienne Rich, Randall Jarrell, Karl Shapiro, and Richard Wilbur. With the formation of the Writer's Workshop at the University of Iowa, creative writing became a disciplinary area in itself, employing writers to teach and instructing young writers how to emulate their teachers. The popularity of modern literature classes and creative writing brought new constituencies to the English department but fostered a division between literature and writing that would have profound repercussions in the 1960s and 1970s.

Being Exegetical: Postwar Poetry and the Linguistic Turn

If New Critical detachment implied a populist access to the understanding of poetry, New Critical cultural theory was a good deal less egalitarian. To Robert Penn Warren's remark in "Pondy Woods," "Nigger your breed ain't metaphysical," the African-American poet, Sterling Brown replied, "Cracker, your breed ain't exegetical." (Baker 1987: 149). Brown's riposte is more than verbal sparring; it recognizes that when metaphysics can be used to validate racism, exegesis – interpretation – needs to be applied to rhetoric. During the 1950s, a younger generation of poets – both black and white – subjected parent figures like Warren to a severe exegesis, exposing the older generation's elitism while redeeming a spirit of romantic testimony. The most obvious version of this spirit could be found among the Beat poets who adopted a nose-thumbing attitude toward US official culture – academic, political, cultural – introducing lifestyle and personal biography in direct opposition to the academic orthodoxy of the day. Against the formal social, religious, and political philosophies of the parent generation (Marxism, Anglo-Catholicism, Fascism, Agrarian fundamentalism) the Beats substituted anarchism, Zen Buddhism, Dadaism, and existentialism as alternatives. Moreover, unlike the parent generation, they courted popular culture – rock 'n' roll, comics, television – in ways that troubled their predecessors.

The Beat poets (Allen Ginsberg, Gregory Corso, LeRoi Jones, Bob Kauffman and others) eschewed a reflective poetics and extended William Carlos Williams's faith in the validity of ordinary experience. Against the ironic impersonal poetics of Eliot they substituted a directly confessional testamentary style. "First thought, best thought," was Ginsberg's succinct formula, and Robert Creeley concurred: "as mind is a finger,/ pointing, as wonder/ a place to be" (Creeley 1982: 387). This expressivism – or what Frank O'Hara called personism – was the salient feature of numerous schools of poetry of this era and marks a distinct break with the modernist crisis of solipsism. Instead of the distancing personae of Pound and Eliot, postwar poets developed more intimate modes of address or else returned to bardic vatic postures. Many of these poets were featured in Donald Allen's 1960 anthology, *The New American Poetry*, which first categorized them according to affinities (Black Mountain, New York School, Beat, San Francisco Renaissance). And beyond the work of the New American Poets, a generation of writers who had grown up with existentialism and psychoanalysis began to focus more directly on highly personal intimate experiences. The Confessional Poets (Robert Lowell, Sylvia Plath, Anne Sexton, John Berryman, etc.) fused the New Critical emphasis on strict control of the medium with charged personal content.

Charles Altieri characterizes the ethos of many poets during the postwar years as a "poetics of immanence" (Altieri 1979: ch. 1). He distinguishes between the symbolist poet's faith in the ordering powers of the mind and the postmodern poet's faith in the mind's ability to discover order in nature, a natural supernaturalism versus the miraculist fusion described by Ransom. Charles Olson's idea of "Projective Verse," for example, treats the poem as a dynamic field of energies and kinetic forces that replicate or embody cognitive acts. "From the moment [the poet] ventures into FIELD COMPOSITION – puts himself in the open – he can go by no track other than the one the poem under hand declares, for itself" (Olson 1997: 240). Olson seeks an immediacy by which each element of the poem registers a new act of mind, and because the line derives from the body and breath (and not the counting of syllables or feet) it embodies the mind's speculative workings. In a similar vein, Robert Creeley speaks of writing as a form of knowing: "One knows in writing . . . writing makes its own demands, its own articulations, and is its own activity – so that to say, 'Why, he's simply telling us the story of his life,' the very fact that he is telling of his life will be a decisive modification of what that life is" (Creeley 1973: 103). Denise Levertov treats this poetics of immediacy in religious terms. Drawing on romantic notions of organic form, she insists that poetry involves intuiting "an order, a form beyond forms, in which forms partake, and of which man's creative works are analogies, resemblances, natural allegories" (Levertov 1973: 7). All of these formulations insist that poetry is a dynamic open-ended form that claims a world of value by authenticating the mind's speculative powers.

Such an unabashed reprise of romanticism was combined, in the 1960s and 1970s, with new social movements. What had been the academic poet-critic of the 1940s and 1950s became the social critic of the antiwar, feminist, environmentalist, and black nationalist movements. Poets were among the most significant public intellectuals of the period. Adrienne Rich, Allen Ginsberg, Gary Snyder, LeRoi Jones/Amiri Baraka, Denise Levertov, and Robert Lowell all participated actively in forms of social protest and political activism. With the exception of Lowell, none were associated with English departments and they were regular presences at rallies and public debates. The phenomenon of the "public poet" had not been seen in such vivid array since Whitman or Whittier, leading more conservative culture critics like Daniel Bell and Irving Howe to conflate the "barbaric yawp" of their poetry with the strident nature of their polemic. Neoconservative criticisms of the new poets reflected a Cold War era distrust of ideology and a desire to keep the realms of culture and art separate from social criticism.

The first attempt to theorize these various poetic tendencies came in the mid-1970s through critics such as William Spanos, Charles Altieri, Gerald Bruns, Paul Bové, and Joseph Riddel, who saw in the poetics of "field" a new postmodern aesthetics of temporality. Drawing on Martin Heidegger's existential hermeneutics in *Being and Time*, critics writing in the journal *boundary 2* saw Olson's field poetics as posing a crucial alternative to modernism, based neither on an autotelic text nor on a spatial metaphysics of truth. The *boundary 2* critics argued that truth is not prior to experience but comes into being in momentary acts of attention. The new poetry of spontaneous testimony seemed an ideal test case for such a hermeneutics. David Antin's talk pieces, Jerome Rothenberg's ethnopoetics, Gary Snyder's naturalist lyrics, Robert Creeley's intimate confessionalism, Robert Duncan's ideas of "open form," Denise Levertov's organic poetics – these were all read as exemplars of what Heidegger called *aletheia*, the uncovering of truth as a temporal process. The fact that many of these poets wrote long – often *very* long – poems reinforced the proposition that truth-as-revelation had to occur over a long duration. Whereas Bergsonian ideas of temporality had stressed the continuity of Self through duration, the New American poets stressed the discovery *of* time within consciousness. The New Critics had valued an organic ideal of poetry that was spatial in its centripetal organization of thematic elements; the ethical charge of the poem was its ability to contain and balance ambiguities against the tensions of historical causation. The new American poets valued a temporal centrifugal poetics of discovery that challenged spatial form; value could be achieved by keeping the form open to new experiences and sudden shifts of attention.

The hermeneutic reading of postmodern poetry opened the way for more theoretical approaches launched in the late 1970s and 1980s as Theory, with a capital T, came more and more into the academy. Translations into English of French structuralists such as Roland Barthes, Claude Lévi-Strauss, and Ferdinand de Saussure;

the publication of major figures of the Russian Formalist and Prague Linguistic groups; and the various extensions of hermeneutics from Heidegger, Gadamer, and Dilthey brought European theory into the academy in ways that announced a "linguistic turn" in philosophy. Equally, analytic philosophy, particularly the work of Wittgenstein, exerted its influence on poetry through its study of the propositional or situated nature of human utterances. This linguistic focus offered a series of challenges to positivistic thinking about language based on the idea that words, in some way or another, "contain" meanings that exist prior to them. Rather, as de Saussure points out, meanings are arbitrarily attached to phonemes, constructed within linguistic conventions and usage. Meaning is conferred through social use of language, either through ritualized forms (as described by Marcel Mauss and Claude Lévi-Strauss) or speech acts (as formulated by Ludwig Wittgenstein). The so-called "arbitrary nature of the sign" as defined by de Saussure, and the dialogic theories of M. H. Bakhtin, challenged the idea that words express innate inherited meanings. Rather, words are conventions within a social matrix, organized along the twin axes of combination (metonymy) and selection (metaphor).

Traditional humanists and literary scholars found such attitudes threatening in their implications. Structuralist and post-structuralist thought suggested, among other things, that much of humanism since the Enlightenment is based on a rather unsteady scaffolding. If, as semioticians held, everything is a text, then what is the purpose of genres, styles, canons – the traditional categories of poetics? How could one evaluate poetry – or, indeed, any work of literature – according to fixed standards of value if those standards are historically contingent? And what about the role of the Humanities as a civilizing force? What function do the human sciences fulfill if they are simply institutions of class privilege and educational background. Perhaps the most damaging question for poetry raised by new textual theories is the idea that identity itself is a linguistic function, the "I" as a grammatical position in a sentence as formulated by the linguist, Emile Benveniste, or the psychoanalyst, Jacques Lacan. Such ideas defied many of the ideals and aspirations of modernism as a forward-looking movement of improvement and change, yet many of these ideas were underwritten by attitudes toward language that experimental modernist poets had been deploying for years. This latter fact was not lost on post-structuralist philosophers like Julia Kristeva or Roland Barthes who vaunted modern poetry's "intransitive" nature as an alternative to rationalist or "logocentric" thought.

Although the linguistic turn in theory was to exert a powerful impact on the Humanities in academic contexts, it provoked an ambivalent response among poets. If the oral or "phonocentric" nature of poetry is now revealed to be a product of a debased metaphysical view, what were poets to do with treasured ideas like "voice" and "meter" and "speech"? More significantly, if language is not a window onto the soul but merely a set of grammatical functions, how can poetry claim any originating function? Some, such as Joseph Epstein or Dana Gioia, blamed Creative Writing departments and the professionalization of literary study for this impasse for encouraging a formulaic, standardized, lyric model of poetry. Conservative critics saw the turn towards language as a sign of the debasement of Western cultural institutions that had unconsciously subscribed to ideas of "diversity" and "pluralism." Such criticisms led to a series of "culture wars" that pitted academic theorists against traditionalists. Poets were among the combatants in the culture wars, often deploring but occasionally defending the linguistic turn in theory.

Among the latter were Language Writers who took the premises of post-structural linguistics and Russian Formalism to heart and aligned these theories with European avant-garde movements such as Surrealism and Dadaism. In journals such as *L=A=N=G=U=A=G=E*, *This*, *Tottel's Miscellany*, *Hills*, and *Poetics Journal*, these poets developed a critique of the expressivist premises that dominated so much poetry of the 1950s and 1960s. Both expressivism and the creative writing workshop lyric were based, they felt, on a unitary "I" and a speech-based poetics of the voice. "I hate speech," Robert Grenier said in the first issue of *This*, indicting not the oral tradition so much as the metaphysical assumptions behind a speech-based poetics. The Language Poets' response included extensive experiments with non sequitur, collaboration, and radical disjuncture to reveal the semiotic and grammatical functions of language. They also experimented extensively in prose forms, the basic unit of which is what Ron Silliman calls "The New Sentence." In an essay by that name, Silliman contrasts the French prose poem, which organizes its units around a more traditional narrative progress, and the "new sentence" of poets such as Bob Perelman, Clark Coolidge, or Lyn Hejinian (Silliman 1987). In the latter, the organization of sentences repudiates "syllogistic logic," the organization of grammatical units according to rhetorical or logical means. Rather, the poet continually torques or diverts meaning into new semantic areas. The result is a form of prose poetry that builds on small elements within each sentence rather than subordinating language to a narrative denouement. Like the Objectivists before them, the Language writers are interested in returning the materiality of writing to poetry so that it would lose its subservient relationship to ideas and identity. Language writers share the political hope that the open-ended textual structure of their work would encourage the reader to participate in the writing process and become an active collaborator in meaning making rather than a passive consumer of meanings.

A less theoretical response to theory occurred among more mainstream poets who turned from the testamentary styles of Deep Image and Confessional verse and developed a considerably more muted expressive style that Charles Altieri characterizes as "the scenic mode." Where poets of the 1950s and 1960s had celebrated "Experience in capital letters," the poets of the 1970s and 1980s, in Altieri's terms, use voice as "an index of how we can register the complexity of the given and thus develop our personal powers for responding to experience" (Altieri: 1984: 37). In the work of Robert Hass, Louise Gluck, Jonathan Holden, Stanley Plumly, Steven Dunn, and John Ashbery, the subtle manipulation of tone modulates around seemingly mundane experiences – washing dishes, riding a bike, bird watching, shopping – that eventually leads to a discrete apotheosis. What validates this desultory lyricism is the subtle deployment of tone to map various positions and postures. Where Language writing flattened expressive speech through extensive use of non sequitur, these poets developed a conversational, sometimes narrative mode, that meanders around momentary acts of reflection, memory, resignation. The poet maintains a voice that is relatively self-effacing, preferring indirection and nuanced understatement to prophetic statement. Yet like both Confessional and Deep Image poets before them, these poets use the lyric mode to draw out subterranean content.

The Cultural Turn

Thus far, I have described two "turns" in philosophical inquiry as it was represented within poetics: first, a modernist epistemological crisis around the existence of other minds; second, a postmodernist "linguistic turn" framed as the problem of the sign. The last two decades of the twentieth century have seen a shift that could be described as a "cultural turn" marked by the emergence of new constituencies, canons, and cultural traditions. Critical race theory, queer theory, diaspora studies, critical legal studies, disability studies – these are some of the terms within which this change is being experienced and within which new poetries are emerging. To some extent this shift in emphasis has brought together the two discourses already covered – the problem of "other minds" is now revealed to be a problem not between the self and other but between socially constructed notions of otherness reinforced by social institutions. The shift from a foundationalist or essentialist view of self and culture is made possible by appropriating the critique of the sign and showing how identity is produced within discursive situations. Influential in this respect have been Michel Foucault's historical studies of sexuality and penal institutions, Franz Fanon's writings on imperialism and racism, Antonio Gramsci's writings on culture and hegemony, Stuart Hall and Gayatri Spivak's writings on postcoloniality, and Judith Butler's theory of identity as performance. Many of these tendencies have focused on narrative as the embodiment of a socially significant text (culture as "story," narrative as "national allegory") and partly in response to poetry's hegemony within the ahistorical New Criticism and structuralism. Nevertheless, there have been important forays into a "cultural poetics" by younger theorists who seek to situate poetry within constituencies for whom it is a value. While it would be difficult to generalize how cultural studies apply to new poetry, one could look at several innovative trends in US poetry that show a shift from issues of personal confession to constituencies and cultural formations.

The first trend that displays this culturalist emphasis could be the idea of hybridity or *mestizaje* as it is discussed within minority discourse. The poet/critic Gloria Anzaldúa has introduced the concept of *mestiza* consciousness to describe the contributions of many in the Unites States who straddle several cultures, for whom a "tolerance for ambiguity" is a response to white, masculinist, monolingual culture (Anzaldúa 1987: 79). A poetics of hybridity implies both a formal investment in new genres and structures but also a theoretical investment in cross-cultural identities. Chicana/o poets who write both in Spanish and English (and idioms combining both), deaf poets who create poems in ASL (American Sign Language), diasporic poets like Teresa Hak Kyung Cha or Edward Kamau Brathwaite who write in multiple dialects and voices of the cultures they traverse, queer performance poets like Luis Alfaro or Terry Galloway who use performance to critique gender and ethnic stereotypes – these would be some of the forms that a poetic *mestizaje* takes. Anzaldúa's own essays are a crossing of poetry, manifesto, and social polemic, laced with references to New World religion, and gender politics. In all of this work, issues of expression are framed around communal or collective identities rather than personal confession. And unlike cultural nationalist poetries of the early 1970s, the new poets tend not to form around single identities but to combine and sample from a number of cultural zones.

One of the salient features of this hybridic representation of cultural forms is its development of collaborative and dialogical models for poetry. Stand-up poets, rap poets, and performance poets depend on a complex interweaving of cultural idiolects and argots to create works meant to perform culture while sedimenting audience collaboration. Such events also blur the boundary between popular cultural forms (rock concerts, MTV) and poetry. Henry Louis Gates's influential term, "signifyin(g)," describes features of African-American literature that could be applied to many contemporary poets. Gates distinguishes between Western cultural values that depend on signification or representation in forging cultural hegemony and Afro-American verbal play or "signifyin'" that relies on a speaker's ability to control several levels of signification at the same time (Gates 1988: 46). Signifyin(g) builds upon an oral tradition shared by many black poets but also upon Afrocentric origins (Yoruba mythology, Haitian *Vaudou*) and the grim heritage of New World slavery. The recent phenomenon of standup or slam poetry could be seen as verification of this impulse in its competitive frontal public address, although it applies as well to more textual poetry such as that of Harryette Mullen, Nathaniel Mackey, or Mark McMorris, who construct their works out of subtle modulations of voice and idiolect.

One implication of both ideas of hybridity and signifyin(g) is to challenge the authority of canonical versions of "literariness" and to question the putative criteria for poetry. Where critics of the 1970s and 1980s could speak of a "dominant style" in US poetry, the sheer range and vitality of writing today defies such categorizations. To some extent this has led to a complete revisioning of a modernist canon in relation to residual and emergent traditions. Thus we might read the work of Chicano/a poets such as Lorna Dee Cervantes or José Montoya in relation to the late nineteenth-century heroic *corrido* and romance as much as to the postwar personalism made possible through the Beat poets. We might read African-American cultural nationalist poetry by Amiri Baraka and Haki Madhubuti through the saxophone of Charles Parker and Ornette Coleman as much as through Charles Olson's "Projective Verse." The multimedia work of Theresa

Hak Kyung Cha or Walter Lew could be explained by the explosion of new electronic technologies of reproduction, but it could also be linked to the diasporic history of Asian Americans through various "ethnoscapes" of immigration, relocation, language instruction, and formal pedagogy. Although these are largely formal issues relating to cultural sources and models, they must be framed in terms of new cultural theories of national, racial, and ethnic origin.

A final word must be said about the role of technology in changing poetry from a genre based on text or voice to one based on virtual spaces of pixel, microchip, and website. The early formulation of postmodernism by Jean-François Lyotard and Jean Baudrillard diagnosed a world powerfully changed by cybernetic knowledge, a replacement of unifying narratives of history, identity, and culture by local situated knowledges. And while this aspect has worried cultural critics who fear a loss of grounded knowledge or history to endless repetitions of the same, for young poets the possibilities of creating hypertext poetry, sound texts through voice modification, verbal collage through websites with visual links have been productive. No longer is the poem consigned to the page or an oral recitation of the page; it now exists on multiple planes at once and is accessible to a public outside traditional publishing venues. Voice recognition software has been used by the sight-impaired Canadian poet Ryan Knighton, and by the British deaf performance artist Aaron Williamson, to create works that complicate the idea of vision and voice as self-evident values in poetry. The performance artist Laurie Anderson has used an electronically modified voice in creating ambiguous gender roles in her performances, and Steve Benson has used multiple tape loops to "interrupt" and alter the trajectory of his readings. Numerous poetry magazines and zines are published on line, and new websites, blogs, and chatlists for specific poetry movements and groups are blurring the boundary between text and context. Most spectacular in this regard is the UbuWeb website, curated by Kenneth Goldsmith, himself a visual artist and experimental writer. UbuWeb features a vast archive of early avant-garde artists and sound poets as well as contemporary work in digital media, sound art, radio art, and the like. A visitor to the website may click on audio tapes and hear sound poetry by Kurt Schwitters, Raoul Helsenback, or the Four Horsemen, or listen to early experimental radio plays. The reader/listener may also access critical articles, bibliographies, documentary sources, and interviews on a wide range of topics – from Brazilian concrete poetry to contemporary deaf performance and documents of ethnopoetics.

This brief survey of the "cultural turn" in poetry shows a shift of emphasis from the singular poet to the collective and collaborative community – from the question of "literariness" and the specific properties of the medium to the blurring of generic boundaries and a fruitful amalgamation with other technologies. While these developments may not seem "philosophical" in the traditional sense, they imply an epistemological shift from knowledge bound by national traditions (Kant, Hegel) or formal media (Adorno, Heidegger) or identity (Freud, James). They also give new meaning to the modernist truism that poetry defamiliarizes reality so that we can see it anew. If reality can no longer be described as something empirically "out there" to which the mind addresses itself, then many of the oppositions upon which modernism is based – mind/reality, singular/plural, individual/society – cease to function. The problematic of the Self – both the modernist anxiety over solipsism and the recovery of the prophetic "I" in the 1950s – is no longer as salient in an era of multiculturalism and globalization What seems the most pressing issue for a volume devoted to US poetry in the twentieth century, however, is the question of the United States as an organizing category for cultural meaning. In an age of globalization and postnational formations, the ability of national boundaries to determine literary or philosophical categories seems in question as we contemplate a postnational moment. What these changes will imply for poetry are hard to tell, although Lyn Hejinian seems to have an intuition of what they will look like: "I receive things at this address, but I don't seem to be/ here in the usual sense" (Hejinian 2003: 55).

References and Further Reading

Altieri, Charles (1979). *Enlarging the Temple: New Directions in American Poetry During the 1960s*. Lewisburg, PA: Bucknell University Press.

— (1984). *Self and Sensibility in Contemporary American Poetry*. Cambridge, UK: Cambridge University Press.

Anzaldúa, Gloria (1987). "*La conciencia de la mestiza*: Towards a New Consciousness." In *Borderlands: La Frontera*. San Francisco: Aunt Lute Books, pp. 77–98.

Baker, Houston (1987). *Modernism and the Harlem Renaissance*. Chicago: University of Chicago Press.

Brooks, Cleanth (1971). "Irony as a Principle of Structure." In Hazard Adams (ed.), *Critical Theory Since Plato*. New York: Harcourt Brace Jovanovich, pp. 1041–8.

Creeley, Robert (1973). *Contexts of Poetry: Interviews, 1961–1971*. Bolinas, CA: Four Seasons Foundation.

— (1982). *The Collected Poems of Robert Creeley, 1945–1975*. Berkeley: University of California Press.

Eliot, T. S. (1962). *Collected Poems*. New York: Harcourt Brace.

— (1975). "The Metaphysical Poets." In Frank Kermode (ed.), *The Selected Prose of T. S. Eliot*. New York: Harcourt Brace, pp. 59–67.

Gates, Henry Louis (1988). *The Signifying Monkey: A Theory of African-American Literary Criticism*. New York: Oxford University Press.

Hejinian, Lyn (2003). *The Fatalist*. Berkeley, CA: Omnidawn Publishing.

Levertov, Denise (1973). "Some Notes on Organic Form." In *The Poet in the World*. New York: New Directions Press, pp. 7–13.

Olson, Charles (1997). "Projective Verse." In Donald Allen and Benjamin Friedlander (eds.), *Collected Prose*. Berkeley: University of California Press, pp. 239–49.

Oppen, George (1969). "Interview with George Oppen," *Contemporary Literature*, 10(2): 159–77.

— (2002). *The New Collected Poems of George Oppen*, ed. Michael Davidson. New York: New Directions.

Silliman, Ron (1987). "The New Sentence." In *The New Sentence*. New York: Roof Books, pp. 69–93.

Stein, Gertrude (1957). "Portraits and Repetition." In *Lectures in America*. Boston: Beacon Press, pp. 165–206.

Stevens, Wallace (1968). *The Collected Poems of Wallace Stevens*. New York: Knopf.

Whitehead, Alfred North (1967). *Science and the Modern World*. New York: The Free Press.

Zukofsky, Louis (1967). "An Objective." In *Prepositions: The Collected Critical Essays of Louis Zukofsky*. Berkeley: University of California Press, pp. 12–18.

Index

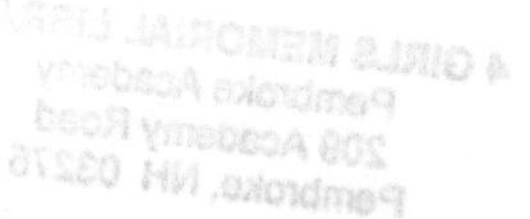